T0296819

Heterogeneous System Architecture

Heterogeneous System Architecture
A New Compute Platform Infrastructure

Edited by

Wen-mei W. Hwu

AMSTERDAM • BOSTON • HEIDELBERG • LONDON
NEW YORK • OXFORD • PARIS • SAN DIEGO
SAN FRANCISCO • SINGAPORE • SYDNEY • TOKYO
Morgan Kaufmann is an imprint of Elsevier

Acquiring Editor: Todd Green
Editorial Project Manager: Charlie Kent
Project Manager: Punithavathy Govindaradjane
Designer: Maria Inês Cruz

Morgan Kaufmann is an imprint of Elsevier
225 Wyman Street, Waltham, MA 02451, USA

ISBN: 978-0-12-800386-2

British Library Cataloguing in Publication Data
A catalogue record for this book is available from the British Library

Library of Congress Cataloging-in-Publication Data
A catalog record for this book is available from the Library of Congress

For information on all MK publications
visit our website at www.mkp.com

Working together
to grow libraries in
developing countries

www.elsevier.com • www.bookaid.org

Contents

Foreword ix
Preface..xi
About the Contributing Authors xiii

CHAPTER 1   Introduction 1

CHAPTER 2   HSA Overview.. 7
    2.1 A Short History of GPU Computing: The Problems
        That Are Solved by HSA..7
    2.2 The Pillars of HSA...12
        2.2.1 HSA Memory Model 13
        2.2.2 HSA Queuing Model 13
        2.2.3 HSAIL Virtual ISA..14
        2.2.4 HSA Context Switching...14
    2.3 The HSA Specifications..14
        2.3.1 HSA Platform System Architecture Specification..............14
        2.3.2 HSA Runtime Specification...15
        2.3.3 *HSA Programmer's Reference Manual*—a.k.a.
             "HSAIL Spec" 15
    2.4 HSA Software 15
    2.5 The HSA Foundation 17
    2.6 Summary 18

CHAPTER 3   HSAIL - Virtual Parallel ISA..................................... 19
    3.1 Introduction...19
    3.2 Sample Compilation Flow 20
    3.3 HSAIL Execution Model 21
    3.4 A Tour of the HSAIL Instruction Set...24
        3.4.1 Atomic Operations...24
        3.4.2 Registers...25
        3.4.3 Segments..26
        3.4.4 Wavefronts and Lanes..28
    3.5 HSAIL Machine Models and Profiles..29
    3.6 HSAIL Compilation Flow 30
    3.7 HSAIL Compilation Tools...32
        3.7.1 Compiler Frameworks 32
        3.7.2 CL Offline Compilation (CLOC) 32
        3.7.3 HSAIL Assembler/Disassembler...33
        3.7.4 ISA and Machine Code Assembler/Disassembler..............34
    3.8 Conclusion 34

CHAPTER 4   HSA Runtime **35**

4.1 Introduction..35

4.2 The HSA Core Runtime API......................................38

4.2.1 Runtime Initialization and Shutdown 38

4.2.2 Runtime Notifications...39

4.2.3 System and HSA Agent Information.....................40

4.2.4 Signals...40

4.2.5 Queues 41

4.2.6 Architected Queuing Language 42

4.2.7 Memory...44

4.2.8 Code Objects and Executables..............................45

4.3 HSA Runtime Extensions 47

4.3.1 HSAIL Finalization 47

4.3.2 Images and Samplers 48

4.4 Conclusion 50

References...51

CHAPTER 5   HSA Memory Model **53**

5.1 Introduction..53

5.2 HSA Memory Structure 55

5.2.1 Segments...55

5.2.2 Flat Addressing..57

5.2.3 Shared Virtual Addressing....................................57

5.2.4 Ownership 58

5.2.5 Image Memory..59

5.3 HSA Memory Consistency Basics................................59

5.3.1 Background: Sequential Consistency 60

5.3.2 Background: Conflicts and Races...........................60

5.3.3 The HSA Memory Model for a Single Memory Scope.......62

5.3.4 HSA Memory Model Using Memory Scopes 65

5.3.5 Memory Segments 69

5.3.6 Putting It All Together: HSA Race Freedom....................70

5.3.7 Additional Observations and Considerations 71

5.4 Advanced Consistency in the HSA Memory Model....................71

5.4.1 Relaxed Atomics...72

5.4.2 Ownership and Scope Bounding 73

5.5 Conclusions...74

References...75

CHAPTER 6   HSA Queuing Model **77**

6.1 Introduction..77

6.2 User Mode Queues 77

6.3 Architected Queuing Language 82
    6.3.1 Packet Types 82
    6.3.2 Building Packets 86
6.4 Packet Submission and Scheduling 88
6.5 Conclusions.. 96
    References.. 96

CHAPTER 7 Compiler Technology 97
7.1 Introduction.. 97
7.2 A Brief Introduction to C++ AMP 98
    7.2.1 C++ AMP *array_view* 99
    7.2.2 C++ AMP *parallel_ for_each,* or Kernel
        Invocation 100
7.3 HSA as a Compiler Target.. 102
7.4 Mapping Key C++ AMP Constructs to HSA 102
7.5 C++ AMP Compilation Flow.. 104
7.6 Compiled C++ AMP Code 107
7.7 Compiler Support for Tiling in C++AMP 107
    7.7.1 Dividing Compute Domain... 109
    7.7.2 Specifying Address Space and Barriers........................... 110
7.8 Memory Segment Annotation... 111
7.9 Towards Generic C++ for HSA 113
7.10 Compiler Support for Platform Atomics 116
    7.10.1 One Simple Example of Platform Atomics 118
7.11 Compiler Support for New/Delete Operators 123
    7.11.1 Implementing New/Delete Operators with Platform
        Atomics... 124
    7.11.2 Promoting New/Delete Returned Address to Global
        Memory Segment.. 126
    7.11.3 Improve New/Delete Operators Based on Wait
        API/Signal HSAIL Instruction 126
7.12 Conclusion 128
    References.. 129

CHAPTER 8 Application Use Cases: Platform Atomics.............. 131
8.1 Introduction... 131
8.2 Atomics in HSA... 132
8.3 Task Queue System... 134
    8.3.1 Static Execution 135
    8.3.2 Dynamic Execution.. 135
    8.3.3 HSA Task Queue System... 136
    8.3.4 Evaluation 140

8.4 Breadth-First Search 142
　8.4.1 Legacy Implementation 145
　8.4.2 HSA Implementation 147
　8.4.3 Evaluation 148
8.5 Data Layout Conversion 151
　8.5.1 In-place SoA-ASTA Conversion with PTTWAC
　　　　Algorithm... 153
　8.5.2 An HSA Implementation of PTTWAC 155
　8.5.3 Evaluation 155
8.6 Conclusions.. 157
　Acknowledgment 157
　References.. 157

CHAPTER 9　HSA Simulators **159**
9.1 Simulating HSA in Multi2Sim 159
　9.1.1 Introduction.. 159
　9.1.2 Multi2Sim-HSA... 161
　9.1.3 HSAIL Host HSA 162
　9.1.4 HSA Runtime... 164
　9.1.5 Emulator Design 165
　9.1.6 Logging and Debugging 167
　9.1.7 Multi2Sim-HSA Road Map................................... 168
　9.1.8 Installation and Support 168
9.2 Emulating HSA with HSAemu.. 169
　9.2.1 Introduction.. 169
　9.2.2 Modeled HSA Components.................................... 170
　9.2.3 Design of HSAemu 171
　9.2.4 Multithreaded HSA GPU Emulator....................... 174
　9.2.5 Profiling, Debugging and Performance Models 176
9.3 SoftHSA Simulator.. 177
　9.3.1 Introduction.. 177
　9.3.2 High-Level Design... 178
　9.3.3 Building and Testing the Simulator 179
　9.3.4 Debugging with the LLVM HSA Simulator............ 180
　References.. 182

Index 185

Foreword

We are at the dawn of the heterogeneous computing era. With virtually all applications being power-limited, all future computing platforms will likely embrace heterogeneity. The Barcelona Supercomputing Center is one of the pioneers in heterogeneous supercomputing. Our Mt. Blanc project explored the use of low-power CPUs with high-throughput GPUs to address the power consumption challenges associated with the design of our future supercomputers. Throughout the project, we experienced many of the problems that the Heterogeneous System Architecture (HSA) is designed to solve.

This book explains how HSA addresses these problems. One such problem is the need to use specialized interfaces in order to program the GPUs in the Mt. Blanc system. I am glad that the HSA features have enabled the development of a standard C++ compiler for both the host and the GPUs. Moreover, I expect to see other mainstream languages such as FORTRAN become available on HSA systems in the future. This will thereby allow programmers to use standard languages to program all compute devices in a heterogeneous computing system, which would greatly reduce software costs. Another challenging problem is the lack of platform-wide synchronization support for coordinating collaborative activities of multiple compute devices. I am pleased to see the case studies that show how some frequently used computation patterns can benefit from the collaborative execution between the CPU and GPU that is enabled by HSA platform atomics.

The chapters of this book are written by the experts who helped create the HSA architecture and software stacks. Their writings provide the historical context and rationale for the various aspects of HSA. Such insights are of great value for graduate students, software developers, and system implementers. Indeed, the publication of this book marks a major milestone for the heterogeneous computing movement.

Mateo Valero,
Director,
Barcelona Supercomputing Center,
September 2015

Preface

I am proud to introduce *Heterogeneous System Architecture—A New Compute Platform*. Heterogeneous System Architecture (HSA) is the outcome of a multivendor collaboration to define a new system architecture that provides essential support for CPUs and specialized compute devices to efficiently and productively collaborate on demanding tasks. This book is a collection of writings by the experts who helped create HSA and its associated software stack. These writings explain the rationale and insight behind the specifications and artifacts that cannot be easily gleaned from reading the manuals and documents. These authors, some from industry and others from academia, are identified in the individual chapters. I am truly privileged to have the opportunity to work with these world-class experts.

There are many people who made significant contributions that are not in the form of chapters. The first person who I would like to acknowledge is Manju Hegde (AMD), who convinced me to serve as the editor of this book and remained a key partner throughout the process. Manju provided the original vision for the book and helped recruit many of the authors and reviewers. He also personally reviewed the chapters and provided valuable comments.

The material of this book grew out of two successful conference tutorials at HotChips 2013 and the ACM/IEEE International Symposium on Computer Architecture (ISCA) 2014. Most of the presenters became chapter authors for this book. However, Chien-ping Lu (MediaTek), Hakan Persson (ARM), and Ian Bratt (ARM), who presented the original HSA queuing model tutorial, could not participate in the writing projects due to other demands on their time. I would also like to acknowledge J.P. Bordes (AMD), who contributed significantly to the HSA applications tutorial.

I would also like to give special thanks to five special individuals. Greg Stoner (AMD), Chief Evangelist of HSA, provided invaluable support to the creation of this book from the HSA foundation. Anton Lokhmotov (ARM) worked diligently with me on the original outline of the book. Tom Jablin (MulticoreWare), who is a leading expert in HSA, gave me invaluable technical support during the editing process. Marty Johnson (AMD) and Sui Chi Chan (AMD) reviewed the chapters and provided valuable feedback to me and the authors.

Finally, I would like to thank Bob Whitecotton (AMD), who served as the project manager for the book. He was the one who kept me and all the authors on track. His project management skills saved me from many pitfalls. Without his help, I would not have been able to complete this project.

About the Contributing Authors

Wen-Mei W. Hwu is a professor and holds the Sanders-AMD Endowed Chair in the Department of Electrical and Computer Engineering at the University of Illinois at Urbana-Champaign. His research interests are in the areas of architecture, implementation, compilation, and algorithms for parallel computing. He is the chief scientist of the Parallel Computing Institute and director of the IMPACT research group (www.impact.crhc.illinois.edu). He is a co-founder and CTO of MulticoreWare. For his contributions in research and teaching, he received the ACM SigArch Maurice Wilkes Award, the ACM Grace Murray Hopper Award, the Tau Beta Pi Daniel C. Drucker Eminent Faculty Award, the ISCA Influential Paper Award, the IEEE Computer Society B. R. Rau Award, and the Distinguished Alumni Award in Computer Science from the University of California, Berkeley. He is a fellow of IEEE and ACM. He directs the UIUC CUDA Center of Excellence and serves as one of the principal investigators of the NSF Blue Waters Petascale computer project. Dr. Hwu received his Ph.D. degree in computer science from the University of California, Berkeley.

At the time of this writing, **Phil Rogers** was a corporate fellow with AMD, the lead architect for the Heterogeneous Systems Architecture, and President of the HSA Foundation. Phil is channeling his expertise into designing highly efficient GPUs to drastically reduce the power consumed when running modern applications on heterogeneous processors. After joining ATI Technologies in 1994, Phil served in increasingly senior architecture positions in the development of DirectX® and OpenGL® software. Phil was instrumental in the development of all of ATI Radeon GPUs since the introduction of the Radeon series in 2000. Phil joined AMD with the ATI acquisition in 2006 and has played a lead role in heterogeneous computing, APU architecture, and programming models during his tenure. Phil began his career at Marconi Radar Systems, where he designed digital signal processors for advanced radar systems. Phil earned his Bachelor of Science degree in electronic and electrical engineering from the University of Birmingham in England.

Ben Sander is a senior fellow at AMD and was the spec editor for the 0.95 version of the *HSAIL Programmer's Reference Manual*. Ben joined AMD in 1995 and has served in various technical and managerial roles on the CPU and GPU development teams. He previously led the CPU performance team at AMD and was deeply involved in the development of the CPU and Northbridge architectures for AMD Opteron processors. In 2009, Ben switched into an individual contributor role in GPU software, optimizing OpenCL™ performance and workloads. Ben's strong background in both CPU and GPU performance architecture led into his current role as the lead software architect for AMD's Heterogeneous System Architecture program. Ben's interests include compilers, programming models (including the Bolt C++ template library), performance, and computer architecture. Ben received his Master of Science and Bachelor of Science degrees from the University of Illinois in Champaign, IL.

Tony Tye is a fellow at AMD and was the specification editor for the 0.99, 1.0, and 1.1 versions of the *HSAIL Programmer's Reference Manual*. Tony joined AMD in 2007 to work on dynamic binary optimization and has been working on AMD's Heterogeneous System Architecture program since 2012. Tony's interests include compilers, runtimes, debuggers, memory models, programming languages, and computer architecture. Tony received his Ph.D. from UMIST in Manchester, UK.

Yeh-Ching Chung received a B.S. degree in information engineering from Chung Yuan Christian University in 1983, and M.S. and Ph.D. degrees in computer and information science from Syracuse University in 1988 and 1992, respectively. He joined the Department of Information Engineering at Feng Chia University as an associate professor in 1992 and became a full professor in 1999. From 1998 to 2001, he was the chairman of the department. In 2002, he joined the Department of Computer Science at National Tsing Hua University as a full professor. His research interests include parallel and distributed processing, cloud computing, and embedded systems. He is a senior member of the IEEE Computer Society.

Benedict Gaster is a researcher at the University of West England, where he works on programming models and system architecture for highly parallel systems. He was one of the developers of the OpenCL programming model and was co-author of two books on the topic. He also contributed to the design of HSA and is one of the lead authors on its memory model. Benedict has a Ph.D. from the University of Nottingham in language design and type theory.

Lee Howes is a senior staff engineer in Qualcomm's GPU architecture organization. He has been working on heterogeneous computing for a number of years at AMD and at Qualcomm, with a recent focus on improving the state of the art for heterogeneous memory consistency models. Lee currently serves as specification editor for the OpenCL and SYCL standards. He did his Ph.D. in software performance optimization at Imperial College London, studying intermediate representations for performance-portable heterogeneous computing.

Derek R. Hower is an architect at Qualcomm, where he works on next-generation SOCs (Systems on a chip). Derek previously worked at AMD, where he developed the foundation for heterogeneous-race-free memory models. Since then, he has been actively involved in adapting that framework to the HSA memory model. Derek earned his Ph.D. degree in computer science from the University of Wisconsin-Madison.

Wen-Heng (Jack) Chung is a solution architect of MulticoreWare, Inc. He is the lead developer of Kalmar, an open source C++ compiler for heterogeneous devices. He began his career at Aplix International Inc., where he optimized Java virtual machine for mobile phones and embedded systems, and engaged in Bluetooth IoT devices. His interests include compilers, embedded systems, and industrial automation. Wen-Heng received his Master's degree in computer science from National Chiao Tung University in Taiwan.

I-Jui (Ray) Sung is a solution architect of MulticoreWare, Inc. He was the architect and lead developer of MulticoreWare C++ AMP compiler, MulticoreWare MxPA OpenCL stack, and LibreOffice Calc 4.2 GPU acceleration. His interests include compilers, domain-specific languages, programming models, and GPGPU. I-Jui received his Ph.D. degree in computer engineering from the University of Illinois.

Yi-Hong Lyu is a software engineer at MulticoreWare, Inc. He is the main developer of the new/delete operator on HSA and also a maintainer of Kalmar (C++ compiler for HSA). He is not only a user of LLVM/Clang but also a contributor. Yi-Hong earned his Bachelor degree in information management from the National Taiwan University.

Yun-Wei Lee is an intern software developer of MulticoreWare, Inc. He was one of the pioneering developers of Kalmar, an open source C++ compiler for heterogeneous devices. In addition to his interests in compilers, computer security, and programming languages, Yun-Wei also acts as the head of the mountaineering club in National Chiao Tung University. He received his Bachelor's degree in computer science from National Chiao Tung University in Taiwan.

Juan Gómez-Luna received his B.S. and M.S. degrees in telecommunication engineering from the University of Sevilla, Spain in 2001, and his Ph.D. degree in computer science from the University of Córdoba, Spain in 2012. Since 2005, he has been a lecturer at the University of Córdoba. His research interests focus on the parallelization and optimization of applications, such as image and video processing, as well as on GPUs and heterogeneous systems.

Antonio J. Lázaro-Muñoz received the B.S. degree in Computer Science in 2010 and the M.S. degree in 2011 from the University of Córdoba, Spain. He is currently a PhD candidate in the Department of Computer Architecture of the University of Málaga, Spain. His research topics are GPU computing and tasks scheduling on heterogeneous and discrete systems.

José María González-Linares received his B.S. and Ph.D. degrees in telecommunication engineering from the University of Málaga in Málaga, Spain in 1995 and 2000, respectively. Since 2002, he has been an associate professor at the University of Málaga. He has published more than 30 papers in international journals and conferences. His research interests are parallel computing, and video and image processing.

Nicolás Guil received his B.S. degree in physics from the University of Sevilla, Spain in 1986, and his Ph.D. degree in computer science from the University of Málaga in 1995. Currently, he is a full professor with the Department of Computer Architecture at the University of Málaga. He has published more than 60 papers in international journals and conferences. His research interests are parallel computing, and video and image processing.

Shih-Hao Hung is currently an associate professor in the Department of Computer Science and Information Engineering at National Taiwan University. His research interests include parallel processing, heterogeneous computing, hardware-software co-design, performance tools, and virtual prototyping. Shih-Hao has been working with top companies, including IBM, AMD, NVIDIA, Oracle, and MediaTek to optimize application performance on the latest IoT, cloud, and big data systems with heterogeneous multicore architectures, GPGPU, and FPGA. He worked on high-performance server systems for Sun Microsystem Inc. in California (2000-2005). He received Ph.D. and M.S. degrees from the University of Michigan, Ann Arbor in 1998 and 1994, respectively. He graduated from National Taiwan University with a BS degree in electrical engineering in 1989.

Wei-Chung Hsu is a professor in the Department of Computer Science and Information Engineering at National Taiwan University (NTU). His research interests are in the areas of optimizing compilers, binary translation, virtual machines, and high-performance computer architectures. He was a computer architect at Cray Research, a technical lead at Hewlett Packard, and a professor at University of Minnesota at Twin Cities. He worked alongside Professor Chung at NTHU to create an HSA emulator called HSAemu (hsaemu.org). Dr. Hsu received his Ph.D. degree in computer science from University of Wisconsin at Madison.

Thomas B. Jablin is a solution architect working at MulticoreWare, Inc., where he helps design solutions to address the challenges created by the intersection of compilers, parallelization, and GPUs. He received a B.A. in computer science from Amherst College in 2006. He received his M.A. and Ph.D. in computer science from Princeton University in 2008 and 2013, respectively, for his work on fully automatic compiler-driven parallelization for GPUs. He has co-authored critically reviewed publications covering topics from compilation strategies to exploiting automatic parallelization of GPUs. His research interests include automatically parallelizing compilers, automatic compilation for GPU targets, and profiling for dynamic optimization.

David Kaeli received his B.S. and Ph.D. in electrical engineering from Rutgers University, and his M.S. in computer engineering from Syracuse University. He is a COE Distinguished Full Professor on the ECE faculty at Northeastern University in Boston, MA. He is the Director of the Northeastern University Computer Architecture Research Laboratory (NUCAR). Prior to joining Northeastern in 1993, he spent 12 years at IBM, the last 7 years at T.J. Watson Research Center in Yorktown Heights, NY. He has published over 250 critically reviewed publications, 7 books, and 13 patents. His research spans a range of areas, including microarchitecture to back-end compilers and database systems. His current research topics include information assurance, graphics processors, virtualization, heterogeneous computing and multilayer reliability. He is an associate editor of the ACM Transactions on Architecture and Code Optimization, IEEE Transactions on Parallel and Distributed Systems, and the *Journal of Parallel and Distributed Computing*. He is an IEEE Fellow and an ACM Distinguished Scientist.

Yifan Sun is a computer engineering Ph.D. candidate at Northeastern University. He is a member of the Northeastern University Computer Architecture Research (NUCAR) group and works under the advisory of David Kaeli. He received his Master of Science in electrical engineering from the University at Buffalo in 2013, and his Bachelor of Science in electrical engineering from Huazhong University of Science and Technology in 2011. His research interests include heterogeneous computing, performance modeling, and processor simulation.

Rafael Ubal obtained his Ph.D. degree in computer engineering in 2010 from Universidad Politécnica de Valencia, Spain. He works currently as a teaching professor in the Electrical and Computer Engineering Department at Northeastern University. He's a member of the Northeastern University Computer Architecture Research (NUCAR) group. His research topics of interest include multicore CPU and GPU architecture, heterogeneous computing, and processor simulation.

Introduction

1

W.-M. W. Hwu

University of Illinois at Urbana-Champaign, Urbana, IL, USA

We are experiencing a disruptive revolution in computing. After many decades of evolution, Central Processing Units (CPUs) have reached a plateau in computation speed per Watt. At the same time, many innovative applications demand much higher speeds for their given budget of power consumption. Most of these demanding applications process a large amount data and exhibit a high level of parallelism. As a result, all computing systems, from mobile devices to supercomputers, are quickly becoming heterogeneous. They employ nontraditional computing devices such as Graphics Processing Units (GPUs) and Digital Signal Processors (DSPs) that achieve high computation throughput at a low power through the exploitation of massive parallelism. By using CPUs on latency sensitive, serial parts of an application and GPUs on richly parallel, throughput friendly parts, a heterogeneous computing system can achieve much higher application performance and energy efficiency than traditional systems.

An example application area that benefits from heterogeneous computing is video manipulation. Today, manipulating HD TV videos is a demanding and very parallel process, as are 3D imaging and visualization processes. New functionalities such as view synthesis and high-resolution display of low-resolution videos will demand even more computing power in the TV computing platform. These functionalities are increasingly implemented with GPUs or even special hardware accelerators. At the consumer level, we have already witnessed a quickly growing number of video and image processing applications that improve the focus, lighting, and other key aspects of pictures and videos. Much of the heavy lifting in such applications is done by GPUs in mobile phones and cloud services.

Another example is in the area of consumer electronic gaming. In the past, driving a car in a game followed a prearranged sequence of scenes. If your car bumped into an obstacle, the condition of your car or the course of driving did not change; only the game score changed. Your wheels were not bent or damaged, and it was no more difficult to drive, regardless of whether you bumped your wheels. With increased computing speed, games can now be based on dynamic simulation rather than prearranged scenes. We can expect to see more of these realistic effects in the future: accidents will damage your wheels, and your online driving experience will be much more realistic. Realistic modeling and simulation of physical effects are known to demand very large amounts of computing power and benefit greatly from heterogeneous computing.

Many applications that benefit from heterogeneous computing involve simulating a physical, concurrent world in different ways and at different levels, with large amounts of data being processed. And with this large quantity of data, much of the computation can be done on different parts of the data in parallel, although these parts will have to be reconciled at some point. In most cases, effective management of data delivery can have a major impact on the achievable speed of a parallel application.

While many applications in areas such as computational financing, oil-gas exploration, molecular dynamics, computational fluid dynamics, medical imaging, and computational photography have successfully migrated to heterogeneous computing, others have experienced less success. The lack of success is often due to the high levels of overhead involved in initiating a task on a non-CPU computing device, as well as moving data to and from such a device. These overheads arise from the fact that nontraditional computing devices have been architected as I/O devices in modern computing systems. Much of the work in task initiation and data movement has been carried out by the software drivers of these computing devices. Such software-heavy implementation incurs significant overhead. As a result, application developers must ensure that the cost of each task initiation and data movement activity is overcome by speeding up a large amount of computation on the device. Otherwise, the overhead can outweigh the benefit.

A more subtle problem is that the I/O device model has been exposed in the vendor programming interfaces for heterogeneous computing systems. In OpenCL and CUDA, task initiation and data movement are exposed through API calls in much the same way as file and network I/O devices. Such programming styles that require explicit definition of kernels can disrupt the software architecture of modern applications. As a result, GPU code often resides off the main path of applications, causing maintenance problems. Programmability through mainstream languages such as C++ would be a major step forward for heterogeneous computing.

Heterogeneous System Architecture (HSA) is a new hardware platform and associated software stack that allows different types of processors to work together efficiently and cooperatively through shared memory. Its primary implementation vehicles are modern Systems on a Chip (SOCs) and Accelerated Processing Units (APUs), which have become prevalent in the last ten years. These SOCs and APUs feature many specialized processing units such as GPUs, DSPs, Codecs, DMA engines, and crypto engines in addition to CPU cores. HSA enables seamless cooperation between these different processing unit types in executing demanding applications. It provides a consistent, unified application programming interface to complex, heterogeneous computing systems that consists of diverse processors from multiple major vendors.

The main idea for this book is to have the leading experts who helped create the HSA architecture and software stacks give the reader the historical context and rationale for the various aspects of HSA that cannot be easily gleaned from reading the specifications and software documents. The book is targeted at software developers, university researchers, and students. The goal of the book is to equip this audience with the insights needed to improve their applications and to help advance the design and implementation of future heterogeneous computing systems.

The book elaborates on the most relevant parts of the specification, so that the reader will understand how HSA has been architected to make performance available in an easily accessible way and at a low power. It also explains the software stack innovations for compiling and executing applications on a wide variety of hardware dynamically. Then it presents case studies to examine how applications would benefit from a mapping to the HSA architecture. The chapters of the book are organized as follows.

In Chapter 2, Phil Rogers, President of the HSA Foundation and AMD Fellow, presents the historical context, main goals, and important features of HSA. Rogers is a pioneer of GPU computing and a leader of the heterogeneous computing movement. He gives the historical context for the creation of HSA and its main objectives. More importantly, he articulates how the four major pillars of HSA (the memory model, the queuing model, virtual ISA, and context switching) support its objectives. Rather than focusing on the details of these features, this chapter focuses on why these features are in the HSA and how they contribute to the objectives.

In Chapter 3, Ben Sander of AMD and Tony Tye of AMD present the rationale for the HSA Intermediate Language (HSAIL). These are the individuals who led the creation of HSAIL and its associated software infrastructure. HSAIL defines the virtual HSA ISA, and serves as the main vehicle for software distribution for HSA systems. HSAIL is designed for expressing parallel regions of applications. Its binary form, called BRIG, can be embedded in traditional binary object files. To maximize portability, HSA requires vendors to provide a lightweight code generator called a finalizer to translate HSAIL into vendor ISAs. Like traditional physical ISAs such as X86, HSAIL is a stable format that is forward compatible to future hardware generations. That is, HSAIL binaries will run correctly on future generations of hardware. This chapter explains the key concepts behind the most important facets of HSAIL: the parallel execution model, expressiveness, machine models and profiles, compilation flows, and useful tools.

In Chapter 4, Yeh-Ching Chung of National Tsing Hua University highlights the most important aspects of the HSA runtime. Prof. Chung led the development of the first version of the HSA runtime. The core (required) functionalities of the HSA runtime are to manage the compute devices (called HSA agents) in an HSA system, launch compute kernels on available HSA agents, allocate/deallocate HSA memory, report kernel execution to the user process, and support communication between HSA agents. The chapter discusses how these primary functionalities are implemented as core HSA runtime APIs, and how they are related to each other. It also explains the concept of two types of HSA runtime extension APIs. The HSA-approved extensions are optional but have a standardized specification approved by the HSA foundation. Most vendors will likely support these HSA-approved extension APIs. The vendor-specific extensions will likely be supported by one of a few vendors and not standardized. Understanding these different types of APIs and how they will likely evolve helps a developer to take full advantage of the current implementation and future evolutions of the HSA runtime.

In Chapter 5, Lee Howes of Qualcomm, Derek Hower of Qualcomm, and Ben Gaster of University of the West England present the main ideas behind the HSA memory consistency model. They are the experts who led the specification of the HSA memory model. The chapter starts by introducing the major HSA memory segment types. It then explains how the concept of ownership can be used to improve the performance and energy efficiency of memory locations that need to be accessed by a particular device within a time window. Finally, the chapter explains the two views of the HSA memory consistency model. The sequential consistency view holds when the executing program does not have any data races, which are defined as unsynchronized data access conflicts. The behavior of programs under this view is easier to understand but excludes some important hardware and software optimizations. An application developer can restrict the scope of atomic operations to improve performance and reduce power consumption. The scope of atomic operations is a powerful knob in the HSA memory model that can be tricky to use if the application developer does not fully understand the concepts behind it. The authors conclude the chapter with an explanation of the relaxed atomic operations, and how they can be used to allow better performance and/or reduced power consumption.

In Chapter 6, Ben Gaster, Lee Howes, and Derek Hower present the main innovations of the HSA queuing model. An important innovation is that the HSA queues are in the user space and can be manipulated without involving the operating system. Keeping the HSA queues in the user space reduces the often significant kernel overhead of traditional queue mechanisms in CUDA and OpenCL systems. The authors first highlight the API functions for manipulating HSA queues in the user space. They then describe the HSA architected queuing language that defines the types of command packets that applications can submit to the HSA agents through these queues. The authors conclude the chapter with a detailed explanation of the states of a packet as it goes through the life cycle of submission, scheduling, and execution.

In Chapter 7, Wen-Heng (Jack) Chung, Yi-Hong Lyu, I-Jui (Ray) Sung, Yun-Wei Lee, and Wen-Mei Hwu of MulticoreWare present a C++ compiler with HSAIL as one of its targets. The MulticoreWare team built the first C++ compilation path for HSA. The authors explain the process of lowering C++ AMP parallel_for_all constructs into HSA kernels and HSAIL queue commands, with detailed mapping as well as compiler implementation flow. They further explain how the MulticoreWare compiler maps the C++ data into HSA memory segment types. The authors conclude the chapter with a more advanced compiler support for tiling algorithms, platform atomics, and memory management. The chapter is designed to give compiler writers of other high-level languages the level of insight needed to target their language to HSA.

In Chapter 8, Juan Gómez-Luna, I-Jui (Ray) Sung, Antonio J. Lázaro, Wen-Heng (Jack) Chung, José María González-Linares, and Nicolás Guil show three application cases that demonstrate the benefit of HSA platform atomics using a real HSA system. The first case study is a histogram calculation for frames from a video sequence where the tasks to be processed by the GPU are dynamically identified by the CPU. The consumer and producer synchronization is done through the HSA platform atomic operations. The authors show that the dynamic queue approach, enabled by HSA platform atomic operations, achieves a much better load balance than static task distribution schemes and a lower kernel launch overhead than the traditional dynamic task distribution schemes. The second case study is a graph breadth-first search application that dynamically switches the tasks between GPUs and CPUs depending on the workload characteristics, such as the number of tasks in the queue. The switching allows the application to use the CPU or the GPU on a dynamic basis in each phase of the execution. The third case study is a matrix transposition application where the CPU and GPU collaborate closely through platform atomics and coherent virtual memory. This improves the execution time, compared to using only one of them.

Chapter 9 contains descriptions of three simulation tools for HSA by their creators. David Kaeli, Yafan Sun, and Rafael Uba describe Multi2Sim-HSA, an HSAIL instruction emulator that provides HSAIL-level tracing and debugging support. Shih-Hao Hung describes HSAemu, a full-system emulator that models HSA system components such as HSA queues, HSA shared virtual memory, and HSA agents. It is designed to run arbitrary HSA applications. This emulator can be used by system designers to study the behavior of their designs when running applications. Thomas Jablin describes softHSA, a high-performance, debuggable HSAIL simulator that allows compiler writers and application developers to debug full applications. This tool provides better debugging support than real hardware. These simulation tools have complementary functionalities. Most readers will find at least one of them useful.

The chapters are ordered to give a logical flow. Each chapter introduces concepts that will likely be used in subsequent chapters. For example, the HSAIL, HSA runtime, memory model, and queuing model chapters all provide background knowledge for the compilation technology chapter. It is therefore beneficial for the reader to follow the chapter order.

The book is designed to be self-sufficient. It is designed as a textbook for computer architecture courses, so that graduate students can learn the major concepts of HSA with this book. Compiler writers can learn how to target HSA with this book, referring to the specifications as a reference. System designers will find this book a good introduction to the specifications. The reader should not have to go to the HSA specifications in order to understand any of the chapters. Nevertheless, please keep in mind that the authors intentionally focus on the key concepts rather than the full details. Interested readers are encouraged to read the specifications after reading the relevant chapters, if they are interested in implementing future HSA systems or port software to HSA systems.

HSA Overview

2

P. Rogers
Austin, TX, USA

Heterogeneous System Architecture (HSA) is a new hardware platform and associated software stack that allows processors of different types to work efficiently and cooperatively together in shared memory. This is an architecture that is applicable to smart phones, tablets, PCs, workstations, and even the HPC nodes in a supercomputer. HSA has roots in the shared-memory system architectures that have bound CPU cores and CPU sockets together for the last 30 years. HSA takes many of those lessons from homogeneous multiprocessor systems and applies them to today's heterogeneous Systems on a Chip (SOCs) and Accelerated Processing Units (APUs), which have become prevalent in the last 10 years. These SOCs and APUs feature many specialized processing units such as GPUs, DSPs, Codecs, DMA engines, and crypto engines, in addition to CPU cores. Prior to HSA, such an architectural integration for seamless operation between the different processing unit types had not been attempted.

HSA was originally focused on using the GPU efficiently as a parallel co-processor to the CPU. As we developed HSA, we realized that the architectural features necessary for efficient operation on GPUs were also applicable to many different types of specialized processing units, many of which are already present in SOCs. Nevertheless, it is instructive to view the development of HSA through the steps necessary to architecturally integrate the GPU for computation.

GPUs were originally attached to CPUs as I/O devices. At that time, they were on separate silicon and used purely for graphics. This I/O heritage has caused multiple challenges to using them as a co-processor for general-purpose computation (initially called "GPGPU compute"). The problem persisted when GPUs were brought on chip in early SOC designs. When the HSA Foundation was founded in 2012, the GPU cores inside of SOCs were still very hard to program. The HSA Foundation was established to solve this problem and to pave the way for architectural integration of all types of processing units on the SOC.

2.1 A SHORT HISTORY OF GPU COMPUTING: THE PROBLEMS THAT ARE SOLVED BY HSA

GPU computing started in the early 2000s when the GPU was still on a peripheral card (typically in a PC) attached to the CPU via a PCI bus, as shown in Figure 2.1.

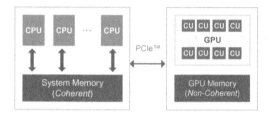

FIGURE 2.1

Legacy GPU compute on discrete GPU cards.

In a legacy system with a discrete GPU, the CPU cores operate in system memory, which is where the operating system and application programs reside. GPU cores typically have their own GPU memory pool that they must use to get full performance. These separate memory pools create a lot of headaches for the programmer, as data must be moved between the pools of memory, depending on which processor will operate on it next. The system memory is typically large, but does not offer very high bandwidth. The GPU memory is typically much smaller, but has significantly higher bandwidth. The CPU can operate coherently and with high bandwidth to the system memory; however, it can only operate non-coherently and with much lower bandwidth to the GPU memory. Conversely, the GPU typically operates non-coherently to both pools of memory, with high bandwidth to the GPU memory and much lower bandwidth to the system memory. A system with multiple pools of memory in a multi-processing environment is often referred to as NUMA—Non-Uniform Memory Access. In multi-socket CPU systems (Symmetric Multi-Processing or SMP), there is typically an identical memory pool attached to each socket. Such SMP systems are called NUMA, because a CPU core in socket A experiences longer latency to memory on socket B than on socket A. The degree of non-uniformity in such NUMA SMP systems is relatively low. In contrast, the legacy GPU compute system has what we call severe NUMA characteristics.

In addition to the problem of multiple memory pools, legacy GPUs used a completely different virtual address space from the CPU for the same application or within the same process. This means that when a piece of data in system memory is located at address A for the CPU, the same memory is accessed by a completely different address B by the GPU. This means that an address cannot be passed between the CPU and the GPU, and cannot be immediately dereferenced in either place. Instead, software must intervene and perform an address conversion. Worse still, early GPUs worked entirely from offsets within memory buffers, rather than using full addresses or pointers. The CPU often works with data structures that contain embedded pointers. When GPU compute first started, all such embedded pointers had to be changed to offsets, and data structures had to be completely "flattened" prior to sending from the CPU to the GPU.

The next problem to be tackled was memory paging. Some recent systems allow GPUs to access system memory, but with some restrictions. CPUs can operate at will in all of system memory, and if the OS had removed a page from system memory, the CPU would notify the OS to retrieve the page before continuing. GPUs, by contrast, could only operate in system memory pages that had been previously "page locked" or "pinned" by the OS. This meant that earlier the application had to make an OS call to pin such memory pages to prevent the OS from paging them out. Operating systems typically have a policy not to allow more than half of system memory pages to be pinned in this way, in order to keep the system responsive. This limits the amount of system memory that can be used by the GPU and puts the burden on the programmer to identify, ahead of time, all pages that might be accessed later by the GPU and lock them down.

The final memory problem for the GPU was coherency. The legacy systems lacked the ability of multiple threads to share data in memory through hardware visibility rules, rather than relying on software to flush caches at visibility boundaries. CPU cores in a multicore CPU, or across SMP sockets, are cache coherent with each other. That means if data has been written to address A by one CPU and the data is in its cache, not all the way out to memory, and then another CPU core reads from address A, the system hardware will ensure that the read sees the updated data. Typically, this is done by one CPU probing the caches of the other CPU cores to check if there is updated data, before fetching data from memory. When HSA was conceived, GPU compute units (CUs) were capable of probing CPU caches, but the CPU was not capable of probing the GPU CU caches. In fact, the GPU CUs were not capable of even probing each other's caches. Instead, software was responsible for running GPU jobs in batches and remembering to flush the GPU caches between jobs or batches to make results visible to the rest of the system. This meant that GPUs were only capable of very coarse-grained coherency, which limited the types of job they could run. This was a very difficult paradigm for programmers who were used to programming multi-processing CPUs, where they never had to worry about caches for correctness.

The next problem faced by early GPU compute developers was the overhead inherent in initiating a GPU task. Typically, any data to be processed by the GPU comes from the CPU. All data input buffers have to be copied from the CPU's system memory to the GPU memory. Next, the commands to execute the task on the GPU must be assembled and converted into a form in memory that the GPU can fetch and decode. This happens through a queuing API function in OpenCL or CUDA that converts a generic command packet into final hardware, from which it is proprietary to the GPU vendor. Then an operating system call is used to put the command packet into a single queue to the hardware that is shared by all application processes. Finally, the hardware executes the job to completion and produces a CPU interrupt. Subsequently, any results generated would be copied back from the GPU memory to the CPU memory to make them available to the rest of the application running on the CPU. Typically, this overhead was very high. This meant that even if the GPU were much faster at parallel processing (e.g., 10 times faster), the offload to the GPU was only a net win if the amount of computation to be done was very large. This overhead restricts the type of work that can be offloaded.

Because legacy GPU compute systems were so specialized, they were not directly programmable using C++, Python, Java, or any other popular programming language used by application developers. Instead, new languages and programming models were created like Brook+, CUDA, and OpenCL. These programming models typically included two elements: a runtime library with an API and a GPU "kernel language" based on a very limited subset of the C language. Most programmers are only interested in writing code in their first language of choice for a given application and are quite resistant to writing modules in a second language within the same project. This has further limited the adoption of GPU compute to those willing to learn and include a new language, especially one that lacked many convenient features, such as pointers, templates, recursion, memory allocation, and exceptions.

A subtle but important effect of requiring a specialized language for GPU compute was that it led to a requirement for "dual source programming," which turned out to be a very big problem. Most applications that have the potential to accelerate through GPU compute must also be capable of running on systems that do not contain a suitable GPU. This means that all modules which may be offloaded to the GPU have to be coded *twice*—once in the main language of the application to run on the CPU (e.g., C++), and then again in the GPU kernel language for opportunistic offload (e.g., OpenCL). These two copies of source code typically reside in different source files but must be maintained to contain the same functionality and always produce the same results for the same input data. This means that if a bug is found in one routine and fixed, it must be checked for in the other routines and fixed there, too, if present. Also, if any change is made in functionality, it must be coded in both places. Such dual source development is expensive, tiresome, and hard to get right.

Finally, some of the legacy GPU compute programming models are proprietary and only run on GPUs from a single vendor. Most application developers are unwilling to write different code for different vendors, further limiting adoption of GPU compute.

The early GPU compute landscape was a very hard environment where only expert programmers who were willing to deal with these problems were able to succeed. At the HSA Foundation, we set out to fix *all* of these problems, eliminate the many barriers to the GPU being a true co-processor to the CPU, and enable simple "single source" programming for GPU compute to mainstream programmers.

It is a testament to just how much acceleration was available through the GPU, from which, through the first 10 years of GPU compute, we saw hundreds of commercial GPU accelerated programs. These were written by the estimated pool of 10,000 programmers worldwide who had the expertise to write programs for legacy GPU compute. Many of these commercial programs are in areas like CAD, CAM, CAE, Image Processing, Oil and Gas Exploration, financial modeling, weather modeling, biosciences, and other HPC applications. Indeed, the whole area of Deep Neural Networks (DNN) for image, voice, and video classification would not have become financially viable without the computational throughput of GPUs.

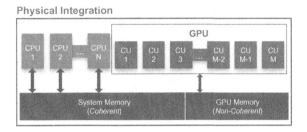

FIGURE 2.2

Legacy GPU compute on SOCs.

So what would happen if we could make the benefits of GPU compute as easy as programming for a multicore CPU? What would happen, and what is happening, is that we bring the benefits of GPU compute acceleration to the 10 million programmers in the world already writing code in C, C++, Java, Python, and OpenMP.

The next innovation to make GPU compute programming easier was the creation of the SOC, or APU, as shown in Figure 2.2.

The physical integration of the GPU onto the same silicon as the CPU and the memory controller was a very important step. It placed the GPU on the same system memory as the CPU, but unfortunately it did not architecturally unite the memory spaces of the CPU and the GPU. In many cases, a physically contiguous "carve out area" of the system memory was reserved at boot time as GPU memory—perhaps 512 MB on a 4 GB system. GPU cores often could operate faster into this carve out GPU memory than in the rest of the system memory, and the application did not need to page lock it before use. This GPU memory pool was non-coherent for the CPU. The GPU caches remained non-coherent, and the system still had completely separate virtual address spaces for the two memory pools and different bandwidths to each memory pool. Despite the fact that the GPU was on the same memory controller as the CPU, a NUMA system architecture still existed. The GPU was still limited to accessing a small amount of memory, and copies were common between system memory and GPU memory, even though the memory cells were in the exact same DRAM chips.

Without full memory coherency, a common address space, and the ability of GPUs to dereference pointers, programmers could only program in OpenCL and CUDA, leaving them in "dual source hell." Also, in these early SOCs, GPU cores typically had only a single command queue that continued to be managed through operating system calls to ensure atomicity of queue access. This meant that dispatch overhead had not come down; only large compute jobs could be considered for offload.

So, despite a very good step forward with physical integration, programming GPU compute on these devices remained the domain of experts and, to date, has not attracted mass adoption.

Figure 2.3 shows how an HSA enabled SOC is configured to memory. Now we truly have a single memory pool, where a "carve out" for the GPU is no longer necessary, and the GPU cores are designed to deliver full performance into the system memory. Furthermore, the GPU hardware is upgraded to use the same address space

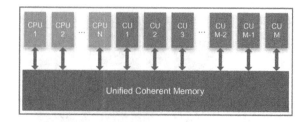

FIGURE 2.3

An HSA enabled SOC.

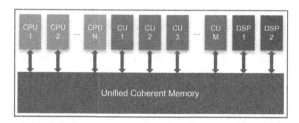

FIGURE 2.4

An HSA enabled SOC featuring multiple processors beyond CPU.

as the CPU, be fully coherent with the CPU, operate into pageable memory, handle page faults, and use real addresses rather than offsets within a memory buffer. Finally, we have **a pointer is a pointer** on whichever processor it is accessed. This is incredibly powerful as it allows the GPU to operate directly on a CPU data structure that came from a high-level language. In turn, this leads to the high-level language being compiled directly to both CPU and GPU code. There is no longer a need to use a GPU-specific language—the nirvana of single source programming!

Figure 2.4 shows that HSA is not limited to GPU compute. In the future, we expect DSP cores and other accelerators to participate in the HSA architecture. One of the great aspects of HSA is that the operating system support for it is generic. This means that once support for HSA has been added to an OS for one processor type, say GPU compute, further OS changes are not needed in order to add additional processor types, such as the DSP, codecs, FPGAs, and other accelerators. HSA is truly heterogeneous, and not limited to just two processor types.

2.2 THE PILLARS OF HSA

HSA includes dozens of features and hundreds of requirements, but the architecture stands on a small number of pillars that differentiate it from previous architectures, enable single source program development, and, for the first time, make GPU computing accessible to mainstream programmers.

2.2.1 **HSA MEMORY MODEL**

Some of the HSA memory model features have already been discussed. They include unified addressing, pageable memory, full memory coherence, and the ability to pass pointers between processors of different types. This section discusses the synchronization feature that further enables direct collaboration between processors.

The HSA model includes a definition of platform atomic operations, meaning a required set of operations into shared memory, which are atomic with respect to all processors that access the memory. These platform atomics are key to allowing different processor types to interoperate in managing queues, synchronizing work, and implementing lock-free data structures.

The HSA memory model is a relaxed consistency memory model, in order to allow high-throughput parallel performance, and is synchronized with store-release and load-acquire semantics, barriers, and fences. Acquire and release semantics are rules that affect the visibility of loads and stores between threads of execution. A "load-acquire" in a sequence of loads is guaranteed not to be re-ordered with respect to any load that follows it within a thread of execution. A store-release is guaranteed not to be re-ordered relative to any store that precedes it within a thread of execution. This allows ordinary loads and stores to be re-ordered within a thread of execution, by compilers or hardware, for best performance. The load-acquire and store-release operations provide ordering synchronization, allow lock-free programming, and enable reliable interactions in memory between independent threads.

The HSA memory model is compatible by design with all of the major high-level language memory models including the C++14, Java, OpenMP, and .Net memory models.

2.2.2 **HSA QUEUING MODEL**

The HSA queuing model was designed to allow low latency dispatch of work between HSA agents, which is the terminology for an HSA-capable processor. There are two fundamental parts to this.

The first is user mode scheduling. This means that the HSA agents (such as GPU compute cores) are able to fetch from multiple separate queues under the control of a scheduler. The design of the user-mode queues enables a separate queue to be created for each application, or even multiple queues per application. Each application can place dispatch packets directly in its own queue(s) without needing to use a runtime API or OS service to manage a shared queue. The user-mode queues significantly reduce the latency involved for applications to submit work. Furthermore, they also better support advanced schedulers to enforce a different quality of service policies.

Second, we created a standard packet format for initiating parallel compute, called Architected Queuing Language (AQL). This means that any HSA agent, from any hardware vendor, can now execute AQL. This is in contrast to legacy systems, which required a device driver or other software layer to convert an API packet format to a vendor-specific format.

By implementing these two steps, typical dispatch times have gone from milliseconds to a few microseconds, drastically increasing the efficiency of the system and allowing smaller parallel jobs to benefit from acceleration.

2.2.3 HSAIL VIRTUAL ISA

Heterogeneous System Architecture Intermediate Language (HSAIL) is a virtual ISA for parallel compute routines or kernels. HSAIL is a low-level intermediate representation, typically generated by a high-level language compiler, which is vendor- and ISA-independent. Prior to execution, a finalizer is executed to translate HSAIL into the ISA of the machine on which it will execute. HSAIL is key to making HSA "ISA agnostic" and compatible across vendors.

Note that the HSA finalizer may be run at different times to suit the situation. It can be run "just in time" (JIT), at first application run time, at application install time, or even at compile time. The choice of when to finalize is left to the application developer and will depend on whether an application is built for an open hardware platform that supports plug and play devices, such as a PC, or for a closed hardware platform, such as a phone or an HPC installation.

2.2.4 HSA CONTEXT SWITCHING

For heterogeneous computing to become truly ubiquitous, HSA applications need to work well in systems where multiple applications or processes are running simultaneously. Legacy GPU compute systems have suffered from quality of service issues when more than one program is scheduling work to the GPU. This is especially severe if one of those programs employs compute kernels that do not yield the machine for long periods of time, or use large amounts of pinned memory.

For this reason, HSA includes specifications for preemption and context switching to enable the OS to preempt a long running job, save its state for later resumption, and switch to a different job, just like what it does for a CPU. The context switching requirements in the HSA specifications differ for different machine models.

2.3 THE HSA SPECIFICATIONS

The specifications that completely define the HSA are located here:
http://www.hsafoundation.com/standards/
There are three specifications:

2.3.1 HSA PLATFORM SYSTEM ARCHITECTURE SPECIFICATION

This specification documents the hardware requirements for HSA, including shared virtual memory, coherency domains, signaling and synchronization, atomic memory operations, system time stamping, user-mode queuing, AQL, agent scheduling, context switching, exception handling, debug infrastructure, and topology discovery.

2.3.2 HSA RUNTIME SPECIFICATION

This specification documents a thin runtime library, to which HSA applications link to use the platform. The runtime includes APIs for initialization and shutdown, system and agent information, memory management, signals and synchronization, architected dispatch, and error handling.

One of the aspects of the HSA Runtime that distinguishes it from all previous compute runtimes is that there is not a required API for job dispatch. Instead, the runtime enables the application to set up its own user-mode queues, to which it can dispatch work at will, with low latency. By design, the HSA Runtime is not called at all during parallel processing, and therefore should not appear in profiler traces, if used as intended.

2.3.3 *HSA PROGRAMMER'S REFERENCE MANUAL—A.K.A. "HSAIL SPEC"*

This specification documents the HSA virtual machine and the HSA Intermediate Language. The majority of HSAIL will be generated by the code generators of open source compilers, such as LLVM and gcc. While it is not recommended for general programmers, it is possible to hand code in HSAIL, and some high-performance libraries may be optimized in this way.

This specification also specifies an object format for HSAIL called BRIG. This enables "fat binaries" to be generated from single source programs. Here, for parallel routines, a compiler will generate both CPU object code and HSAIL code into the same binary. At load time, choices are made for what path to execute based on discovery routines in the HSA Runtime. It is this ability to compile a function or method twice, once for the CPU and once for HSAIL, that delivers the promise of "single source programming."

2.4 HSA SOFTWARE

The HSA platform architecture leads to a more efficient software execution stack, as shown in Figure 2.5.

In this figure, the broad vertical arrows represent the heavily used command and execution paths. In the legacy driver stack, every command from the application to the hardware must go through several software layers, including runtime, user-mode drivers, kernel mode drivers, and the operating system, before delivering a command packet to the hardware. By contrast, in the HSA software stack, applications can write command packets to the hardware queues directly, without having to call through any additional software layers. There is still a runtime in this architecture and a kernel

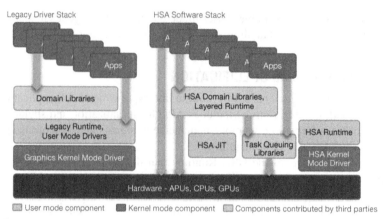

FIGURE 2.5

The HSA software execution stack.

mode driver, but they sit off to the side and are called much less often to handle things like initialization, queue creation, memory allocation, and exception handling. The HSA Runtime does not have to be called for GPU task dispatch.

There are two major advantages to this software stack:

1. The overhead for dispatching work to the GPU is much smaller.
2. The application has more control of execution and is much less susceptible to finding that its performance profile changed after a driver update.

Both of these characteristics are very attractive to application developers.

In addition to a more efficient execution stack, HSA opens the door to programmers using their language of choice for writing the code to be executed on the GPU compute engines, as shown in Figure 2.6.

The HSA software stack lends itself to an open source implementation and much of the HSA software stack is being released in open source form by AMD and is

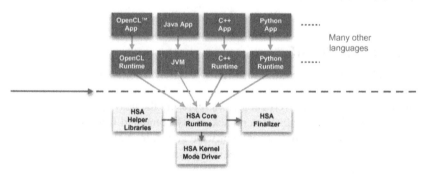

FIGURE 2.6

Programming language choices on HSA.

publically available already. While the finalizer and kernel mode drivers are hardware vendor specific, other components such as the HSA runtime, HSA helper libraries, and the LLVM compiler HSAIL code generator are hardware independent and can be used across all hardware vendors.

There are several advantages to an open source stack for heterogeneous computing:

1. A single open source version of common components avoids divergent implementations of the same functionality, creating a more uniform software environment for application developers.
2. Many customers prefer open source software, so that they can contribute to performance optimizations, perform their own maintenance, and not feel locked to a single vendor.
3. Open source software opens the door for university researchers to explore this exciting new area and make their own contributions.

2.5 THE HSA FOUNDATION

The HSA architecture was created by, and is managed by, the HSA Foundation, a nonprofit industry consortium. The HSA Foundation has a very diverse membership, including hardware IP companies, semiconductor manufacturers, OEMs, operating system companies, software companies of every type, government laboratories, and universities.

The HSA Foundation can be found on the web at www.hsafoundation.com and the full specifications are at www.hsafoundation.com/standards. If you are at a company or a university who are involved in heterogeneous computing and not yet a member, please consider joining the foundation. It is a very inclusive body and has membership levels tailored to every situation. By joining the foundation, you get a stake in influencing the future of computer architecture.

2.6 SUMMARY

This chapter presented an overview of HSA, covering:

- What problems are solved by HSA
- How HSA works at a high level
- The major features of HSA
- The benefits of using HSA
- The main features of the HSA software stack

The following chapters will delve deeper into each topic and also explore real world examples where HSA delivers high performance, low power, and ease of programming. They are designed to provide readers with insights that will help them to better understand the specification documents.

HSA is an important step forward in computer architecture and is finding its way rapidly into phones, tablets, PCs, workstations, and supercomputers.

HSAIL - Virtual Parallel ISA

3

B. Sander*, T. Tye†,

AMD, Austin, TX, USA*; AMD, Boston, MA, USA†

3.1 INTRODUCTION

Heterogeneous system architecture intermediate language (HSAIL) is a low-level compiler intermediate language, designed to express parallel regions of code and be portable across multiple vendor platforms and hardware generations. It also serves as a vehicle for application distribution for HSA systems.

HSAIL is typically generated by a high-level compiler. The developer writes a program in a user-friendly language such as C++, C, or Python, and identifies parallel regions of code using the natural syntax of the language (e.g., directives or parallel_for loops). The compilation produces host code for the CPU and HSAIL for the identified parallel regions. HSAIL defines a binary format (called "BRIG"), which can be embedded in HSA application binaries. A just-in-time (JIT) compiler called the "finalizer" extracts the embedded BRIG and translates it to the target instruction set for the heterogeneous device. Depending on the usage model, the finalizer may be run at build time, install time, or runtime.

One of the benefits of HSAIL is its portability across multiple vendor products. Unlike CPU instruction set architectures (which have stabilized to just a handful, including ARM, ×86, and MIPS), parallel instruction sets for GPUs and DSPs demonstrate significant variation, even from the same vendor. Thus a standard for a portable, multi-vendor intermediate language for compute is an important contribution. Compilers that generate HSAIL can be assured that the resulting code will be able to run on a wide variety of target platforms. Likewise, HSAIL-based tools (debuggers, profilers, etc.) will also support many target platforms. Full-fledged compiler and tools environments are challenging to develop independently. Sharing this infrastructure across multiple vendors provides a more consistent approach for developers, and allows vendors to leverage common components and focus energy on the truly product-specific parts of the tool chain.

HSA is an open foundation with broad industry support, including vendors who ship products in mobile devices (such as phones and tablets), personal computers (such as notebooks and desktop PCs), and servers (such as are found in

High-Performance Computing). HSAIL is a stable format that is forward compatible to future hardware revisions (so applications that contain BRIG will continue to run on future hardware). We expect that HSAIL will evolve with the addition of new operations primarily driven by workload analysis, but at a controlled pace of one revision approximately every couple of years—similar to modern CPU architectures. We might also expect some expansion of HSAIL in future releases to exploit and differentiate between classes of domain processors. Such additions would be provided as extensions to HSAIL, would be optional, and would rely on core HSAIL instructions to program the fundamental parallelism common to many devices.

HSAIL is a low-level intermediate language, just above the machine instruction set. It is designed for fast and robust compilation; the conversion from HSAIL to machine code, the finalization step, is more of a translation than a complex compiler optimization process. The simplicity of this finalization step reduces the chance for errors to creep into the design, and also reduces performance variations due to changes in the finalizer. Instead, most optimizations are intended to be done in the high-level compiler, which has a larger time budget and more scope to implement complex optimizations. For example, HSAIL provides a fixed-size register file, so the high-level compiler performs register allocation, which is traditionally one of the more complex, error-prone, and time-consuming parts of the compilation process. In some implementations, the finalizer may simply map the HSAIL registers to the target ISA registers. It may spill some of the registers, if the number of available registers in the target ISA is smaller than what is used in the HSAIL code.

3.2 SAMPLE COMPILATION FLOW

Figure 3.1 shows a typical compilation flow from a high-level language to code that can be executed on the host and target HSA agent. An HSA agent is a device that participates in the HSA memory model and could be a GPU, a CPU, or some other domain processor or specialized hardware. In this case, the program is written in OpenMP, a common programming language for expressing parallel computation for shared-memory multi-processors. The parallel region (the small highlighted "for" loop) is preceded by the "#pragma omp" line, which is an indication from the programmer that the following loop can be executed in parallel. This parallel code will be converted to BRIG (the binary format of HSAIL) by the high-level compiler. The host CPU code (i.e., the main function and the data allocation for the arrays, shown in white) is contained in the same source file. The high-level compiler will compile this source code into object code in the host CPU instruction set. The resulting executable image will thus contain a mixture of CPU and BRIG code. The compiler will also generate CPU code associated with the for loop, which will load the BRIG code, finalize it for the target machine, and dispatch the resulting code to the target machine. At runtime, this code executes when the loop is encountered in the CPU instruction flow. Typically, BRIG is finalized only once, and the resulting code object is saved in memory. The HSA code object that is output from the finalizer contains object code for the target HSA agent instruction set.

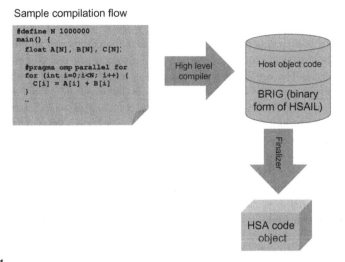

Sample compilation flow

```
#define N 1000000
main() {
  float A[N], B[N], C[N];

  #pragma omp parallel for
  for (int i=0;i<N; i++) {
    C[i] = A[i] + B[i]
  }
  ...
```

High level compiler

Host object code

BRIG (binary form of HSAIL)

Finalizer

HSA code object

FIGURE 3.1

Compilation flow from source to code object.

The example code does not contain any specific commands to control data transfer or copies. These are not needed when targeting the shared virtual memory of an HSA agent. More details on the shared virtual memory can be found in Chapter 5.

This simple example shows how parallelism, expressed with OpenMP pragmas, can be executed on an HSA agent. Other languages use different syntax to mark the parallel region, but the remainder of the compilation flow is similar:

- The same source file contains both parallel and host CPU code.
- The parallel regions are explicitly identified by the programmer, using the syntax of a familiar programming language such as C++. In many cases, the same syntax designed for multi-core CPU acceleration can also be used for acceleration on HSA agents.
- Object file output from the compiler contains both host CPU object code and BRIG.
- At execution time, the generated code calls into the HSA runtime to finalize the BRIG and dispatch it to the target HSA agent.

Chapter 7 shows an example of compilation flow for C++ AMP, a parallel extension of C++.

3.3 HSAIL EXECUTION MODEL

HSAIL and the HSA execution model are designed for parallel execution. However, they cleanly present the parallelism as a single-threaded HSAIL program coupled with a parallel grid that is specified at dispatch time, and describes the shape of the parallel execution. More specifically, the HSAIL program is called a "kernel," and specifies the instruction flow for a single "work-item" of execution. When the HSAIL kernel is dispatched, the dispatch command specifies the number of work-items that should be executed (the "grid" dimension); each work-item is a single point in the grid. The organization of the grid is often influenced by the shape of the data being processed. For example, to process a two-dimensional 1920×1080 high-definition video frame, we may form a 1920×1080 grid where each work-item processes one pixel in the frame. Alternatively, we may form a 960×540 grid where each work item processes a 2×2 patch of pixels.

Figure 3.2 shows the different levels of the HSAIL execution model. This model will likely be familiar to experts in graphics or GPU computing. First, note that the grid consists of a number of work-items. Each work-item, thus, has a unique identifier (specified with x, y, z coordinates). HSAIL contains instructions so that each work-item can determine where it is within the grid (its unique coordinates), and thus on which part of the data the work-item should operate. Grids can have 1, 2, or 3 dimensions—the picture here shows a 3D grid, but the previous video frame example would use a 2D grid.

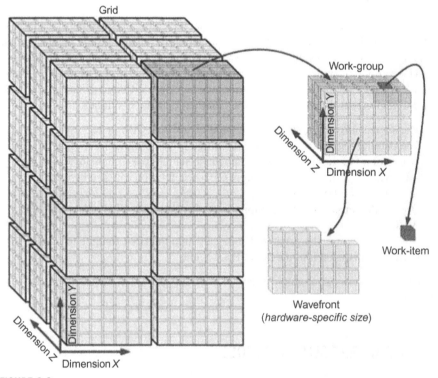

FIGURE 3.2

An HSA grid and its work-groups and work-items.

Grids are divided into one or more "work-groups." Work-Items in the same work-group can efficiently communicate and synchronize with each other through a high-bandwidth "group memory." Work-groups can provide opportunities for extracting peak performance from the machine through the use of group memory. The last work-group in each dimension of a grid may be only partially filled, providing developers with some flexibility in the grid size.

The "wavefront" is a hardware concept that indicates the number of work-items that are scheduled together and that execute in lock-step fashion. Different hardware may have different wavefront widths, and thus most programs do not need to be aware of the wavefront width (although HSAIL does support this for the intrepid expert). HSAIL also provides cross-lane operations that combine results from several work-items in the same wavefront.

When a grid executes, work-groups are distributed to one or more compute units in the target HSA agent. The grid is always scheduled in work-group-sized granularity. Work-groups thus encapsulate a piece of parallel work, and performance naturally scales for higher-end devices with more compute units.

The work-items in the HSA execution model provide a familiar target for programmers, because each work-item represents a single thread of execution. HSAIL code thus resembles a sequential program. Each work-item appears to have its own program counter, and control-flow can be represented with condition-checks and branch instructions, rather than as explicitly specified execution masks. Parallelism is expressed by the grids and work-groups (which specify how many work-items to run), rather than inside the HSAIL code itself. This is a powerful lever to make the model portable across a wide range of parallel hardware with different vector widths and numbers of compute units. Contrast this with CPU models, which often require expressing thread parallelism (i.e., between CPU cores) and SIMD parallelism (within each core) using different, incompatible mechanisms. Furthermore, SIMD parallelism is often hard-coded into the programs and difficult to scale as the SIMD width increases. Ironically, wide-vector CPU architectures are sometimes believed to be easier to program. This is because they are extensions of existing, popular CPU architectures. However, expressing that parallelism can be challenging, and often requires developing directly in assembly or intrinsics and further hard-coding the assembly for a specific vector width and instruction set generation. HSAIL code, which looks like a familiar sequential program, is a significant improvement over wide-vector assembly coding in terms of usability and scalability.

Finally, the HSA execution model specifies that work-items can execute in parallel, and any communication between work-items must be explicitly specified with group memory and barriers, atomics, or with special cross-lane instructions. Also, work-groups are allowed to execute in parallel, and in any order. Both of these restrictions allow HSA binaries to have excellent scalability as hardware for parallel compute is added, without requiring expensive dependency-checking hardware. A classic issue with some languages is that, by default, the language permits implicit memory aliasing and cross-loop dependencies. The compiler must determine when these are not present in order to enable good parallel performance scalability.

HSAIL compilers for these languages have a similar responsibility—they must disambiguate the pointers and cross-loop dependencies, and then generate HSAIL, which the hardware will naturally execute in a massively parallel fashion. Some languages (i.e., OpenCL™ and CUDA) have a similar weak execution model like HSA, and thus can naturally map to the HSA execution model without sophisticated compiler analysis.

3.4 A TOUR OF THE HSAIL INSTRUCTION SET

Writing in HSAIL is similar to writing in a CPU assembly language: the language uses a load/store architecture, supports fundamental integer and floating point operations, branches, atomic operations, multi-media operations, and uses a fixed-size pool of registers. The example below shows two HSAIL operations that load a 64-bit value into HSAIL register "$d0," and then add the immediate "42" to the value in $d0:

```
ld_global_u64    $d0, [$d6 + 120]   ; $d0= load[$d6+120]
add_u64          $d1, $d0, 42       ; $d1= $d2+42
```

HSAIL supports approximately 150 opcodes; for comparison, Java bytecode provides 200. The instruction set defines floating point doubles (64-bit), singles (32-bit), and halves (16-bit). HSAIL not only has the features for implementing existing GPU programming models such as OpenCL™ and C++ AMP, but also adds more to support programming models which have traditionally targeted only CPUs such as C++, Python, and OpenMP. Thus, HSAIL can support function pointers, virtual functions, shared virtual memory, system atomics, and signals for efficient cross-device communication.

Additionally, HSAIL defines group memory, hierarchical synchronization primitives (e.g., work-group, agent, and system scope synchronization), and wavefronts that can be useful for achieving peak performance. Many of these features will look familiar to GPU programmers who are experienced with current-generation GPU programming languages such as OpenCL. The HSAIL specification provides a detailed explanation for the rich set of operations available in HSAIL. The remainder of this section describes a few of the interesting features in HSAIL, which distinguish it from other compiler intermediate languages.

3.4.1 ATOMIC OPERATIONS

The atomic operations are part of the HSA memory model, which defines how work-items and host threads synchronize memory accesses to control memory visibility (also known as memory coherency). Memory visibility is controlled by memory ordering in conjunction with memory scope. Memory ordering specifies how atomic operations in different work-items and threads synchronize with each other, and memory scope controls the levels of the memory hierarchy over which this synchronization can take place.

The HSA memory model defines both sequentially consistent acquire/release and relaxed atomic memory ordering. The memory scope can be specified as either system, agent, work-group, or wavefront. On some machines, limiting the memory scope can improve performance. See Chapter 7 for more information.

Atomic operations can specify system memory scope, to enable HSA agents to communicate with each other in a fine-grained fashion. For example, an HSA agent such as a GPU can generate data into a work queue, then use an atomic operation with sequentially consistent release memory ordering and system memory scope to move the tail pointer on the queue. The CPU or another HSA agent can then use an atomic operation with sequentially consistent acquire memory ordering and system memory scope to see the data in the queue. All this can be done without exiting the HSAIL kernel. Likewise, the CPU in this example could use sequentially consistent release memory ordering and system memory scope atomics to move the tail pointer on the queue to perhaps send a response data back to the GPU in another queue. The kernel dispatch executing on the GPU could use an atomic operation with sequentially consistent acquire and system memory scope to see the result.

The HSA memory model allows HSA agents to act as true peers to the CPU. The resulting paradigms for communication between HSA agents are the same as those used for communication between CPU cores. Legacy GPU models tend to treat the GPU as a "slave" to the CPU, with communication allowed only at coarse-grained kernel dispatch boundaries. HSA support for fine-grained coherency with a well-defined, multi-vendor memory model is a significant improvement over existing GPU systems that support only heavyweight, coarse-grain synchronization at kernel dispatch boundaries.

The *HSAIL Programmer's Reference Manual 1.0* describes atomic operations (Section 6.6) and HSAIL support for the HSA memory model (Section 6.2). Some examples:

```
// system scope atomic add with release synchronization
atomic_add_global_screl_system_b32 $s1, [&x], 42
```

```
// agent-scope atomic add with acquire synchronization
atomic_add_global_scacq_agent_b32 $s1, [&x], 42
```

3.4.2 REGISTERS

A key design point for HSAIL is the use of a fixed-size register pool. This allows the register allocation to be moved to the high-level compiler, and allows the finalizer to run faster and with less complexity. HSAIL provides four classes of registers, defined by their sizes:

- C: 1-bit predicate registers that can be used to contain the output of comparison operations.
- S: 32-bit registers that can contain values such as 32-bit integers or single-precision floating point numbers.

- D: 64-bit registers that contain values such as 64-bit integers or a double-precision floating point numbers.
- Q: 128-bit registers that contain packed values. Several packed formats are supported. Each packed element can range from 8 bits to 64 bits in size.

HSAIL provides up to 128 C registers. The S, D, and Q registers share a single pool of resources, which supports up to 2048 32-bit register "slots." Each S register consumes one register slot; each D register consumes 2 register slots, and each Q register consumes 4 register slots. The high-level compiler must ensure that the "1*S+2*D+4*Q" is less than 2048 in the generated HSAIL code. This pool is designed to be large enough to represent a wide variety of parallel machine targets, but also has a known finite size to simplify the finalization step. If the high-level compiler consumes all available registers, it will utilize the HSAIL "spill" segment to shuffle live values in and out of the registers. If the HSAIL code contains more registers than are supported on the target architecture, the finalizer can use a simple spilling heuristic. Or, optionally, can invest more time and complexity to minimize the register pressure.

3.4.3 SEGMENTS

HSAIL partitions the address space into seven "segments": global, group, spill, private, arg, readonly, and kernarg. In some cases, the segments map to special hardware structures. Or, they provide the compilation stack with means to store information that can be used for optimization or clarity. HSAIL memory operations specify the desired segment in the instruction. For example:

```
ld_global_u64    $d0,[$d6]
ld_group_u64     $d0,[$s6+24]
st_spill_f32     $s1,[$s6+4]
```

The seven HSAIL memory segments are described in the following:

Global segment: The global segment is visible to all HSA agents (including the host CPU). This is the main segment for HSA agents to exchange information such as task queues, platform atomics, and shared virtual memory.

Group segment: Provides high-performance memory shared by the work-items in the work-group. Group memory can be read and written by any work-item in the work-group, and made visible to other work-items in the work-group with the HSAIL barrier instruction combined with a memory fence. Work-items cannot see the group memory of other work-groups.

Spill, private, and arg segments: These three segments represent different regions of a per-work-item stack and may share a single contiguous memory region. Memory references to these segments are typically generated by a compiler, rather than being explicitly specified by the programmer. The spill segment is used for register spills. The private segment is used to store data that is private to the work-item, such as variables not allocated into registers. Finally, the arg segment is used to hold parameters that are passed to an HSAIL function.

Readonly segment: The readonly segment remains constant during the execution of the kernel, and may map to special hardware on some machines.

Kernarg segment: The kernarg segment is used to pass arguments into a kernel. For example, the HSA agent that is dispatching the kernel will write the arguments into the kernarg segment and pass a pointer to the kernarg segment in the kernel (specified in the AQL packet). Then, the kernel will use loads from the kernarg segment to access the kernel arguments. The in-memory format of the kernarg segment is specified in Section 4.21 of the *HSAIL Programmer's Reference Manual 1.0* guide, and includes the size and alignment requirements for all types that can be passed to the kernel. Therefore, the layout, size, and alignment of all kernel parameters can be statically determined, in a device-independent manner, by examining the kernel's signature. This property is critical for enabling portability across vendors, and is also useful for simplifying finalizer implementation and enabling library developers to write low-level assembly code that can easily access kernel parameters.

The code below shows the header for a simple kernel that adds two vectors together. The kernel has four arguments—three array pointers (a, b, and c) passed as 64-bit values to the kernel, and a 32-bit-sized N. Note the load instruction uses the kernarg segment to load from the kernarg segment to an HSAIL register, which can then be accessed by the HSAIL instructions later in the kernel (not shown).

```
kernel &vec_add (
    kernarg_u64 %arg_a,
    kernarg_u64 %arg_b,
    kernarg_u64 %arg_c,
    kernarg_u32 %arg_N)
{
    ld_kernarg_u64  $d0, [%arg_a];
    ld_kernarg_u64  $d1, [%arg_b];
    ld_kernarg_u64  $d2, [%arg_c];
    ld_kernarg_u32  $s0, [%arg_N];
...
```

Finally, HSAIL also supports a "flat" memory address. This is the memory address used when the instruction does not explicitly identify a segment. For example:

```
ld_u64      $d1,[$d0+24]; flat
```

A flat address maps to either the global, group, or private segment based on the virtual address. This capability is very useful for writing an HSAIL function that accepts flat pointers, as opposed to requiring multiple specializations of the function to cover all possible combinations of explicitly specified global/group/private segments. For example, consider a member function in C++ class which references a parameter from a "this" pointer. Flat addressing allows a single finalized version of that kernel to be used, regardless of whether the containing class is allocated in global memory, group memory, or private memory.

3.4.4 **WAVEFRONTS AND LANES**

The wavefront is a hardware concept indicating the number of work-items that are scheduled together. Recall that an HSAIL program represents the program flow for a single work-item, with the appearance that each work-item has its own independent program counter. On many parallel machines, the actual hardware executing a wavefront "behind the scenes" is SIMD, where each lane in the vector represents a work-item. All lanes in the wavefront always execute the same instruction, but some lanes may be "inactive." This means they consume hardware resources but don't produce any results or do any useful work. The hardware uses execution masks to present the appearance of independent program counters. Each lane is associated with a bit in the execution mask; the bits for inactive lanes are cleared, while those for active lanes are set.

Figure 3.3 shows how a simple program (which would map to a portion of an HSAIL kernel) is executed on the lanes in a wavefront. Note that the "if" statements are represented as branches in HSAIL ("cbr" is the HSAIL conditional branch instruction), without exposing the details of the hardware implementation. The finalizer and hardware may use hardware-based execution masks (typical on GPU hardware) or explicit masking instructions (typical on CPU hardware).

HSAIL defines several "cross-lane" instructions (see Section 9.4 of the *HSAIL Programmer's Reference Manual 1.0*) that perform work across the lanes in a wavefront. For example, the "activelaneid" HSAIL instruction returns the number of earlier active work-items within the same wavefront. This can be useful for compaction algorithms. For example, when only a subset of work-items should produce a result, and the programmer wants the results to be densely packed in memory without holes for inactive lanes, this can be used.

The cross-lane "activelanepermute" instruction allows a work-item to read a result produced by another lane without going through group memory and the associated barrier. Activelanepermute is useful for reduction operations (including the classic sum-of-all-elements), where the final steps of the algorithm involve combining the results from all work-items in a wavefront into a single result. More details on these instructions, as well as other cross-lane operations, are available in the *HSA HSAIL Programmer's Reference Manual 1.0* (Section 9.4).

Pseudo-Code	HSAIL	Hardware Execution Comment
		Assume all lanes are active at this point.
C = A + B;	add $s2, $s0, $s1	Executed on all lanes.
if (C < 0)	cmp_ge_b1_u32 $c0, $s2, 0 cbr_b1 $c0, @label1	Note HSAIL uses branch instructions. The execution mask is set by the finalizer and hardware, depending on the vendor implementation.
A++;	add $s0, $s0, 1 br @label2	Executed only on lanes where C<0.
else	@label1:	Finalizer and hardware invert execution mask.
B++	add $s1, $s1, 1	Executed only on lanes where C>=0.
	@label2:	

FIGURE 3.3

Example showing how wavefront lanes execute on hardware.

Many programs can deliver excellent scalability through an HSAIL kernel and a large grid to specify the parallelism, without worrying about the details of work-group dimensions or wavefront widths. Specifying work-group dimension provides an opportunity for optimization, in particular when work-items in a group can benefit from the high-speed communication mechanisms (group memory and work-group barriers). Programs that use specific work-group dimensions are portable across HSA vendors (at least for work-group dimensions up to 256, which is the minimum required by HSA). Programming at the wavefront level typically is not portable, because each vendor architecture only supports a single wavefront width. The cross-lane HSAIL instructions are portable in the sense that they can be finalized for any HSAIL kernel agent, and the WAVESIZE macro returns the wavefront width for the target agent. However, typically the algorithms that use these instructions are inherently targeted for a specific wavefront width. Nevertheless, for some algorithms, wavefront-aware programming provides a significant performance boost, and HSAIL does allow this performance to be exploited.

3.5 HSAIL MACHINE MODELS AND PROFILES

HSAIL is intended to support a wide range of devices from a big iron in a computing farm to a small gadget in your hands. To make sure that HSAIL can be implemented efficiently for multiple market segments, the HSA Foundation introduced the concepts of machine models and profiles. Machine model concerns the sizes of the data pointers; profiles focus on features and precision requirements.

Having too many machine models and profiles would fragment the ecosystem, and make it difficult for both the infrastructure and the community to evolve and grow. For this reason, there are currently only two machine models: Small for 32-bit address and Large for 64-bit address space. Likewise, there are only two profiles: Base and Full.

A process executing with a 32-bit address space size requires the HSAIL code to use the Small machine model. A process executing with a 64-bit address space requires the HSAIL code to use the large machine model. The Small model is appropriate for mobile applications, which today are predominately 32-bit, or a legacy PC application with some portion rewritten as data-parallel kernels. The Large model is appropriate for modern PC applications running on predominately 64-bit PC environments. As mobile application processors evolve into 64-bit, the Large model might be adopted in the mobile space.

HSAIL profiles are provided to guarantee that implementations support a required feature set and meet a given set of program limits. The strictly defined set of HSAIL profile requirements provides portability assurance to users for whom a certain level of support is present. The Base profile indicates that an implementation targets smaller systems that provide better power efficiency without sacrificing performance. Precision is possibly reduced in this profile to improve power efficiency. The Full profile indicates that an implementation targeting larger systems will have hardware that can guarantee higher-accuracy results without sacrificing performance.

The Full profile follows the IEEE-754 rules for floating point operations. Notably, this requires mathematically accurate results for addition, subtraction, multiplication, division, and square root operations. Also, the Full profile supports a rich set of IEEE-754 rounding modes. The Base profile relaxes the accuracy requirements for division and square root, and only supports a single floating-point rounding mode, which can be either round-to-nearest or round-to-zero.

The following rules apply to profiles:

- A finalizer can choose to support either or both profiles.
- A single profile applies to the entire HSAIL program.
- An application is not allowed to mix profiles.
- Both the large and small machine models are supported in each profile.

3.6 HSAIL COMPILATION FLOW

Figure 3.4 shows how the HSA runtime generates code from HSAIL that can be executed on HSA kernel agents. The figure shows two distinct stages:

- Finalization: Creates code for a specific instruction set architecture.
- Loading: Manages the allocation of global and readonly segment variables, and the installation of the finalized code onto specific HSA kernel agents.

The finalization flow (in green (dark gray in print versions)) is cleanly separated from the loading flow (shown in orange (light gray in print versions)), and, in fact, the finalizer APIs are an optional extension that is not required to be included in an HSA runtime implementation. Runtime finalization is optional to support systems that perform finalization at build-time or install-time, and thus have no need for runtime finalization. The compilation flow allows a *code object* to be generated offline, perhaps by an offline compiler that generates HSAIL and then calls the finalizer tool, or perhaps by an offline compiler that generates the target ISA (instruction set architecture or machine code) directly. Both paths are supported, as well as a full online finalization flow where the BRIG is generated and then finalized at runtime.

The optional finalization flow starts by constructing a program from one or more input modules. All BRIG code is contained in modules (BRIG is defined in Chapter 18 of the *HSA HSAIL Programmer's Reference Manual 1.0*). Programs may contain multiple BRIG modules that share function code and data. The program is passed to the finalizer to generate ISA for the target platform, and the output of the finalizer is a code object. The code object can be either passed directly to the loading flow or serialized and saved to a disk file.

The loading flow starts with a code object, which can come directly from the output of the finalizer (runtime finalization) or from deserializing a disk file (offline finalization). The code object is then loaded, which allocates memory for global variables, resolves offsets to global symbols in the code, and prepares the code for execution on the target HSA agent. The output of the load step is an "executable,"

31

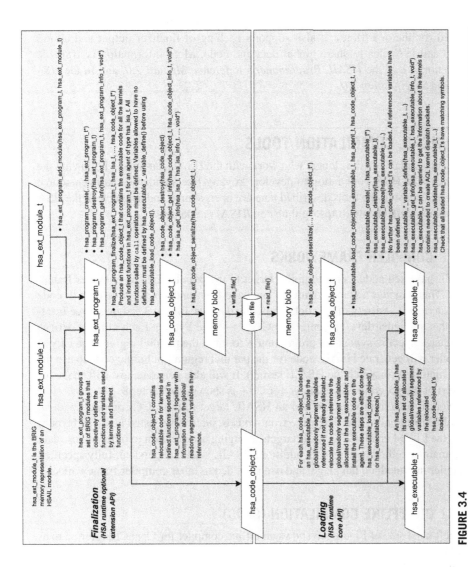

FIGURE 3.4

HSA runtime support for HSAIL life cycle.

which may contain the code for multiple kernels and associated functions. The HSA runtime provides APIs to extract handles for "kernel objects" from the executable, and the kernel object handles can be passed in the AQL packet to execute the desired kernel code.

The HSAIL compilation process involves several data structures and separate steps, but provides significant flexibility in controlling when compilation is performed (online or offline). It also supports caching of finalizer output and allows BRIG and ISA files to share global data and code. More information is available in Section 4.1 of the *HSAIL Programmer's Reference Manual 1.0*, and in the *HSA Runtime Specification 1.0*.

3.7 HSAIL COMPILATION TOOLS

Tools are available to developers who work with the HSAIL language. Following the charter of the HSA Foundation to develop "royalty-free standards and open-source software," most of the tools described here are open-source and available at the HSA Foundation GitHub site (https://github.com/HSAFoundation).

3.7.1 COMPILER FRAMEWORKS

HSAIL has been added as a compiler target to the popular LLVM compiler framework. This provides a smooth path for language front-ends to generate HSAIL code that can run on a variety of parallel computing devices. Figure 3.5 shows three front-ends that are under development: OpenCL, C++, and Python. Each of these defines a language-specific syntax for programmers to mark the parallel region. The LLVM compiler will generate HSAIL code for the parallel region (including code to use the HSA runtime to dispatch the HSAIL kernel). It will also generate host CPU code for the rest of the program. An example for C++ is shown in Chapter 8.

Work is also in progress to add an HSAIL target to the GCC compiler, with an OpenMP front-end. Other language front-ends besides those listed here can be built upon the LLVM and GCC HSAIL targets, bringing acceleration to other mainstream or domain-specific languages. In addition, HSAIL is an independent, fully specified compiler intermediate language, and can be added to other compiler frameworks.

3.7.2 CL OFFLINE COMPILATION (CLOC)

The left-hand side of Figure 3.5 shows an offline compiler for OpenCL, referred to as "CLOC." This parses the OpenCL kernel syntax, runs through LLVM compiler, and generates HSAIL/BRIG as the output. Offline compilation for OpenCL is useful in its own right, because it shows error messages at compile-time rather than run-time and can facilitate rapid development flow. This also provides a convenient way to generate BRIG serialized files that can be used directly with the HSA runtime. These can be useful when generating test cases, porting code, or developing libraries for use in other

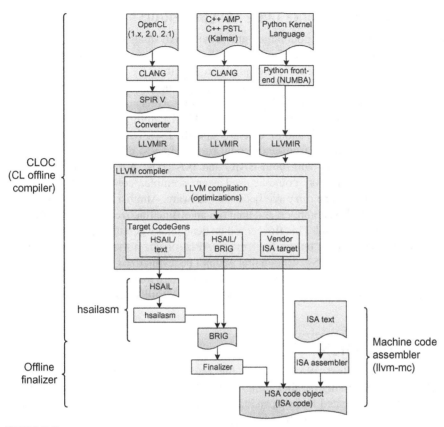

FIGURE 3.5

HSAIL compilation tools.

languages. OpenCL defines a rich kernel language, which supports many features, including group memory and barriers, extensive math libraries, and images. It is much simpler to write in a high-level language like OpenCL kernel languages (based on C99) than code directly in HSAIL text. Note that when executed directly with the HSA runtime, CLOC-generated BRIG kernels do not have access to a full OpenCL runtime. This means that OpenCL kernel language features that require OpenCL runtime support (such as printf, device enqueue, and pipes) are not available. Nevertheless, many kernels do not require these features, and CLOC can be a useful development tool.

3.7.3 HSAIL ASSEMBLER/DISASSEMBLER

BRIG is the binary form of HSAIL text. The "hsailasm" tool translates HSAIL text to BRIG or visa-versa. The binary and text forms are two representations for the same information, and can be converted between each other. Both text HSAIL and binary BRIG are described in more detail in the *HSAIL Programmer's Reference Manual 1.0*.

3.7.4 ISA AND MACHINE CODE ASSEMBLER/DISASSEMBLER

HSAIL is a low-level compiler target, and provides advantages in portability to other vendors and to future hardware from the same vendor. In some cases, developers may prefer to generate ISA for the target platform directly. This is useful, for example, when performance or binary stability is a primary concern. Compilers can choose to create "fat binaries" that contain both ISA for some targets and BRIG for portability.

Figure 3.5 shows an example where the LLVM compiler contains target code generators for both HSAIL and for a vendor-specific ISA. With proper compiler support, any of the language front-ends could run the LLVM compiler multiple times to generate a fat binary with both BRIG and ISA code. Additionally, the LLVM "machine-code" framework could be used as an assembler, converting ISA text into object code that could be run directly on the hardware. Another option is to generate BRIG from the LLVM compiler, and then run an offline finalizer to generate ISA for the selected target agents. This flow could be beneficial when the target system does not support the optional online finalization APIs, or when the developer wants to lock in a fully finalized ISA version that will not be re-finalized on the target system.

The flexible HSAIL compilation framework and finalizer interfaces provide many options to developers, and support portability, stability, and performance goals.

3.8 CONCLUSION

This chapter described HSAIL—a portable, low-level compiler intermediate representation for expressing parallel computation. The *HSAIL Programmer's Reference Manual 1.0* was created by an open standards body and ratified in March of 2015. Other examples in this book show how existing languages can use the compilers that generate HSAIL to target a variety of parallel computing devices.

HSA will fundamentally change the way that people program heterogeneous devices. We can already see the potential in the examples in this book—compilers for existing, popular programming models can generate HSAIL. Programmers will continue to program in the languages they are already using; they can use pointers and data structures as they expect; and the resulting HSAIL code is portable and will run on many different parallel targets. HSAIL on HSA will enable programmers to achieve massive performance gains without the traditional pain of accelerator programming.

HSA Runtime

4

Y.-C. Chung
National Tsing Hua University, Hsinchu, Taiwan, ROC

The HSA runtime is a thin, user-mode applications programming interface (API) that provides the interface necessary for the host to launch compute kernels to the available HSA agents. It can be classified into two categories: core and extension. The HSA core runtime API is designed to support the operations required by the HSA system platform architecture specification, and must be supported by any HSA-compliant systems. The HSA extended runtime API can be HSA-approved or vendor-specific, and is optional for HSA-compliant systems. In this chapter, we will first describe the HSA core runtime API, including initialization and shutdown, notifications, system, and HSA agent information, signals, queues, memory, and code objects and executables, followed by the HSA-approved runtime API, including HSAIL finalization and images.

4.1 INTRODUCTION

The HSA standard integrates CPU, GPU, and other accelerators into a single platform with a shared, high-bandwidth memory system to support a large variety of data-parallel and task-parallel programming models. To achieve this goal, three specifications, namely, HSA platform system architecture [1], HSAIL [2], and HSA runtime [3], were proposed by HSA Foundation.

The specification of HSA platform system architecture, from a hardware point of view, defines a set of system architecture requirements, such as HSA platform topology discovery, signal and synchronization, queuing model, Architecture Queuing Language (AQL), memory model, etc., to support the HSA programming model and system software infrastructure. By programming to the HSA programming model, developers can build portable HSA applications that reap the power and performance benefits of the dedicated HSA agents. Many of these HSA agents, including GPUs and DSPs, are capable and flexible processors that have been extended with special hardware for accelerating parallel code. Historically, these devices have been difficult to program due to their specialized or proprietary programming languages. HSA aims to bring the benefits of these agents to mainstream programming languages, such as C++ and Python.

The specification of heterogeneous system architecture intermediate language (HSAIL) defines a portable and low-level compiler intermediate language to represent an intermediate format of GPU compute kernels. A high-level compiler handles most of the optimization processes and generates the HSAIL for the parallel regions of code. A low-level and lightweight compiler, called the finalizer, translates the HSAIL to target machine code. The finalizer can be invoked at compile-time, install-time, or runtime. Each HSA agent provides its own implementation of the finalizer.

The specification of the HSA runtime defines a low-overhead, user-mode API that provides the interface necessary for the upper-level language runtime, such as OpenCL runtime to launch compute kernels to the available HSA agents. The overall goal of the HSA runtime design is to provide a high-performance dispatch mechanism that is portable across multiple HSA vendor implementations. To achieve high-performance dispatch, the argument setting and kernel launching mechanisms are architected at the hardware and specification level defined in HSA platform system architecture. The HSA runtime API is standardized such that languages built on the HSA runtime can run on different vendor platforms that support the API.

The HSA runtime API can be classified into two categories: core and extension. The purpose of the HSA core runtime API is to support the operations required by the HSA System Platform Architecture specification. The HSA core runtime API is required for any conforming HSA implementation. Key sections of the HSA core runtime API include

- Runtime initialization and shutdown
- Runtime notifications
- System and HSA agent information
- Signals
- Queues
- AQL packets
- Memory

The HSA extended runtime API can be HSA-approved or vendor-specific. The HSA-approved extensions are optional for conforming HSA implementations, but are expected to be widely available. Currently, there are two HSA-approved extensions, HSAIL finalization and image. The HSAIL finalization API allows the application to compile a set of HSAIL modules in binary format (BRIG), generate vendor-specific code objects, and retrieve these code objects. The image API allows the application to specify the image loaded from a picture and store information about its resource layout and other properties in the memory. With the image API, the application can control the allocation of the image data and manage memory more efficiently. Extensions approved by the HSA Foundation could be promoted to the core API in future versions of the standard. When such promotion occurs, the extension specification is added to the core specification. Functions, types, and enumeration constants that are part of a promoted extension will have their extension prefix removed. However, HSA implementations of such later revisions must also continue to declare and expose the original versions of the functions, types, and enumeration constants as a transition aid.

The implementation of the HSA runtime may include operating system kernel-level components (required for some hardware components) or may only include user-space components (e.g., simulators [4] or CPU implementations). The API for the HSA runtime is standard across all HSA vendors, that is, language implementations that use the HSA runtime can be executed on different platforms that support the API. Vendors are responsible for supplying their own HSA runtime implementations that support all the HSA agents provided in their platforms. HSA does not provide a mechanism to combine runtimes from different vendors.

Figure 4.1 shows the position of the HSA runtime in the HSA software architecture stack. At the top of the stack is a programming model or language such as OpenCL™, C++, C++AMP, OpenMP, or a domain-specific language (DSL). The programming model must include some way to indicate a parallel region that can be accelerated. For example, OpenCL has calls to a function named clEnqueueN-DRangeKernel() with associated kernels and grid ranges. For another example, as described in Chapter 7, C++ AMP provides a *parallel_for* construct that delineates parallel execution regions in method functions. In the language runtime layer, each language includes its runtime; the implementation of which may build on the HSA runtime. (In the future, it will be possible for some languages to choose to expose HSA runtime directly.) When the language compiler generates code for a parallel region, the language runtime will set up and dispatch the parallel region to HSA agents by calling the corresponding HSA runtime routines. The language runtime is also responsible for calling the appropriate HSA runtime API functions for initializing the HSA runtime, selecting target devices, creating execution queues, managing memory, etc. The finalizer is an optional component of the HSA runtime. An application can call the finalizer via HSAIL finalization routines to convert the HSAIL modules to target binary during the execution of the application.

The rest of chapter is organized as follows. In Section 4.2, the HSA core runtime APIs will be described in some detail. The HSA-approved extensions, HSAIL finalization, and images, will be given in Section 4.3.

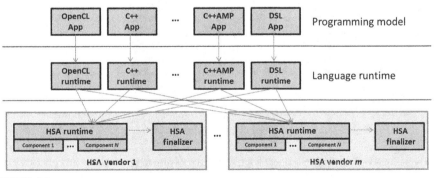

FIGURE 4.1

The software architecture stack with HSA runtime.

4.2 THE HSA CORE RUNTIME API

As the required portion of the HSA runtime, the HSA core runtime API includes runtime initialization and shutdown, runtime notifications, system and HSA agent information, signals, queues, AQL packets, and memory. Understanding the specified functionalities of these features helps both hardware architects and language implementers in their work. In the following, we describe each section in more detail.

4.2.1 RUNTIME INITIALIZATION AND SHUTDOWN

Before the HSA runtime can be used by an application, it must be first initialized. The purpose of the initialization is to create a runtime instance and to allocate resources to the created runtime instance. The runtime instance is implementation specific. A typical runtime instance may contain information on platform, topology, reference count, queues, signals, etc. Figure 4.2 shows an example of the runtime instance used in IISAemu [4]. The initialization routine defined in HSA runtime is **hsa_init**. When **hsa_init** is invoked for the first time in a given process, a runtime instance is created; the reference count associated with the runtime instance is set to one. Whenever the initialization routine is invoked thereafter, the reference count is increased by one. The reference count is used to record the number of times the initialization API was invoked in a given process. Only a single runtime instance will exist for a given process.

When a runtime instance is no longer needed, the application that creates the runtime instance calls a shutdown routine to close the runtime instance. The shutdown routine defined in HSA runtime is hsa_shut_down. When **hsa_shut_down** is invoked, the reference count associated with the runtime instance is decreased by one. If the reference counter of the current HSA runtime instance is less than one, then all the resources associated with the runtime instance (queues, signals, topology information, etc.) are considered invalid. Invocation of any HSA runtime

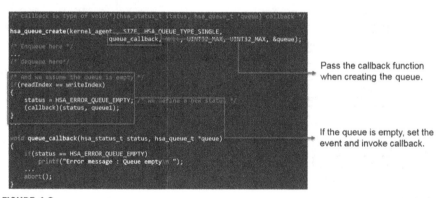

FIGURE 4.2

An example of associating a user-defined callback function with a queue.

routines other than **hsa_init** in subsequent API calls results in undefined behavior. When hsa_shut_down is called more times than hsa_init, the HSA runtime will return status code HSA_STATUS_ERROR_NOT_INITIALIZED to inform the users that the HSA runtime is not initialized. Depending on the implementation, the invalid resources allocated to the runtime instance can be released or wait until another **hsa_init** is invoked to activate the HSA runtime instance again. This way, a single runtime instance is maintained for all HSA clients in the same process until all of them have called the shutdown routine.

4.2.2 RUNTIME NOTIFICATIONS

HSA applications report errors and events using runtime notifications. The HSA runtime defines two kinds of notifications: synchronous and asynchronous. The synchronous notification is used to indicate whether the invoked HSA runtime routine is executed successfully. The HSA runtime uses the return values of HSA runtime routines to pass notifications synchronously. The HSA runtime defines a status code as an enumeration (**hsa_status_t**) to capture the return value of any HSA runtime routine that has been executed, except for some queue index or signal value APIs. The notification is a status code that indicates either success or an error. A success status is represented by HSA_STATUS_SUCCESS, which is equivalent to zero. An error status is assigned a positive integer and its identifier starts with the HSA_STATUS_ERROR prefix. The status code can help determine a cause of the unsuccessful execution. In addition to **hsa_status_t**, the HSA runtime also defines a routine, **hsa_status_string**, for applications to query additional explanation information associated with the status code.

When the HSA runtime detects the occurrence of asynchronous events or errors, it passes asynchronous notifications by calling appropriate callback functions provided by applications. An example is shown in Figure 4.3. In Figure 4.2, the

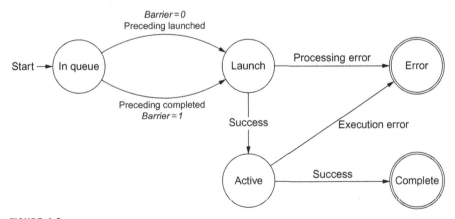

FIGURE 4.3

Packet state diagram.

tasks queued by an application are asynchronously consumed by the packet processor. When the packet processor is instructed to retrieve packets from *queue1* but finds *queue1* empty, the runtime detects this error and calls the callback function, **queue_callback**, with a status code and a pointer to the erroneous queue. The callback function **queue_callback** is associated with *queue1* when **hsa_queue_create** is invoked. The HSA runtime does not implement any default callbacks. That is, all callbacks are user-defined. One needs to be careful when using blocking functions within the callback implementation. For example, a callback that does not return can render the runtime state to be undefined.

4.2.3 SYSTEM AND HSA AGENT INFORMATION

According to the HSA platform system architecture specification, a HSA system can be implemented as either a little or big endian. The machine model can be implemented as either a 32-bit small system or a 64-bit large system. The shared virtual memory can be implemented as either base or full profile, etc. In order for an application to query the implementation type of a given HSA system, the HSA runtime defines an enumerator, **hsa_system_info_t**, for all HSA system attributes. The HSA runtime also defines a routine, **hsa_system_get_info**, for an application to get the value of a specified system attribute.

One important attribute of a HSA agent is whether it is a kernel agent or not.

In order for an application to access HSA agents in a given system, the HSA runtime defines an opaque handle of type **hsa_agent_t** to represent a HSA agent and an enumerator, **hsa_agent_info_t**, for agent attributes. The HSA runtime also defines a routine, **hsa_iterate_agents**, for applications to traverse the list of HSA agents that are available in the system. In addition, it defines a routine, **hsa_agent_get_info**, for applications to query HSA agent-specific attributes. Examples of agent attributes include: name, type of backing device (CPU, GPU), and supported queue types. Implementations of **hsa_iterate_agents** are required to at least report the host (CPU) agent. The applications can inspect the HSA_AGENT_INFO_FEATURE attribute in order to determine if the agent is a kernel agent. A HSA agent is a kernel agent if it supports the HSAIL instruction set and supports execution of the AQL kernel dispatch packet format. A kernel agent can dispatch commands to any kernel agent (including itself) using memory operations to construct and enqueue AQL packets. A kernel agent is composed of one or more compute units and exposes a rich set of attributes related to kernel dispatches, such as wavefront size or maximum number of work-items in the grid. It is possible for a system to include agents that are neither kernel agents nor host CPUs. Dedicated encoders/decoders and specialized encryption engines are examples of non-kernel agents.

4.2.4 SIGNALS

HSA agents can communicate with each other by using coherent global memory, or by using signals. In the HSA platform system architecture specification, the properties and operations of signals are well defined. A HSA signal value must only be manipulated by kernel agents using the specific HSAIL mechanisms, and by the host CPU using the HSA runtime mechanisms. The required mechanisms for HSAIL and the HSA runtime are:

- Allocate a HSA signal
- Destroy a HSA signal
- Read the current HSA signal value
- Send a HSA signal value
- Atomic read-modify-write to a HSA signal value
- Wait on a HSA signal to meet a specified condition
- Wait on a HSA signal to meet a specified condition, with a maximum wait duration requested

The HSA runtime uses an opaque signal handle **hsa_signal_t** to represent a signal and **hsa_signal_value_t** to represent the true value. With the opaque signal handle mechanism, the signal value can only be manipulated by the HSA runtime routines or HSAIL instruction, thus satisfying the restrictions on its usage.

The HSA runtime defines a routine, **hsa_signal_create**, to create a HSA signal and a routine, **hsa_signal_destroy**, to destroy a HSA signal. Because a signal value may be simultaneously manipulated by multiple agents, each read or write signal operation must support memory ordering semantics. The possible memory ordering semantics include relaxed, release, acquire, and acquire-release. The HSA runtime defines routines **hsa_signal_load_acquire** and **hsa_signal_load_relaxed** to read the current HSA signal value atomically. For the operation of sending a HSA signal value, updating the value of a signal is equivalent to sending the signal value. The HSA runtime defines routines **hsa_signal_store_release** and **hsa_signal_store_ release** relaxed to set the value of a HSA signal atomically. The signal atomic read-modified-write operations include AND, OR, XOR, Add, Subtract, Exchange, and CAS. The HSA runtime defines routines for the combinations of atomic read-modified-write update and memory ordering operations for signals. For example, **hsa_signal_add_release** is a routine to increment a signal value by a given amount with the atomic memory fence release. The combinations of actions and memory orders defined in the HSA runtime match the corresponding HSAIL instructions. For the operations of waiting on a HSA signal to meet a specified condition with or without a maximum wait duration, the routines **hsa_signal_wait_acquire** and **hsa_signal_wait_relaxed** are defined.

4.2.5 QUEUES

In the HSA platform system architecture specification, the types, features, attributes, and operations of queues are well defined. A HSA-compliant platform supports the allocation of multiple user-level queues. A user-level queue (or queue for short) is characterized as runtime-allocated, user-level accessible virtual memory of a certain size, containing packets defined in the Architected Queuing Language, referred to as

AQL packets [1]. A queue is associated with a specific HSA agent, but a HSA agent may have more than one queue attached to it. HSA software manipulates memory-based structures to configure the hardware queues. It does this to allow for efficient software management of the hardware queues of the HSA agents. The queue's memory is processed by the packet processor as a ring buffer, with separate memory locations defining the write and read state information of that queue. The packet processor is logically a separate agent. Its primary responsibility is to efficiently manage the queues on behalf of the corresponding kernel agent.

A queue is defined as a semi-opaque object that contains a visible part and an invisible part. The visible part includes the type, feature, and attributes of a queue. The invisible part contains the read/write indices. The type of a queue can be either single-producer or multiple-producer. The HSA runtime defines an enumerator, **hsa_queue_type_t**, for all types of queues. A queue can be either kernel dispatch or agent dispatch. Kernel queues are used to dispatch kernels to an agent, whereas agent queues are used to dispatch built-in functions to an agent. The HSA runtime defines an enumerator, **hsa_queue_feature_t**, for the features of queues. The attributes of a queue include type, feature, base address, doorbell signal, size, and identifier. The HSA runtime defines a data structure, **hsa_queue_t**, for the attributes of a queue. Queues are read-only data structures as far as the user code is concerned. Writing values directly to a queue structure by the user code results in undefined behavior. However, HSA agents can directly modify the contents of the buffer pointed by base address. They can also use HSA runtime routines to access the doorbell signal or the agent dispatch queue.

The operations defined for queues include allocating a queue, destroying a queue, deactivating a queue, and managing queue read/write indices. The HSA runtime defines a routine, **hsa_queue_create**, to allocate a HSA queue; a routine, **hsa_queue_destroy**, to destroy a HSA queue; and a routine, **hsa_queue_inactive**, to change the queue to a non-active state. The difference between inactivate and destroy is that any operation to a destroyed queue is invalid, but to an inactive queue is valid. The read and write indices of a queue cannot be directly exposed to the user code. Instead, the user code can only access the queue read/write indices by using dedicated HSA runtime routines. The HSA runtime defines routines for the combinations of the read/write index operations, including load, store, add, and CAS, and memory orders. For example, **hsa_queue_store_write_index_release** is a routine to assign a given value to the write index with the release memory order (store-write-index-release).

4.2.6 ARCHITECTED QUEUING LANGUAGE

The Architected Queuing Language (AQL) provides a standard binary interface for dispatching agent commands. AQL allows HSA agents to build and enqueue their own command packets, enabling fast, low-power dispatch. AQL also provides support for kernel agent queue submissions. An AQL packet is a user-mode buffer with a specific format that encodes one command. The HSA runtime does not provide any routines to create, destroy, or manipulate AQL packets. Instead, the application uses user-level allocators (e.g., malloc) to create a packet and performs regular memory operation to access the contents of packets. Applications are not required to explicitly reserve storage space for packets, because a queue already contains a command buffer where AQL packets can be written.

In the HSA platform system architecture specification, there are six types of AQL packets:

- Kernel dispatch packet
- Agent dispatch packet
- Barrier-AND packet
- Barrier-OR packet
- Vender-specific packet
- Invalid packet

The HSA runtime uses an enumerator, **hsa_packet_type_t**, to enumerate all types of AQL packets; a data structure, **hsa_kernel_dispatch_packet_t**, to define the format of kernel dispatch packet; a data structure, **hsa_agent_dispatch_packet_t**, to define the format of agent dispatch packet; a data structure, **hsa_barrier_add_packet_t**, to define the format of barrier-AND packet; and a data structure, **hsa_barrier_or_packet_t**, for the format of barrier-OR packet. All packet formats share a common header, **hsa_packet_header_t**, which describes their type, barrier bit (which forces the packet processor to complete packets in order), and other properties. An application uses a kernel dispatch packet to submit a kernel to a kernel agent; it uses an agent dispatch packet to launch built-in functions in a HSA agent.

The barrier-AND packet allows an application to specify up to five signal dependencies and requires the packet processor to resolve those dependencies before proceeding. The packet processor will not launch any further packets in that queue until the barrier-AND packet is complete. A barrier-AND packet is complete when all of the dependent signals have been observed with the value 0 after the barrier-AND packet launched. The barrier-OR packet is similar to the barrier-AND packet, but it becomes complete when the packet processor observes that any of the dependent signals have a value of 0.

The packet format for vendor-specific packets is vendor-defined. The behavior of the packet processor for a vendor-specific packet is implementation-specific, but must not cause a privilege escalation or break out of the process context. The packet format for all queue entries is set to invalid when the queue is initialized. Whenever a queue entry is read, its packet format is set to invalid and the read index of the queue is incremented.

After a packet is submitted, it can be in one of the following five states: *in queue*, *launch*, *active, complete*, or *error*. A packet is in the *in queue* state if the packet processor has not started to parse the packet. A packet is in the *launch* state if the packet is being parsed, but it has not started execution. A packet is in the *active* state if the execution of the packet has started. A packet is in the *complete* state if a memory release fence is applied with the scope indicated by the release fence scope field in the header, and the completion signal (if present) decremented. A packet is in the *error* state if an error was encountered during the launch or active phases. When a packet enters the error state, no further packets will be launched from the queue. The queue cannot be recovered. It can only be deactivated (if it is shared by many processes) or destroyed (if it is not shared by other processes). Figure 4.3 shows the packet state diagram.

The HSA runtime defines two error codes for the launch phase and one for the active phase. For the launch phase, the error code **HSA_STATUS_ERROR_INVALID_PACKET_FORMAT** is used to inform the users that there is a malformed AQL packet. The error code **HSA_STAUS_ERROR_OUT_OF_RESOURCES** is used to inform the users that the system cannot allocate enough resources to the packet. For the active phase, the error code **HSA_STATUS_ERROR_EXECPTION** is used to inform the users that a HSAIL exception has been triggered during the execution of a kernel. Division by zero is an example. There are five types of exception. For more information please see the HSA PRM section on hardware exceptions.

4.2.7 MEMORY

An important functionality of the HSA runtime is to provide memory management services for HSA agents. A HSA memory region (or region for short) represents a block of virtual memory that is directly accessible by a HSA agent. It exposes properties about the block of virtual memory and how it is accessed from that particular HSA agent. A HSA memory region is partitioned into four different segments: global, readonly, group, and private. The HSA runtime defines a region object, **hsa_region_t**, for region declaration, an enumerator, **hsa_region_segment_t**, for all possible segments that a region can be associated with, and an enumerator, **hsa_region_info_t**, for all attributes associated with a region. A region might be associated with more than one agent. The HSA runtime defines a routine, **hsa_agent_iterate_regions**, for an application to inspect the set of regions associated with an agent. It also defines a routine, **hsa_region_get_info**, for an application to get the current value of an attribute of a region.

The global segment is used to store data that is accessible by all HSA agents. Regions associated with the global segment are divided into two categories, fine-grained and coarse-grained. Memory allocated outside of the HSA runtime routines (e.g., the C language **malloc routine**) is considered fine-grained only for those agents in the system that supports the Full profile. If the allocated fine-grained memory via **malloc** is accessed by a kernel agent, the user is encouraged to *register* the corresponding address range beforehand using the HSA runtime routine **hsa_memory_register**. Registering a buffer indicates to the HSA runtime that the memory might be accessed by a kernel agent in the near future. Registration is a performance hint that allows the HSA runtime implementation to know which buffers will be accessed by some of the kernel agents and do the corresponding optimization ahead of time. While kernels running on kernel agents with Full profile support can access any regular host pointer, a registered buffer can result in improved access performance. In agents that only support the Base profile, fine-grained semantics are constrained to buffers allocated using the HSA runtime routine **hsa_memory_allocate**, which is used to allocate memory in global and readonly segments. The user can only use memory allocated from a fine-grained region to pass arguments to a kernel. The fine-grained memory can be accessed by all the HSA agents in the system at the same time (under the terms of the HSA memory model). The coarse-grained memory can also be accessed by many HSA agents, but only one agent at any point in time. The HSA runtime defines a routine, **hsa_memory_assign_agent**, for an application to assign ownership of a buffer to a specific agent explicitly.

The readonly segment is used to store constant information. The content of a readonly buffer can be initialized or changed by using the HSA runtime routine **hsa_memory_copy**. Regions associated with readonly segments are private to kernel agents. Passing a readonly buffer that is associated with one agent in a kernel dispatch packet that is dispatched for execution by a different agent results in undefined behavior. Kernel agents are only permitted to perform read operations on the addresses of variables that reside in their own readonly segments. The contents of readonly segments are persistent throughout the lifetime of applications.

The group segment is used to store information that is shared by all the work-items in the same work-group. A variable in group memory can be read and written by any work-item in the same work-group with which it is associated, but not by work-items in other work-groups or by other agents. Group memory is live during the execution of the work-items in the work-group of the kernel dispatch with which it is associated, and it is uninitialized when the work-group starts execution.

The private segment is used to store information local to a work-item. Private memory is visible only to a single work-item of a kernel dispatch. A variable in private memory can be read and written only by the work-item with which it is associated, but not by any other work-items or agents. Private memory is persistent across the execution of the work-item with which it is associated, and it is uninitialized when the work-item starts execution.

Memory usage in the group and private segments is similar to that of global and readonly segments. Each kernel agent exposes a group region and a private region. However, the user is not allowed to explicitly allocate memory in these regions using **hsa_memory_allocate**, nor can it copy any contents into them using **hsa_memory_copy**. On the other hand, the user must specify the amount of group and private memory that needs to be allocated for a particular execution of a kernel by populating the *group_segment_size* and *private_segment_size* fields in the kernel dispatch packet. The actual allocation of group and private memory happens automatically, before a kernel starts execution.

4.2.8 CODE OBJECTS AND EXECUTABLES

When a kernel dispatch packet is enqueued, a kernel object must be specified. A kernel object is a handle to the machine code to be executed. The creation of a kernel object consists of two phases. In the first phase, the kernel source is compiled or finalized down to a target-machine-specific representation called a code object. In the second phase, the code object is loaded into a HSA runtime object called an executable.

The HSA runtime defines data structures **hsa_code_object_t** and **hsa_executable_t** to represent the code object handle and executable handle, respectively. The kernel object can be obtained by performing queries on the executable object using the HSA runtime routines hsa_executable_get_symbol, **hsa_executable_iterate_symbols**, and **hsa_executable_symbol_get_info**. Figure 4.4 shows the flow of retrieving a kernel object handle from a code object. The flow is composed of the following steps:

1. Code object generation step: In this step, a program is compiled into one or more HSAIL modules that contain kernel to be executed. The HSA runtime provides HSAIL finalization extension routines (this will be discussed in Section 4.3.1) for users to create and finalize HSAIL modules into a target machine code object. In other words, this enables users to create a code object. Code object handles (**hsa_code_object_t**) are target-machine-specific representations that contain the code for a set of kernels and indirect functions. The details of this step will be given in Section 4.3.1.
2. Code object serialization/deserialization step: This step enables the application to read code objects generated in an offline compilation process, or to write out the code objects generated in step 1 for later use. The HSA runtime provides routines, **hsa_code_object_serialize** and **hsa_code_object_deserialize**, for applications to perform code object serialization and deserialization operations, respectively. Each code object is associated with multiple symbols (**hsa_code_symbol_t**), each of which represents a variable, a kernel, or an indirect function in the original source program.
3. Executable handle generation step: In this step, an empty executable handle of type **hsa_executable_t** is created by invoking the HSA runtime routine

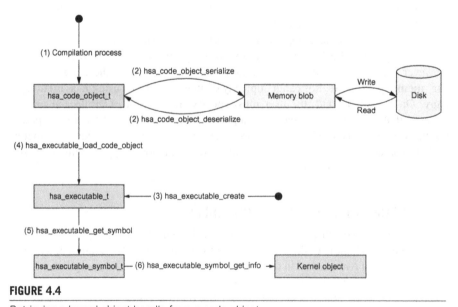

FIGURE 4.4

Retrieving a kernel object handle from a code object.

hsa_executable_create. The HSA runtime will use the executable handle to load a set of code object handles, possibly associated with different target machines, in the next step.

4. Code object load step: In this step, a code object can be added (or loaded) to an executable handle by invoking the HSA runtime routine **hsa_executable_load_code_object**.

5. Retrieve executable symbol step: In this step, the executable symbol corresponding to the given kernel and agent can be retrieved by calling the HSA runtime routine **hsa_executable_get_symbol**. Executable symbols that represent kernels expose the attribute **HSA_EXECUTABLE_SYMBOL_ INFO_KERNEL_OBJECT**, which is a handle to the machine code that is ultimately used to launch a kernel.

6. Retrieve kernel object step: In this step, the kernel object handle associated with an executable symbol can be retrieved by invoking the HSA runtime routine **hsa_executable_symbol_get_info**.

4.3 HSA RUNTIME EXTENSIONS

Although the HSA runtime extension API is not a required part of a compliant implementation, vendors will likely support the HSA-approved extensions. In this section, two HSA-approved extensions, HSAIL finalization and images, will be described in some detail.

4.3.1 HSAIL FINALIZATION

The purpose of HSAIL finalization routines is to finalize a set of HSAIL modules in binary format (BRIG) to a target-machine-specific code during runtime. The target machine code is represented as a code object, as described in Section 4.2.8. Figure 4.4 shows such a finalization flow that consists of the following steps:

1. Source compilation step: In this step, a program is compiled into one or more HSAIL modules. One of the HSAIL modules contains the kernel of interest. This step is performed outside of the HSA runtime. An example of such compilation step for C++ AMP is shown in Chapter 7.

2. HSAIL program handle creation step: In this step, an empty HSAIL program handle with a type of **hsa_ext_program_t** is created by invoking the HSAIL finalization routine **hsa_ext_program_create**.

3. HSAIL module insertion step: In this step, HSAIL modules are added to the HSAIL program handle that was created in step 2 by using the HSAIL finalization routine **hsa_ext_program_add_module**.

4. HSAIL finalization step: After all HSAIL modules are added to the corresponding HSA program handle, the HSAIL program can be finalized by using the HSAIL finalization routine, **hsa_ext_program_finalize**, which creates

a code object handle. The code object handle can be serialized to disk (offline compilation), or further processed in order to launch (online compilation). The further scenario is shown in Figure 4.4 of Section 4.2.8 (Figure 4.5).

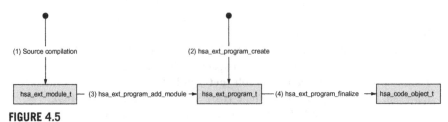

FIGURE 4.5

From source to code object.

4.3.2 IMAGES AND SAMPLERS

Picture image (or image for short) is a feature that shall be optionally provided by the HSA-compliant platform. This feature gives HSA application software the ability to define and use image objects. In the HSA runtime, an image object is defined as an opaque 64-bit image handle (**hsa_ext_image_t**), which can be created and destroyed by the HSA runtime extension routines **hsa_ext_image_create** and **hsa_ext_image_destory**, respectively. The image handle references the image data in memory and stores information about resource layout and other properties. Examples of resource layouts of images were shown in Figure 4.6. Figure 4.6a shows

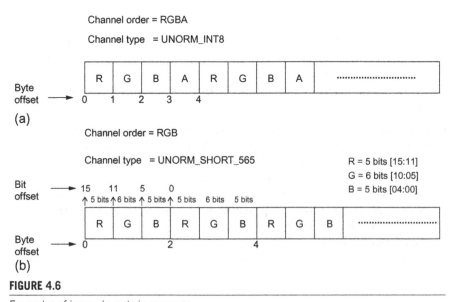

FIGURE 4.6

Examples of image layouts in memory.

an image resource layout with a UNORM_INT_8 (normalized unsigned 8-bit) channel type and RGBA channel order. Figure 4.6b shows an image resource layout with a UNORM_SHORT_565 channel type and RGB channel order. For Figure 4.6a, the value of R, G, B, or A color is represented by one byte (8 bits). For the channel type shown in Figure 4.6b, the value of R, G, or B color is represented by 5, 6, or 5 bits, respectively. HSA decouples the storage of the image data and the description of how to interpret that data. This allows the application to control the location of the image data storage and manage memory more efficiently.

In order to describe an image object, the HSA runtime extension defines an enumerator, **hsa_ext_geometry_t**, for the image dimensions allowed in HSA; a data structure of type **hsa_ext_image_format_t** to represent the image format, which describes channel order (e.g., RGB, sRGBA, ARGB) and channel type (e.g., UNORM_SHORT_565, UNORM_INT8, UNORM_INT16); and a data structure of type **hsa_ext_image_descriptor_t** to describe image dimension, image data size, and image format. The HSA runtime extension provides a routine, **hsa_ext_image_ get_info**, for applications to obtain the specific image data size and image alignment. An application can obtain image format capability through the HSA runtime extension routine **hsa_ext_image_get_capability**. This routine will retrieve the capability defined by **hsa_ext_image_capability_t** for the given combination of geometry and image format. For the image operations, the HSA runtime extension defines routines **hsa_ext_image_export** and **hsa_ext_image_import** to export and import image data with a linear layout in memory. The HSA runtime extension also defines the routine **hsa_ext_image_copy** to copy a portion of an image to another image, and the routine **hsa_ext_image_clear** to clear the image.

As we mentioned before, HSA decouples the storage of the image data and the description of how to interpret that data. A sampler provides the information for image data interpretation. When a sampler handle is created, the coordinate mode, the coordinate addressing mode, and the coordinate filter mode of the sampler must be specified. The sampler coordinate mode specifies whether the image coordinates are normalized or not. The sampler coordinate addressing mode specifies how to process out-of-range image coordinates. The sampler coordinate filter mode specifies how to perform the filtering on image elements (either nearest or linear). With the sampler handle, one can pass the coordinate mode, addressing mode, and filter mode of image data to the kernel. The HSA runtime extension uses a data structure of type, **hsa_ext_sampler_descriptor_t**, to define a sampler; an enumerator, **hsa_ ext_sampler_coordinate_mode_t**, to enumerate the coordinate modes of a sampler; an enumerator, **hsa_ext_sampler_addressing_mode_t**, to enumerate the addressing modes of a sampler; an enumerator, **hsa_ext_sampler_filter_mode_t**, to enumerate the filter modes of a sample; a routine, **hsa_ext_sampler_create**, to create a sampler handle; and a routine, **hsa_ext_sampler destory**, to destroy a sampler handle.

The image handle and the sampler handle is used by the image instructions, such as **rdimage**, **ldimage**, and **stimage**, which are defined in the *HSA Programmer's Reference Manual*. The **rdimage** instruction uses the coordinate, image handle, and the sampler handle to reference the image and load the channel data value, such as

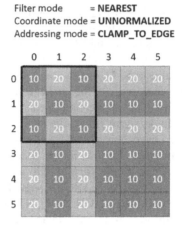

Filter mode   = **NEAREST**
Coordinate mode = **UNNORMALIZED**
Addressing mode = **CLAMP_TO_EDGE**

FIGURE 4.7

An example of image data interpretation using sampler.

Red, Green, Blue, and Alpha, from the referenced image. When the coordinate provided for the **rdimage** is out of bound, the **rdimage** refers the sampler handle and determines how to define the channel data value according to the coordinate mode setting, the coordinate addressing mode setting, and the coordinate filter mode setting. The **ldimage** instruction also uses the image handle to reference the image and load the channel data value. However, the source operand of the **ldimage** instruction does not have the sampler handle. When the coordinate provided for **ldimage** is out of bound, the behavior of the **ldimage** is undefined. The **stimage** instruction uses the image handle, along with the coordinate, to reference the image and store the channel data value back to the image. Because the source operand of the **stimage** instruction does not have the sampler handle, the behavior of the **stimage** is also undefined when the coordinate provided for the **stimage** is out of bound. More specifications related to image instructions can be found in the *HSA Programmer's Reference Manual*.

In Figure 4.7, an example of a sampler interpretation with non-normalized coordinate mode, clamp_to_edge addressing mode, and nearest filter mode is given. In the example, we assume that image boundary (black bold line) is between index 2 and index 3. With the effect of clamp_to_edge addressing mode, the image will repeat the outer edge value (20 or 10) for out of bound coordinates.

4.4 CONCLUSION

In this chapter, we have described some HSA core runtime routines and data types that are designed to support the operations required by the HSA system platform architecture specification and to launch the execution of kernels to the corresponding HSA agents. Some HSA-approved runtime extension routines related to HSAIL finalization and images were also discussed. The purpose of this chapter is to give the reader the conceptual foundation for understanding the HSA runtime APIs. The reader should refer to the HSA runtime specification for details of the core and extension features. Also, HSA vendors are allowed to provide vendor-specific HSA runtime extensions in their systems. The reader is referred to the vendor documentation for details of such vendor-specific extensions. In the github of the HSA Foundation, there is a vector-add example written in C and HSA runtime.

REFERENCES

[1] HSA Platform System Architecture Specification.
[2] HSA Programmer's Reference Manual: HSAIL Virtual ISA and Programming Model, Compiler Writer, and Object Format.
[3] HSA Runtime Programmer's Reference Manual.
[4] J.-H. Ding, B.-C. Jeng, S.-H. Hung, W.-C. Hsu, Y.-C. Chung, HSAemu – a full system emulator for HSA platforms, in: Proceedings of ACM International Conference on Hardware/Software Codesign and System Synthesis (CODES+ISSS), Article 26, 2014.

CHAPTER

HSA Memory Model

L. Howes*, D. Hower†, B.R. Gaster‡

Qualcomm, Santa Clara, CA, USA*; Qualcomm, Raleigh-Durham, NC, USA†; University of the West of England, Bristol, UK‡

5.1 INTRODUCTION

Parallel programming is a notoriously difficult problem. In a parallel shared-memory environment, independent threads of control can race to modify a single location. To ensure that a program behaves in a predictable way, programmers must use synchronization to control those races. A programmer may, for example, use a lock primitive to implement mutual exclusion around a critical section of code.

A "memory consistency model," or just "memory model," defines the ground rules for communication between parallel agents. When those rules are ambiguously defined, or, worse still, entirely absent, a difficult task becomes even harder. In fact, it is generally impossible to write correct, portable code without a well-defined memory model.

To understand the problem more concretely, let's look at a simple example of a critical section. In the syntax, we use {{{ and }}} to bound sequences of operations written in the order the programmer wrote them and | divides sets of operations that occur concurrently.

A simple lock over a shared variable *a* might look like:

```
{{{
    acquire lock;
    temp = a;
    temp = temp + 1;
    a = temp;
    release lock;
}}}
|
{{{
    acquire lock;
    temp = a;
    temp = temp + 1;
    a = temp;
    release lock;
}}}
```

53

In the example, two concurrent tasks increment a. We've broken the increment of a into three operations as a reminder that there are sub-parts to this operation that can be arbitrarily interleaved. The lock is required around a critical section such that only one of the two concurrent tasks is actively incrementing a at any point in time.

Abstractly, such a sequence is relatively simple to understand. However, underneath those lock entities, we have to access memory. So instead, let's use a variable, named "lock," that is stored in memory with an initial value of zero.

```
{{{
    while(compare-and-set(lock, 1)==0);
    temp = a;
    temp = temp + 1;
    a = temp;
    lock = 0;
}}}
|
{{{
    while(compare-and-set(lock, 1) = =0);
    temp = a;
    temp = temp + 1;
    a = temp;
    lock = 0;
}}}
```

In this example, the tasks spin on an atomic update sequence on the lock variable. A task stops spinning when it manages to atomically observe that lock was 0 and then set lock to 1. Otherwise, the task will keep spinning because it is blocked. This is dependent on the update from the first task. At the end of the critical section, we update lock to 0 to release the lock and let the other task continue.

To ensure that this code works correctly, we need to be sure that the update to a has completed before the value of lock returns to zero. Or, to put it another way, the second task has to observe the memory operations in the same order in which the first task intended them. Such ordering guarantees, from one task to another, are provided by a memory consistency model.

While it may seem obvious that any parallel platform should make such ordering guarantees, this is not always the case. For example, neither C nor C++ had well-defined memory models until 2011. Prior to then, implementations relied on compiler-specific or even target-specific operations to order memory. As a result, it was exceptionally difficult to write portable code.

Early heterogeneous programming models have taken a similar path; the first available platforms did not specify a memory model. Early adopters had to rely on knowledge of language and hardware implementations to create code with communications among agents. This target- and implementation-specific approach is clearly impractical when the target is unknown at programming time or compile time, as is the case in portable, standard programming models such as HSA.

For HSA, we define an intermediate layer: a target that a high-level compiler and runtime should use as a portable interface to a range of hardware. In this model, it is vital that this intermediate layer offers a contract to the layers above to guarantee what they can safely do. It is also imperative that implementations of the layer satisfy the requirements they are bound to.

To this end, HSA includes a well-defined, powerful memory model. In the rest of this chapter we'll talk about the features that the HSA memory model offers and why.

5.2 **HSA MEMORY STRUCTURE**

HSA's memory organization will be familiar to anyone who has programmed other heterogeneous programming models that aim for efficient GPU support. It is designed to enable high-performance algorithms with minimal communication to run efficiently, without undue hardware cost or complexity, while enabling powerful memory-ordering guarantees for more demanding algorithms.

The HSA memory organization can be seen as a set of memory regions arranged within a single address space. Each region has slightly different visibility and properties. It is the variation in these policies, combined with some of the memory model features discussed in Section 5.3, that enables tools and hardware to map applications efficiently to the range of target hardware available to HSA toolchains. In addition, multiple segments may use the same address range, yet address entirely separate physical memory locations. The compiler distinguishes between these segments, and hence physical addresses, by the instructions it generates to access the locations.

5.2.1 **SEGMENTS**

HSA's concept of memory is spread over a set of seven different segments. Some of these segments are relevant to developers, and might be exposed in higher-level toolchains such as OpenCL. Others are there to maintain internal information from a high-level compiler, through the HSA Intermediate Language and into the final compiled ISA.

The segments available in HSA are:

- Global
- Readonly
- Group
- Private
- Kernarg
- Spill
- Arg

The first four of these are often directly manipulated by the programmer.

Global represents the large store of memory that is shared across all of the work-items running on a given device, or across multiple devices, depending on the visibility of a particular memory allocation. Readonly is similar, in that it is allocated for shared access across all work-items. The difference is that readonly allocations are, as the name suggests, available only for reading on a device. For the purposes of the implementation, having this information at the intermediate language level is important. This is because some devices are able to use specialized constant buffers to access read-only memory at higher performance or lower power than general caching mechanisms. By exposing this address space as a core HSA feature, compilers may generate special instructions to do so efficiently.

Group memory and private memory have special visibility rules.

A group allocation is shared across work-items in a given work-group and has a lifetime that begins when the work-group is launched and ends when the work-group completes execution. This is similar to the concept of thread-local storage in some traditional programming languages. Group allocations are allowed to map the same virtual addresses to different physical locations in different work-groups, such that an address to group memory that is passed between work-groups may represent either different data or an invalid address when accessed from the other work-group. Thus, the programmer should refrain from passing the address of an object in the group allocation segment from one work-group to another.

Private memory has similar properties to group memory, except that its lifetime and addressability is that of a single work-item. Passing a pointer to a private location between work-items has no defined semantics. Also, the layout of data in the private memory is implementation-dependent to allow flexibility in how private memory is addressed by an implementation. For example, two consecutive private words might be strided in physical memory by the size of an implementation's wavefront to support coalesced vector memory operations to private locations. Private variables may also be easily promoted into registers by the finalizer, because their semantics require them to not be shared. Thus, no further analysis is required.

The final three HSA memory segments are supported to define the underlying ABI of HSA programs compiled to HSAIL.

Kernarg memory represents the set of arguments to a kernel. These are treated as read-only for the execution, and may be copied into separate constant storage by the runtime to make them efficiently visible to all work-items in the dispatch.

Spill memory is a means through which a high-level compiler can allocate into HSAIL registers and communicate with the finalizer any registers that it cannot or does not want to allocate as HSAIL registers. This is done instead spilling them to memory. The finalizer can distinguish between memory operations representing register spills, that are not shared between work-items and that are transient, and other memory operations, which might be shared or have long lifetimes, to optimize the resulting code. Spill memory is not visible through the HSA runtime. For the purposes of memory allocation, it is classified as private memory.

Finally, arg memory represents locations that are used to pass function parameters into called functions. Arg memory communicates to the finalizer that the lifetime of the location is specific to the call/return process and hence allows allocation in various ways depending on the underlying ABI of the device. This is distinct from kernarg memory, in which locations are live throughout a kernel execution.

5.2.2 FLAT ADDRESSING

To ease use, and make the compilation process simpler for high-level languages targeting HSAIL from inputs that do not make address spaces explicit, the HSA memory model supports a flat address space. The flat address space allows addressing of all locations in the global, group, and private address spaces through implementation-defined carved out regions in the address space. We can see this in Figure 5.1. As a result, while the individual address spaces may reuse addresses, such that address 0 in the local address space and address 0 in the global address space map to different locations, the flat address space maps its constituent address spaces into a single 32-bit or 64-bit virtual address space. The benefit of this is that pointers in the high-level language can be reused to map to different segments. Thus, functions may be reused and applied to pointers from any valid segment without change.

Any given operation in the HSAIL code is explicit about what its source address space is. If an operation sources data from the flat address space, then either finalizer-generated conversion operations or hardware must check which sub-range the operation is in and if it is a group or private location. The operations or hardware must then redirect into that segment by subtracting the segment offset if the value is non-null, or converting to the segment-specific null value if it is.

5.2.3 SHARED VIRTUAL ADDRESSING

A core feature of HSA's design is shared virtual memory. The most fundamental part of shared virtual memory is the ability to share virtual addresses between devices. All HSA devices, and the host process, need to be able to pass addresses through

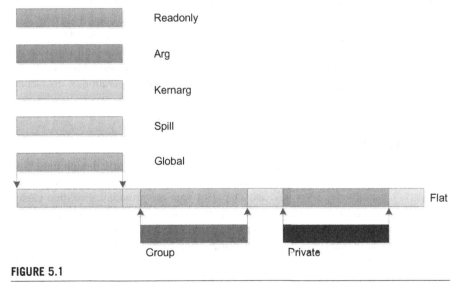

FIGURE 5.1

Segments and flat addressing.

memory. It is necessary for those addresses to be interpreted the same way by all devices in the system. This enables application portability, flexibility, and ease of data structure implementation. Through the avoidance of copies and layout changes, it also increases efficiency.

Sharing virtual addresses allows data structures containing pointers to be passed between HSA devices. It also allows pointers to be stored in memory, without needing to be converted to buffer offsets.

Sharing virtual addresses does not necessarily require memory consistency. However, the transition from data structures containing pointers to data structures containing pointers that can be updated directly is a small step that is discussed in Section 5.3. This step renders modifications immediately visible to other devices.

Even without consistency, sharing virtual addresses can lead to performance benefits. In earlier systems, without the ability to use the same virtual addresses between devices, memory might change address when passed to a device. A memory allocation made on the host CPU would be copied to a GPU's discrete memory. Not only would the physical location change, but the virtual address range referred to might change as well. Any stored pointers referring to locations in this allocation would no longer be valid.

To work around this, pointers were converted to offsets within a single memory allocation. The resulting base + offset addressing scheme could only easily point to a single allocation. This meant that significant restructuring of an application, and possibly significant runtime rearrangement of data, was necessary to massage the data structures into a form that was valid on both the host and accelerator device. Sharing virtual addresses allows that code to become simpler, necessitating fewer data transformations.

In HSA virtual addresses are either 32 bits or 64 bits (only 48 bits are usable) in size, depending on the memory model of the platform and of the compiled code. It is required that the address space of HSA devices matches that of the host. In addition, parts of the virtual address space are carved out by the HSA system software to represent flat addresses into private or group memory on HSA devices. Virtual memory must also satisfy the usual protection mechanisms to ensure separation of data from different processes.

5.2.4 OWNERSHIP

HSA devices in the full profile have access to all system memory, though the HSA runtime software provides allocators that can create memory regions that are more efficiently accessible by HSA devices. The HSA runtime provides allocation capabilities to control regions of memory that can be shared with HSA devices, and this is all that is required to be supported by base profile HSA devices.

Some of these runtime-controlled allocations may be allocated in coarse-grained form. Coarse-grained allocations are memory allocations with shared virtual addressing, but no requirement for coherence. They exist for two primary reasons.

1. The first is that discrete accelerators still exist, even in a world of shared virtual memory and fully controlled memory consistency. On such devices, making every operation consistent across the set of devices may be prohibitively expensive, as the device may be connected to the host via a very low bandwidth or high latency interconnect.
2. The second is to reduce power consumption. HSA is expected to be supported by devices in a range of market segments, from HPC in the high end to mobile and embedded devices in the low end. On very low power devices, memory consistency becomes expensive, even for on-chip accelerators. The additional probe or cache flush traffic of a fine-grained memory consistency system consumes power.

To support these optimizations, coarse-grained memory allows consistency to be restricted to a particular device for some period of time. We call this bounding ownership. Address ranges in the global segment may be bound to a particular device for a period of time. In this case, they are controlled through runtime API calls such that only that device may access the address range. These calls offer the opportunity for driver control to update the virtual memory system, switch off coherence at a page level, migrate data to new physical locations, and update the virtual memory mapping or some combination of these. When an address range is owned by a given device, its memory consistency properties change. This is discussed in Section 5.4.2.

5.2.5 IMAGE MEMORY

The final memory component of HSA's memory model is the image. Images occupy a slightly strange position. They do not fit in the core coherent shared virtual memory model of HSA, and, hence, are not required to be supported by HSA platforms and devices. However, images are a fundamental part of the performance of GPUs, due to the sophisticated filtering, boundary conditions, and compression afforded by fixed-function image hardware. Images are particularly important when an HSA kernel is running on a GPU device and passing data to, or consuming data from, a rendering job written in OpenGL, DirectX, or another related API. These APIs use images or textures as fundamental building blocks.

Image data should be viewed as independent of the other fundamentals of the HSA memory model, excepting that visibility is controlled by fence packets in the HSA queues and runtime API calls.

5.3 HSA MEMORY CONSISTENCY BASICS

HSA has a well-defined memory consistency model that describes the semantics of memory operations in the shared virtual address space. The HSA memory consistency model defines the values that may be observed by load operations, given an HSA program and an input. It is a contract between the program and the system that shows how to write correct HSA programs, how to implement correct finalizer optimizations, and how to build correct HSA-compliant hardware.

There are two equally valid views of the HSA memory consistency model. First, there is a simplified view that only considers the "sequentially consistent" executions (defined below) of an HSA program. This simplified view is the focus of this section, and is the only understanding that a majority of HSA users will need. Second, one can also view the memory consistency model as a complex combination of partial orders in an execution. This more complex view, covered lightly in Section 5.4, is necessary to understand the semantics of HSA "relaxed atomic" operations that may improve performance and/or reduce execution energy in limited circumstances. In the absence of relaxed atomics, the two views are provably equivalent [1].

In the remainder of this section, we will gradually introduce features of the HSA memory model. First, we give the necessary background on sequential consistency and race-free memory models, as HSA builds upon both concepts. Second, we describe the HSA memory model in the simple case when only a single "memory scope" is applied to all synchronization. Memory scopes are features of heterogeneous platforms like HSA that limit the overhead of synchronization in certain circumstances. Finally, we show how programmers can use memory scopes to improve the performance and/or reduce the energy of an HSA execution. We focus in particular on how to write correct programs that use synchronization with different memory scopes.

5.3.1 BACKGROUND: SEQUENTIAL CONSISTENCY

Most memory consistency models, HSA included, preserve sequential semantics within a single unit of execution, thread, or agent. If memory operation (load, store, or read-modify-write) O_1 occurs before memory operation O_2 on agent A, then the effect of O_1 will be visible to O_2. However, memory models vary considerably in how they allow memory operations from different units of executions to interleave with one another. The most intuitive of these models is called sequential consistency.

Sequential consistency guarantees that there is a single, globally observable, interleaving of loads, stores, and read-modify-write operations in any valid execution. It gets its name because it appears as though the entire program is executed by a simple, in-order, sequential processor that multitasks among available threads. Figure 5.2 shows the sequentially consistent executions of a simple concurrent program.

While sequential consistency is intuitive for programmers, it can also limit the optimizations that hardware and/or a compiler can perform. For example, hardware write buffers that coalesce store operations, a common component in graphics processors, could cause the non-sequentially consistent result in Figure 5.2. Because of the limitations, most platforms, including HSA, specify a model weaker than sequential consistency.

5.3.2 BACKGROUND: CONFLICTS AND RACES

In an execution, two memory operations, let's call them C_1 and C_2, "conflict" if they access the same location, and at least one is a write. If C_1 and C_2 are from different threads, then we say that C_1 and C_2 "race," because we cannot always tell whether C_1

```
        Initially,global locations A = B = 0
          {{{
    i1:   A = 1;
    i2:   R1 = B;
          }}}|
          {{{
    i3:   B = 1;
    i4:   R2 = A;
          }}}
```

Valid sequentially consistent outcomes:

R1	R2	Example Instruction Execution Order
1	1	$i1 \rightarrow i3 \rightarrow i2 \rightarrow i4$
0	1	$i1 \rightarrow i2 \rightarrow i3 \rightarrow i4$
1	0	$i3 \rightarrow i4 \rightarrow i1 \rightarrow i2$

A non-sequentially consistent outcome:

R1	R2	Example Instruction Execution Order
0	0	Single order does not exist

FIGURE 5.2

The result R1 = R2 = 0 is not allowed in any sequentially consistent execution of this program.

or C_2 will occur first. For example, in the following program, we cannot say for sure if location A will be 1 or 2 when the program completes because we do not know how the threads will appear to interleave.

```
{{{
A = 1;
}}}
|
{{{
A = 2;
}}}
```

Races can be classified based on whether or not they are "synchronized." A "memory race" occurs when conflicts have been synchronized (e.g., they occur in a critical section protected by a lock). Memory races are typically benign, because the synchronization will ensure they always execute in the correct order. A "synchronization race" occurs when the conflicting operations are part of a synchronization primitive (e.g., the compare-and-set that implements a lock above). Synchronization races are also benign, because they are designed to enforce an order of the operations they protect.

A "data race" occurs when conflicts have not been synchronized and are not part of a synchronization primitive. Data races are often harmful and unintentional in a program, because they lead to unpredictable behavior.

We say an execution is "data-race-free," if it does not contain any data races. We say that a program is data-race-free if all executions of that program are data-race-free. The data-race-free classification is important for the HSA memory model, as it joins a growing list of platforms, including C++, Java, and OpenCL, that define memory consistency in terms of data-race-free executions.

5.3.3 THE HSA MEMORY MODEL FOR A SINGLE MEMORY SCOPE

The HSA consistency model describes how to write a data-race-free HSA programs and then guarantees that any data-race-free program will result in a sequentially consistent execution. This is the fundamental tenant of the HSA memory model, so we will state it again. **The execution of any data-race-free HSA program will appear sequentially consistent.**[1] Furthermore, the execution of any HSA program with a race is undefined.

A race-free memory model framework has several advantages. From a user perspective, programmers can reason in terms of sequential consistency, which most find intuitive. At the same time, because any program containing a race will have an undefined execution, HSA implementations have plenty of optimization opportunities (such as the write buffer described above).

Because the memory model only defines the behavior of data-race-free HSA programs, we must be able to precisely define a data race to write correct programs. To avoid data races, we must ensure that a program has sufficient synchronization. For a basic understanding, we can say that conflicts in a sequentially consistent execution are synchronized, if HSA synchronization (described in the following) appears between the conflicting operations in the observed sequentially consistent order of operations. However, there are some nuances in that definition, and we will spend the next several subsections making that informal description more precise.

5.3.3.1 HSA synchronization operations

In HSA, synchronization happens through atomic memory operations. Synchronization protects non-atomic, or ordinary, memory operations. An HSA atomic is a load, store, or read-modify-write[2] that is qualified as an atomic type with a particular `semantic, memory scope, and segment`. We discuss the atomic semantics next and cover memory scopes and segments later in Sections 5.3.4 and 5.3.5 Until those sections, we will assume examples only use locations from the global segment with system-wide scope visibility.

An HSA atomic can have release, acquire, or `acquire-release`[3,4] semantics. All atomics have side effects that impact how other instructions in the same instruction stream as the atomic appear to other threads. The specifics of those side effects are controlled through the atomic semantics.

---

[1] A sequentially consistent execution is only guaranteed when the program does not contain relaxed atomics. This is an advanced feature of the model that we do not cover in this section.

[2] HSA also supports memory fence operations that have no associated location. However, because fences only have a tangible benefit when combined with relaxed atomics, we defer that discussion until Section 5.4.

[3] For those familiar with C++11 terminology, HSA uses release and acquire differently. An HSA {release, acquire, acquire-release} is analogous to a C++ atomic {`store, load, read-modify-write`} with `seq_cst` memory order. HSA does not support any operation with the same semantics as a C++ atomic with release/acquire memory order.

[4] There is also a relaxed semantic, but because it can result in a non-sequentially consistent execution, we defer that discussion until Section 5.4.

Generally, an atomic with `release` semantics ensures that any operation prior to the atomic is visible to other threads before the atomic completes. In other words, a release prevents an earlier operation, prior to the atomic in program order, from reordering after the atomic (e.g., that may otherwise occur due to a compiler optimization). A release operation should be performed whenever a programmer wants to make a local update visible throughout the system (e.g., as part of an unlock that publishes an update to a data structure).

Acquire is the opposite of release—an atomic with acquire semantics ensures that any operation following the atomic is visible to other threads after the atomic completes. An acquire prevents a later operation after the atomic in program order from reordering before the atomic. An acquire operation should be performed before consuming any updates produced by another thread (e.g., as part of a lock).

An atomic with `acquire-release` semantics behaves like both an acquire and a release, and prohibits any local operation from reordering around the atomic in either direction. For the remainder of this chapter, we will use a "release" to refer to an atomic with `release` or `acquire-release` semantics and an "acquire" to refer to an atomic with acquire or acquire-release semantics.

While the descriptions of the semantics above are helpful, they are not as precise as we would like. The HSA memory model formally defines what has to happen to before two work-items or threads are synchronized. We still need some more background before we can provide a full definition, but we can take a step by introducing the concept of paired release/acquires.

To synchronize ordinary operations from two agents, an atomic with release semantics must be observed by an atomic with `acquire` semantics. According to the memory model, neither the release nor the acquire has any side effect before that observation occurs. It is legal, for example, for an implementation to delay any side effects associated with a release until the moment that the release is observed by an acquire, rather than the moment the release appears to complete locally.

A release can be observed directly if the atomic with `acquire` semantics observes a value produced by the atomic with release semantics. We show a direct observation in Figure 5.3. In any execution, we know that all operations in the Group X1 region are synchronized with operations in the Group Y2 region because the acquire by agent Y will have observed the release by agent X. Operations from Group X2 and Group Y1 are not synchronized. If any ordinary operation in Group X2 or Group Y1 conflicts with another operation from any other group, then this program will contain a race and will result in an unpredictable execution.

5.3.3.2 Transitive synchronization through different addresses
Synchronization in HSA is transitive. If A synchronizes with B and B synchronizes with C, then A is considered to be synchronized with C. We show this in Figure 5.4. In the example program, agents X and Z never directly synchronize through the same atomic location, but because both synchronize with intermediate agent Y, the store and load to *A* does not form a race.

```
                          Initially, global location L = 0
{{{Agent X
    /* Group X1 operations are synchronized with Group Y2 */
    {Group X1}
    atomic_store( L = 1, release )
    {Group X2}
}}} |
{{{Agent Y
    {Group Y1}
    while (atomic_load( L, acquire ) == 0) { /* spin */ }
    /* Group Y2 operations are synchronized with Group Y1 */
    {Group Y2}
}}}
```

FIGURE 5.3

In any execution of this program, all operations in Group X1 are synchronized with all operations in Group Y2. Operations in Group X2 are not synchronized with any operations from agent Y. Operations in Group Y1 are not synchronized with any operations from agent X.

```
                    Initially, global locations A = B = L1 = L2 = 0
{{{ Agent X
    A = 1;
    atomic_store(L1 = 1, release);
}}} |
{{{ Agent B
    while (! atomic_load(L1, acquire)) { /* spin /* };
    B = A+ 1;
    atomic_store(L2, release);
}}} |
{{{ Agent C
    while (! atomic_load(L2, acquire)) { /* spin */ };
    R1 = A;
    R2 = B;
}}}
```

FIGURE 5.4

Transitive synchronization: at the end of this data-race-free program register R1=1 and register R2=2.

Transitive synchronization meets programmers basic intuition on communication. In the example of Figure 5.4, Agent Y produces a result that is dependent on information from Agent X. It would be strange indeed if Z could observe the information from Y that depends on X but could not observe X itself.

5.3.3.3 Finding a race

An HSA program has a race if *any* sequentially consistent execution of that program contains a race. To determine if a program is race-free, programmers must decide that all possible sequentially consistent executions are race-free. It is impossible to exhaustively consider all possible sequentially consistent executions for any non-trivial program. However, in practice, the problem can be managed by identifying program regions where conflicts occur and then ensuring that those conflicts will always be synchronized.

For example, let us revisit the program in Figure 5.2. There is clearly a conflict in that program; both agents read and write both locations. If those reads and writes are ordinary, the program has no synchronization, and therefore the program contains a race. When run on an HSA system, the result would be undefined. If, however, those reads and writes use atomic operations, the conflicting operations do not race (by definition), and so the program is race-free. We cannot say exactly what the result will be at the end, but we know it will be one of the three sequentially consistent executions.

If we assume the program in Figure 5.3 contains many ordinary reads and writes in Groups A1, A2, B1, and B2, then it would represent a program that is difficult to analyze by exhaustively considering the sequentially consistent executions. However, we can easily determine whether the program has a race by looking at the groups as a whole. Groups A1 and B2 are synchronized, so even if they have conflicting operations, there is no race. Groups A2 and B1 are not synchronized, so we only need to determine if any operation in Group A2 or B1 conflicts with any operation from another group. If the answer is no, then we can be confident the program is race-free.

5.3.4 HSA MEMORY MODEL USING MEMORY SCOPES

The HSA memory model includes a concept called "memory scopes," "synchronization scopes," or just "scopes." Every HSA atomic operation specifies a scope. That scope limits the visibility of the atomic operation and its side effects to a subset of work-items or host threads in the system. On many HSA devices, especially GPUs, scopes help programmers write fast and efficient synchronization through shared virtual memory. Before elaborating more on how programmers can use scopes, we will first say a little more on why scopes exist.

5.3.4.1 Scope motivation

Traditionally, shared memory CPU systems have been designed for low-latency, all-to-all communication. Such systems implement coherence protocols that ensure that updates from a unit of execution are automatically propagated to all other work-items or host threads in the system. As a result, synchronization is lightweight. On a high-performance x86 system, for example, an all-to-all synchronization operation only requires flushing a few small internal buffers.

On the other hand, GPUs and other devices targeted by HSA are designed primarily for throughput. Many implementations of GPUs do not have a CPU-style coherence protocol, because of the belief that it would lower throughput. Instead, such devices synchronize through heavyweight cache maintenance operations like flush and invalidate.

A particularly observant reader may wonder which specific caches in the system are flushed and invalidated. After all, in an HSA system, there may be multiple levels (L1, L2, etc.) of cache and multiple instances within a level (e.g., each compute unit has an L1). If the system is unaware of which actors are synchronizing, it must assume the worst-case and flush/invalidate all caches that could be holding stale data. However, the system could reduce the amount of maintenance operations if knew where the synchronizing entities execute in the system. For example, if synchronizing work-items share an L1 cache during execution, then a cache flush/invalidate may be unnecessary when those two work-items synchronize with each other. This fact is the very reason that scopes exist.

Specific implementations of memory scopes will vary, but in general, it is less costly to synchronize work-items or host threads that are closer to each other in the HSA execution hierarchy. It will be faster to synchronize two work-items in the same work-group than two work-items in the same agent but different work-groups. For example, the former may only involve a flush of small internal buffers, similar to a CPU synchronization, while the latter may involve at least a flush and invalidate of L1 caches.

5.3.4.2 HSA scopes

The scope of an atomic is an indication from the programmer that the atomic will only be observed by a subset of work-items or host threads in an execution. For good performance and low power, HSA programs should specify the smallest scope possible. However, care should be taken. If the programmer specifies a smaller scope than the set of work-items or threads that actually observe the atomic or its side effects during execution, then that program contains a data race. We will more precisely define the HSA notion of a race due to incorrect scope below, but first we must discuss the particular scopes defined by HSA and the distinction between scopes and scope instances.

HSA defines five scopes: work-item, wave-front, work-group, agent, and system. These scopes closely mimic the hierarchy of the HSA execution model and are strictly ordered; work-item scope is smaller than wave-front scope, which is smaller than work-group scope, etc. During execution, each static scope name corresponds to exactly one dynamic "scope instance" that corresponds to a particular set of work-items or threads in the execution. We show how scopes map to scope instances during an execution in Figure 5.5.

If every atomic in the program specifies the system scope, then there can be no races that are caused by insufficient scope. Such a program corresponds to the initial description of the HSA memory model that has been discussed until now, as well as languages like C++ aimed at homogeneous CPU targets.

Atomic's Scope	Scope Instance
Work-item	The single work-item performing the atomic
Wave-front	The set of all work-items in the same wave-front as the work-item performing the atomic
Work-group	The set of work-items in the same work-group as the work-item performing the atomic
Agent	The set of work-items in the same agent (i.e., device) as the work-item performing the atomic
System	The set of all work-items and threads in the HSA system

FIGURE 5.5

Scope to scope instance mapping.

5.3.4.3 Using smaller scopes

With the addition of scopes, programmers are faced with the additional choice of which scope to use with synchronizing atomic operations. For the best performance, they should strive to use the smallest scope that still results in race-free executions. We still are not quite ready to define HSA race freedom in the fullest sense, but we can for the simple and common case where all atomics involved in a synchronization specify the same scope. Let's call this case "direct scope synchronization."

To avoid a race with direct scope synchronization, the specified scope instance of an atomic should include all of the work-items and host threads participating in the synchronization. For the best performance, that scope instance should be the smallest possible scope instance.

In Figure 5.6 we show an example of direct scope synchronization involving two work-items. If both work-items, w1 and w2, belong to the same work-group, then both atomic operations specify the same work-group scope instance, and that scope instance includes both work-items. Therefore, we know that this program is race-free. If we assume that w1 and w2 are not in the same wavefront, then the specified work-group scope instance is also the smallest possible scope instance that would still include both w1 and w2.

However, if work-items w1 and w2 belong to different work-groups, then the scope instances specified by the atomics are also different. In this case, neither atomic scope instance contains both w1 and w2. Thus, the program contains a race, and the behavior of the program will be unpredictable.

Direct scope synchronization is a powerful tool to improve the performance of HSA programs. It also is a good match for highly regular, data parallel applications that are commonly run on heterogeneous components like GPUs. However, it can be limiting in the forward-looking systems that HSA targets, because of the restriction that all atomics specify the same scope instance. For that reason, HSA provides two race-free ways to use atomics that specify different scope instances. The first is called "inclusive scope synchronization" and the second is called "transitive scope synchronization."

```
                    Initially, global locations A = L = 0
{{{ work-item w1
   A = 1;
   atomic_store(L = 1, release, work-group);
}}} |
{{{ work-item w2
   while (! atomic_load(L, acquire, work-group)) { /* spin /* };
   R1 = A;
}}}
```

FIGURE 5.6

Direct scope synchronization. This program is race-free when w1 and w2 are in the same work-group.

Scope inclusion

Work-items or threads can synchronize through atomics without causing a race as long as each atomic specifies a scope instance that contains both of the synchronizing actors. When the two scope instances are not identical, we call this scope inclusion. It is so named because, if the two scope instances are not identical, then one must be included in the other due to the strict hierarchy of scope instances defined by HSA. For example, if one atomic specifies work-group scope and the other specifies system scope, then the former scope instance is completely included in the latter scope instance when both are executed by work-items in the same work-group.

We show an example of scope inclusion in Figure 5.7. In this example, if work-items w1 and w2 belong to the same work-group, then the atomics specify inclusive scope instances that contain both w1 and w2. The atomic from work-item w1 specifies the shared work-group of w1 and w2, while the atomic from work-item w2 specifies all work-items and threads in the system. If, on the other hand, w1 and w2 are in different work-groups, then the scope instances are not inclusive. In that case, the scope instance from the w1 atomic does not contain w2.

Scope transitivity

In HSA, synchronization is always transitive. We have already seen an example of this transitivity through different atomic locations, but the principle also extends to different atomics scopes. As a result, it is possible for work-items or threads to synchronize without causing a race, even if they use atomics with non-inclusive scope instances.

In Figure 5.8, if work-items w1 and w2 belong to the same work-group, but work-item w3 belongs to a different work-group. Then the example shows synchronization through scope transitivity. In that case, work-item w3 will observe the update to A by work-item w1 even though work-item w1 uses an atomic scope instance that does not include w3. Work-item w2 forms the bridge between the two by synchronizing in work-group scope between w1 and w2 and system scope between w2 and w3. In effect, work-item w2's release synchronizes all updates from w2 itself, as well as all updates previously synchronized with w2 from a different work-item or thread.

```
                 Initially, global locations A = L = 0
{{{ work-item w1
   A = 1;
   atomic_store(L = 1, release, work-group);
}}} |
{{{ work-item w2
   while (! atomic_load(L, acquire, system)) { /* spin /* };
   R1 = A;
}}}
```

FIGURE 5.7

Inclusive synchronization.

```
                    Initially, global locations A = B = L1 = L2 = 0
{{{ work-item w1
   A = 1;
   atomic_store(L1 = 1, release, work-group);
}}} |
{{{ work-item w2
   while (! atomic_load(L1, acquire, work-group)) { /* spin /* };
   B = 1;
   atomic_store(L2 = 1, release, system);
}}} |
{{{ work-item w3
   while (! atomic_load(L2, acquire, system)) { /* spin /* };
   R1 = A;
   B = 1;
}}}
```

FIGURE 5.8

Transitive scope synchronization.

5.3.5 MEMORY SEGMENTS

In general, HSA atomics are indifferent to the HSA memory segments. An atomic release-acquire pair will synchronize all memory segments in shared virtual memory regardless of where the atomic is located. For example, in Figure 5.9 we show a race-free HSA program where two atomics operate on locations in group memory but synchronize ordinary loads and stores to global memory.

Some atomic segment/scope combinations simply do not make sense. For example, it does not make sense for an atomic to specify group segment and system scope. The group segment is only visible among work-items in a work-group, so there is no actor in the system outside of the work-group that could possible observe that atomic. For that reason, a group atomic can specify a scope less than or equal to work-group, but any scope specification larger than work-group will be implicitly downgraded to work-group.

```
                   Initially, global location A = 0, group location L = 0
{{{ work-item w1
   A = 1;
   atomic_store(L = 1, release, work-group);
}}} |
{{{ work-item w2
   while (! atomic_load(L, acquire, work-group)) { /* spin /* };
   R1 = A;
}}}
```

FIGURE 5.9

HSA atomics synchronize all segments.

5.3.6 PUTTING IT ALL TOGETHER: HSA RACE FREEDOM

With the background on scopes and segments, we can now more precisely define a race-free HSA program. We will do so twice—once for programs that follow two simplifying rules of thumb and once, more generally, for all programs.

5.3.6.1 Simplified definition of HSA race freedom

There are two rules of thumb that can help simplify a HSA race freedom analysis:

- Always apply the same scope to an atomic variable (for example, do not perform a work-group scope release on atomic A and later perform a system scope acquire on A).
- Release/acquire to/from the smallest scope instance that includes all units of execution *directly* involved in a synchronization (i.e., ignoring transitivity). Because HSA supports transitive synchronization, you do not need to consider which units of execution may *eventually* see a conflict because of communication by an intermediate party.

If you apply those two rules of thumb, then determining race freedom in HSA is largely equivalent to determining race freedom in a homogeneous platform such as C++. In particular, a program is race-free if ordinary conflicts can never appear back-to-back in some sequentially consistent total order of execution. In other words, always make sure ordinary conflicts are separated by synchronization.

Without the simplifying rules of thumb, a precise definition is more complex to describe. Without the first rule of thumb, it is actually possible for two atomic operations to become conflicts; without the second, we must apply a more complex analysis to determine proper synchronization.

5.3.6.2 General definition of HSA race freedom

To develop the general definition of race freedom, we must extend the initial definition of a conflict given in Section 5.3.2. In HSA, a conflict is either ordinary or atomic:

- **Ordinary Conflict** describes two operations to the same location. At least one is a write or a read-modify-write, and at least one is an ordinary operation.
- **Atomic Conflict** describes two atomic operations from different units of execution to the same location. At least one is a write or read-modify-write, and they specify non-inclusive scope instances.

A sequentially consistent execution of a HSA program is race-free, if and only if all conflicts are separated by a transitive chain of inclusive atomic synchronization. A HSA program is race-free overall, if and only if all sequentially consistent executions of that program are race-free.

Let's say you are examining whether or not a sequentially consistent execution of a HSA program contains a race. You observe that there are two ordinary operations that form a conflict, C_1 and C_2, executed by different units U_1 and U_2, respectively.

For simplicity, let's assume C_1 comes before C_2 in the total order of all operations that must exist, because the execution is sequentially consistent. To be race-free, those conflicts must be separated by synchronization with sufficient scope. More specifically, there must exist an atomic with release semantics, R, executed by U_1 after C_1, and an atomic with acquire semantics, A, executed by U_2 before C_2. This must be such that either (i) R and A specify inclusive scope instances, and R comes before A in the total order of execution (as in Figure 5.6 or Figure 5.7); or (ii) there is a chain of atomic release-acquire pairs with inclusive scope instances in the total order of execution that begins with R and ends with A, and where every link in the chain consists of an acquire followed by a release on the same unit of execution (as in Figure 5.8).

The general precise definition can be difficult to understand even before considering the complex relaxed atomic operations that we will discuss later.

5.3.7 ADDITIONAL OBSERVATIONS AND CONSIDERATIONS

There are several minor points and subtleties of the HSA memory model that we discuss in this section.

In HSA, atomic operations cannot partially overlap. For example, it is a race in HSA if a 32-bit atomic writes to address A in one unit of execution, and a 64-bit atomic reads from address A in another unit of execution. Partial overlap is allowed for ordinary memory operations, with the caveat that any such overlap constitutes a race if unordered according to the memory model rules.

Note that, unlike homogeneous CPU race-free models, it is not sufficient to simply say an execution is race-free if conflicts are separated by atomics. Rather, those atomics must also correctly use scopes (i.e., specify inclusive scope instances). In fact, in HSA, it is possible for the atomics themselves to conflict if they specify non-inclusive scope. This leads to the unusual (from the homogeneous computing perspective) consequence that a program composed entirely of atomic operations could contain a race. This is a common point of surprise to those familiar with the homogeneous memory models.

In HSA, programs with races will exhibit unpredictable behavior. However, the HSA specification does at least require that certain catastrophic failures, such as a spontaneous privilege level increase, will not occur. This way users can be sure that buggy or poorly written software is generally safe to run, in the sense that it will not spontaneously gain access to the operating system or cause the hardware to catch fire.

5.4 ADVANCED CONSISTENCY IN THE HSA MEMORY MODEL

The HSA memory model extends the basic sequentially consistent race-free model in two further directions. The first is to add relaxed atomics and fences, which will be somewhat familiar to people used to the C++11 model. In addition, it supports coarse-grained memory regions, where coherence may be restricted, as mentioned earlier in Section 5.2.4.

5.4.1 **RELAXED ATOMICS**

The HSA memory model also defines *relaxed atomics* and *fences*. Relaxed atomics differ from other atomics in two ways. First, relaxed atomics have no synchronization side effects. In other words, they cannot, on their own, force the visibility of ordinary loads or stores in the system. Second, relaxed atomics are not guaranteed to be sequentially consistent, even with respect to each other. This second property makes relaxed atomics exceptionally difficult to reason about.

Relaxed atomics are useful in situations where a program needs read-modify-write semantics, but is not attempting to synchronize work-items or threads. Program statistics for profiling are a common example of such a situation. If a user is interested in the total number of times any work-item calls function f(), then she might atomically increment a counter variable using a relaxed atomic at the beginning of f(). Notably, in this situation, the variable is not used to determine causality among work-items; the user is ambivalent to the order in which the work-items increment the variable.

Relaxed atomics can also be used to establish causality among threads. Doing so can be an extremely difficult task, because the basic sequentially consistent view of HSA is no longer valid. However, there may be performance benefits to using relaxed atomics. For example, a relaxed atomic load operation can be performed repeatedly at relatively low cost, while ordering all memory accesses on the system may come at a significantly higher cost.

To ensure correctness, users must reason about the behavior of the program through a set of operation orders that must exist in any race-free HSA execution. These orders also exist in programs without relaxed atomics. They have not been previously mentioned, as each is a subset of the total sequentially consistent order that must exist in any race-free execution of such a program. There are two notable orders:

• There is a total, coherent order of all loads, stores, and read-modify-write updates to a single location.
• There is a total, sequentially consistent order of all release, acquire, and acquire-release atomics.

From these orders, users must then reason about a formal "happens-before" relation to determine if two conflicting operations in a HSA execution race. This is a nontrivial exercise outside the purview of this book. We refer interested readers to the HSA system architecture specification for details.

Relaxed atomics do not synchronize ordinary loads and stores. In programs that use relaxed atomics, one must add fence operations to establish ordering relationships between the relaxed atomic operations and ordinary loads and stores. Relaxed atomics and fences have a special relationship. In fact, when using a relaxed atomic and a fence as a simple pair, one can think of them as the two parts of a standard atomic. A relaxed atomic corresponds to the part of a standard atomic that operates on a single atomic variable. A fence corresponds to the side effects of the standard atomic that synchronize ordinary loads and stores. Unlike atomics, fences are not associated with any particular location.

```
              Initially, group location A = 0, group location L = 0
{{{ work-item w1
    A = 1;
    atomic_store(L = 1, release, work-group);
}}} |
{{{ work-item w2
    while (! atomic_load(L, relaxed, work-group)) { /* spin /* };
    fence(acquire, work-group);
    R1 = A;
}}}
```

FIGURE 5.10

Using relaxed atomics and fences to reduce the cost of synchronization.

By splitting the relaxed atomics and fences, programmers can independently determine causality and enforce synchronization. Doing so could lead to higher performing programs when the check for causality may not always lead to synchronization (for example, when querying a trylock). In such cases, a relaxed atomic may be queried multiple times before success, at which point synchronization becomes necessary.

Take Figure 5.10 as an example. Here we perform a standard atomic store release in one work-item. We only perform this operation once, as we need to order it after the store to A, so this is an appropriate operation. In the second work-item, we have in earlier examples (such as Figure 5.9) used an acquire operation in the loop. Here, instead, we replace the acquire with a relaxed load. Each load no longer has to order all memory operations and thus can be performed at a lower cost. The only order that must be maintained is the order of the relaxed operations to location L, because there is a single coherent order to a single location.

To order the atomic load with respect to the load of A we insert a fence. It is at this fence that full synchronization occurs, which may be higher cost. As a result, if the loop spins through multiple iterations, each iteration has a relatively low cost to the memory system compared with the loop in Figure 5.9.

Because relaxed atomics are used to determine when fences should occur, relaxed atomics will always appear to occur in program order with respect to fences. This has the effect that fences have a stronger ordering property with respect to relaxed atomics than they do with normal operations. While normal operations may only be blocked from moving through a fence in one direction, they can move in the other direction. They may, for example, be able to move up through a release fence, but not down past it. Relaxed atomics are unable to move in either direction through a fence.

5.4.2 OWNERSHIP AND SCOPE BOUNDING

In Section 5.2.4, we introduced ownership. Ownership is a means by which a memory region, marked as coarse-grained, may be passed to a given agent for use by that component for the duration of the period of ownership.

This plays with the rest of the model in two ways:

- System scope atomic operations within an owned region are implicitly downgraded to device scope.
- Accesses to an addressable region that is not owned is a race.

The first point is similar to the behavior of accesses to local memory locations. Any access at a wider scope than makes sense will be implicitly bounded. In particular, consider how memory on a physically disconnected device might be used. Coarse-grained memory would allow copying of data into that memory, and copying it out at the end. During execution, it is simply impossible to make it visible to other devices in the system, so here we see a physical manifestation of the concept of bounding the scope to some limit. However, bounding the scope of atomic operations alone does not guarantee the required semantics because of scope transitivity. We must also bound the visibility side effects of atomic ordering. If we write to local memory, or to that coarse-grained region, and then perform a system scope release write to some shared region, a reader with no access to the local or coarse locations will not see them, even though the happens-before order suggests that they should.

For local memory, it is valid for addresses to be reused from one work-group to another. So, it is almost obvious that whatever updates are made to one local memory region cannot be visible to another work-group, which would be seeing different locations through the same local addresses. Coarse-grained memory does not behave in this way; its addresses must be the same for any device accessing it.

In both cases, we can view this abstractly as a set of locations that are observable to a given device for some period of time. This set of observable locations and the resulting operations is a restriction on the global sequentially consistent and happens-before orders. An update to a location in local memory will never be observable to another work-group. An update to a location in owned memory will not be observable to another agent until ownership is transferred.

For races, we have to view this even more strongly. Any access to an unowned memory region races not with an access by the owner, but with the ownership transfer itself. Think of this as the worst case behavior of a copy. If at ownership transfer that entire memory region is copied from one physical location to another, then every location is accessed by the copying entity as non-atomic operations, beginning with an acquire from one physical region at device scope and a release to the other at device scope. Any access to locations within that region that is not synchronized by the release or acquire is hence a race. That release or acquire must synchronize with the copy itself, and hence this is only possible for runtime-level ownership transfer operations that may synchronize with queue packets.

5.5 CONCLUSIONS

In this chapter, we've summarized the features of HSA's memory model. Memory consistency is a complicated topic, and for full details we refer the reader to the

HSA System Architecture specification. There are also numerous works on memory consistency. One reference that formalizes scoped synchronization, which is a core feature of HSA's memory model, is by the authors [1].

The HSA memory consistency model is a fundamental feature to allow the construction of high-performance portable applications. Chapter 6 describes how the features of the memory model are necessary to support architected queues, and the later examples make use of the features in user code.

REFERENCES

[1] B.R. Gaster, D. Hower, L. Howes, HRF-Relaxed: Adapting HRF to the Complexities of Industrial Heterogeneous Memory Models. In: ACM Transactions on Architecture and Code Optimization (TACO), ACM, New York, USA, 2015.

HSA Queuing Model

6

B.R. Gaster*, L. Howes[†], D. Hower[‡]

University of the West of England, Bristol, UK*; Qualcomm,
Santa Clara, CA, USA[†]; Qualcomm, Raleigh-Durham, NC, USA[‡]

6.1 INTRODUCTION

In previous chapters we have seen examples of HSAIL kernels, which are intended to be executed on a HSA agent. However, for this to be useful we need to understand how such kernels are dispatched or submitted for execution by the HSA system. This is the job of HSA queues, an asynchronous framework for building graphs of potentially dependent kernels for execution on a specific HSA agent. Multiple queues can be created for a single agent or for multiple agents within a HSA system. Dependencies between kernels are controlled with HSA signals. Signals represent a general solution provided by all HSA systems and enable low-latency synchronous and asynchronous communication between different agents.

To enable the implementation of low-latency dispatch, a queue is allocated by the HSA runtime. From then on, the application submits work directly to the queue in the form of Architected Queuing Language (AQL) packets. The API provides a small number of operations for manipulating the queue structure in a way that is portable across a variety of implementations. Queue scheduling is separated from the HSA runtime and instead managed by the corresponding agent's packet processor (PP), as visualized in Figure 6.1. The packet processor coordinates the scheduling of kernels on a specific HSA agent. It reads packets from a set of queues, checks dependence, and dispatches jobs on the corresponding agent's compute units, when resources are available.

The remainder of this chapter describes the process of coordinating kernel execution within the HSA framework. First we look at allocating queues, then at the formal language of packets, the AQL, and finally we consider how AQL packets are submitted by the application and consumed by the packet processor.

6.2 USER MODE QUEUES

In this section, we consider how to create, destroy, and manipulate HSA queues.

The following function creates a user mode queue for a particular agent:

77

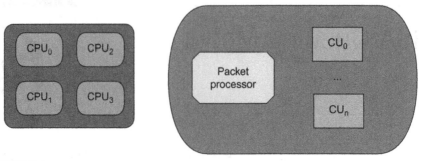

FIGURE 6.1

100 foot view of a HSA system, with host CPU and HSA agent.

```
hsa_status_t hsa_queue_create(
      hsa_agent_t agent,
      uint32_t size,
      hsa_queue_type_t type,
      void (*callback) (hsa_status_t status,
                        hsa_queue_t *source,
                        void *data),
      void *data,
      uint32_t private_segment_size,
      uint32_t group_segment_size,
      hsa_queue_t **queue);
```

A queue is associated with a single HSA agent, described by the parameter *agent*, which can be an agent supporting kernel dispatch or agent dispatch or one that supports both, as described in Chapter 4. An agent supporting kernel dispatch is capable of supporting execution kernels compiled from the HSAIL, as detailed in Chapter 3, or at least matching the HSAIL ABI and execution model. Conversely, agent dispatch queues support execution of functions "native" to that device, and are not required to follow the HSAIL parallel execution model. Figure 6.2 shows this relationship diagrammatically.

It is important to remember that, while Figure 6.2 shows the two queues within the corresponding agent, this is a logical relationship only and there is no requirement that the queue memory is placed within an agent's memory. Instead, HSA requires that this memory is exposed within the process's virtual address space and is accessible to the agent's packet processor. The packet processor is also shown within its corresponding agent, but again, there is no explicit requirement that this be the case. Two different, but equally valid designs for a packet processor exist. It could be implemented in software on the host CPU, calling through a low-level driver to dispatch work onto the underlying device. Or, alternatively, it could be provided on a hardware widget on the device, itself, to handle queue scheduling independent of the host CPU. HSA could be implemented on top of an OpenCL 2.0 implementation supporting SVM with fine-grain atomics [1]. However, it is important to note that allowing the packet processor to be directly implemented using hardware has

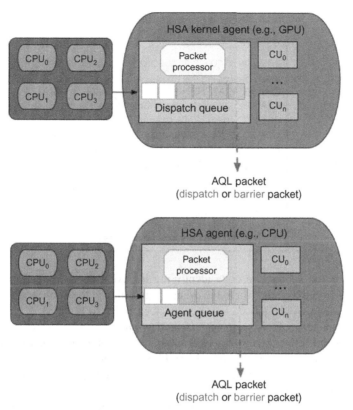

FIGURE 6.2

HSA has two types of queues: one for HSA agents that are capable of executing HSAIL kernels, and one for HSA agents that execute "native" functions.

the potential for HSA implementations that incur less software driver complexity of OpenCL and legacy device drivers.

The *size* of the queue represents the maximum number of packets that can be contained in the queue at any given time. The parameter *type* can be one of the following values:

• HSA_QUEUE_TYPE_MULTI: The queue can support multiple producers, i.e., multiple threads on the host CPU and/or multiple agents.
• HSA_QUEUE_TYPE_SINGLE: The queue supports only a single producer, although there is no specific restriction on the specific producer.

Restricting a queue to only a single producer allows the producer to avoid using (sometimes) costly memory consistency operations when adding packets to the queue, as described below.

The parameter "callback" allows the application to receive information, asynchronously, concerning events related to the queue. The HSA runtime passes three

Table 6.1 User Mode Queue Type: *hsa_queue_t*

Field Name	Description
Type	The type of queue as specified at queue creation time
Features	Mask describing the queues features, can be one of HSA_QUEUE_FEATURE_KERNEL_DISPATCH, or HSA_QUEUE_FEATURE_AGENT_DISPATCH. Its value is determined by the type of agent passed to hsa_queue_create
base_address	Starting address of the memory allocated. The passed value must be aligned to the size of an AQL packet
doorbell_signal	HSA signal object that is used to inform the PP that a packet is ready to be processed
size	Maximum number of packets a queue can hold at any time. Must be a power of 2
reserved0	Not used and will always be 0
ID	An ID that is unique for a given process

arguments to the callback: a code identifying the event that triggered the invocation, a pointer to the queue where the event originated, and the application data. The "data" parameter will be passed to the callback each time it is called.

The parameters *private_segment_size* and *group_segment_size* are hints to the packet processor reflecting the expected maximum size of the private and group segments, respectively. This is a performance hint only and the system is required to work even if this value is exceeded. In the case that the application does not know this size, it should pass UINT_MAX.

On successful creation of a user mode queue, indicated by a return value HSA_STATUS_SUCCESS, a pointer to a readonly queue type, *hsa_queue_t*, is returned in the parameter queue containing the data fields described in Table 6.1.[1] On queue creation, each element of the queue's buffer (i.e., the locations where packets will be submitted) are initialized to the packet type HSA_PACKET_TYPE_INVALID. This is necessary to prevent the associated packet processor from inadvertently scheduling an unintended job. This will become clearer when we introduce AQL packet scheduling in the following section.

It is possible that queue creation might fail (e.g., out of resources), and, in this case, one of the following error codes will be returned:

- HSA_STATUS_ERROR_NOT_INITIALIZED: The HSA runtime has not been initialized.
- HSA_STATUS_ERROR_OUT_OF_RESOURCES: There is failure to allocate the resources required by the implementation.

---

[1] It is important remember that for easy reading we are using the HSA runtime descriptions of queue types. However, queues are architected in HSA, which means that the bit layout of these structures is well-defined and thus portable. For example, the top of Figure 6.3 shows how a queue will appear in memory, as defined by the HSA system architecture (Chapter 2). An implication is that the HSA runtime types are not necessary to generate and manipulate the queue.

- HSA_STATUS_ERROR_INVALID_AGENT: The agent is invalid.
- HSA_STATUS_ERROR_INVALID_QUEUE_CREATION: The agent does not support queues of the requested type.
- HSA_STATUS_ERROR_INVALID_ARGUMENT: Size is not a power of two, size is 0, type is an invalid queue type, or queue is *NULL*.

Because job queues are generally useful, HSA provides the ability to create a "soft" queue, which enables the application to implement HSA style queues using a custom packet processing method of the developer's choice. Soft queues allow the seamless integration with other parts of the HSA runtime, in particular HSA signals. Thus, soft queues enable libraries to be developed in such a way that they are agnostic of the knowledge of whether a corresponding queue is hard or soft. They do this by "emulating" the interface of "hard" queues. This allows code to work independently of being passed a "soft" or "hard" queue, for example.

The following function creates a soft queue:

```
hsa_status_t hsa_soft_queue_create(
    hsa_region_t region,
    uint32_t size,
    hsa_queue_type_t type,
    uint32_t features,
    hsa_signal_t doorbell_signal,
    hsa_queue_t **queue);
```

The parameter "region" is the area of memory that is used to store the packets submitted to the queue. The memory backing "region" must have been previously allocated by a call to the HSA runtime.

The "size" of the queue represents the maximum number of packets that can be contained in the queue at any given time. The parameter "type" is the same as for hard queues, given above, and has the same features.

Unlike hard queues, where the doorbell signal is allocated by the HSA runtime as part of queue creation, a soft queue doorbell is created with a pre-allocated signal, passed in the parameter *doorbell_singal*. This allows the application to customize the doorbell signal according to its own needs.

On successful creation of a soft queue, indicated by a return value HSA_STATUS_SUCCESS, a pointer to a structure of readonly queue type *hsa_queue_t* is returned in the parameter *queue*. This structure contains the data fields described in Table 6.1.

Like hard queues, it is possible that soft queue creation might fail and, in this case, one of the following error codes will be returned:

- HSA_STATUS_ERROR_NOT_INITIALIZED: The HSA runtime has not been initialized.
- HSA_STATUS_ERROR_OUT_OF_RESOURCES: There is failure to allocate the resources required by the implementation.
- HSA_STATUS_ERROR_INVALID_ARGUMENT: Size is not a power of two, size is 0, type is an invalid queue type, the doorbell signal handle is 0, or queue is NULL.

The following function deletes an existing ("hard" or "soft") queue: `hsa_status_t hsa_queue_destroy ( hsa_queue_t *queue );`

The parameter *queue* is a valid queue, previously allocated with call *hsa_create_queue*().

6.3 ARCHITECTED QUEUING LANGUAGE

In this section, we introduce the language of packets, the AQL. The AQL is a binary interface[2] used to describe commands such as a kernel dispatch. An AQL packet is a region of memory containing data laid out with a specific format encoding a single command. The HSA runtime does not provide any specific functionality for creating, destroying, or manipulating AQL packets. This is left to higher-level libraries or the application to directly perform these operations. There is no need for an application to explicitly reserve storage space for packets, because a queue already contains a buffer representing a sequence of AQL packets.

6.3.1 PACKET TYPES

The HSA runtime defines several packet types that designed for the follow situations:

- HSA_PACKET_TYPE_VENDOR_SPECIFIC: Vendor-defined packet, cannot be depended on for portable code.
- HSA_PACKET_TYPE_INVALID: The packet has been processed in the past or never used, but has not been reassigned to the packet processor. A packet processor must not process a packet of this type. All queues support this packet type.
- HSA_PACKET_TYPE_KERNEL_DISPATCH: Packet specifying an HSAIL ABI data-parallel execution to run on a kernel agent.
- HSA_PACKET_TYPE_AGENT_DISPATCH: Packet specifying a general agent dispatch.
- HSA_PACKET_TYPE_BARRIER_AND: Packet used by agents to delay processing of subsequent packets until a boolean AND between a set of dependencies is satisfied.
- HSA_PACKET_TYPE_BARRIER_OR: Packet used by agents to delay processing of subsequent packets until a boolean OR between a set of dependencies is satisfied.

Packets are architected as 512-bit entities, although not all packet types use the allotted amount. All packet types share a common 16-bit header, which includes a type descriptor, a barrier bit, and other properties. The packet header is defined in Table 6.2.

---

[2] Like queues, AQL packets are architected and defined as part of the HSA system architecture. We will continue to mix HSA runtime types with HSA system architecture definitions, as we believe it helps in understanding HSA.

Table 6.2 AQL Packet Header

Bits	Field Name	Description
7:0	Format	AQL packet type
8	barrier:1	If set, then processing of the packet only begins when all preceding packets are complete
10:9	acquire_fence:scope	Determines the scope and type of the acquire memory fence operation for a packet
12:11	release_fence:scope	Determines the scope and type of the release memory fence operation applied after kernel completion, but before the packet is completed
15:13		Reserved and must be 0.

The "format," or packet type, can be one of the types defined above, while the barrier bit states if there is an implicit dependency between earlier packets in the queue and this packet.[3] The acquire and release fences determine if a memory fence, and its corresponding scope as per the HSA memory model (see Chapter 5), should be performed by the packet processor before and after the packet is executed, respectively.[4] Careful use of memory fences, before and after a kernel's execution, can reduce unnecessary memory traffic, while at the same time providing for fine-grain control of memory visibility from an external controller (i.e., outside of the kernel or a set of kernels).

The last 64 bits of any packet is a handle to the (optional) completion signal. The completion signal communicates that a given packet has completed execution, including any corresponding side effects. On completing the main action associated with a given packet, for example executing a kernel, the packet processor will commit to memory any writes, as defined by the release fence specified in the packet. If a non-zero completion signal handle is provided, the PP will decrement the signal's value by one. More details of this process are given in Section 6.4.

The remaining 432 bits are defined by each packet type individually, as highlighted in the following definitions of each packet type.

- **Vendor-specific packet:**
  A vendor-specific packet is defined by a specific implementation and the layout cannot be assumed to be portable.
  The type field for an invalid packet is set to HSA_PACKET_TYPE_VENDOR_SPECIFIC.

---

[3] Barrier bits are a way of implementing a sequence of dependent kernels, without using the more "heavy" weight barrier packets or signals. They only work for dense linear sequences; for more complicated dependencies, graphs signals must be used to explicitly encode dependencies.
[4] As discussed in the following, a corresponding "completion" signal can be used to formalize the informal notion of "after the packet is executed."

Table 6.3 AQL Kernel Dispatch Packet.

Bits	Field Name	Description
15:0	Header	Packet header as described in Table 6.2
17:16	Dimensions	Number of dimensions specified in grid-Size. Valid values are 1, 2, or 3
31:18		Reserved and must be 0
47:32	workgroup_size_x	x dimension of work-group measured in work-items (Chapter 3)
63:48	workgroup_size_y	y dimension of work-group measured in work-items (Chapter 3)
79:64	workgroup_size_z	z dimension of work-group measured in work-items (Chapter 3)
95:80		Reserved and must be 0
127:96	grid_size_x	x dimension of grid measured in work-items (Chapter 3)
127:96	grid_size_y	y dimension of grid (measured in work-items (Chapter 3))
127:96	grid_size_z	z dimension of grid (measured in work-items (Chapter 3))
223:192	private_segment_ size_bytes	Total size in bytes of required private memory allocation per work-item (Chapter 3)
255:224	group_segment_ size_bytes	Total size in bytes of required group memory allocation per work-item (Chapter 3)
319:256	kernel_object	Handle for an object in memory that includes an implementation-defined executable ISA image for the kernel
383:320	kernarg_address	Address of memory containing kernel arguments
447:384		Reserved and must be 0
511:448	completion_signal	HSA signaling object handle used to indicate completion of the job. Can be NULL

- **Invalid packet:**
  The invalid packet is the initial state of all packets in a queue, in which the contents of the 432-bit container is undefined. Setting a packet to the invalid state communicates from the consumer to the producer that the slot is free. Changing it from invalid to some other state communicates from the producer to the consumer that the packet is ready for consumption.[5]
  The type field for an invalid packet is set to HSA_PACKET_TYPE_INVALID.
- **Kernel dispatch packet:**
  Any HSA agent is required to support the HSAIL ABI and its corresponding execution model. HSAIL, like OpenCL [1,2], supports a data-parallel execution model based on grids, work-groups, wavefronts, and work-items, as described in Chapter 3. An HSAIL *kernel* is executed over a 1D, 2D, or 3D grid and is launched via a kernel dispatch packet placed in an HSA queue. Table 6.3 details the format of a kernel dispatch packet.

---

[5] Note that the way the packet processor scheduler is defined, it is not possible for the packet processor to invalidate a packet before the corresponding read offset has been moved on.

Table 6.4 AQL Agent Dispatch Packet.

Bits	Field Name	Description
15:0	Header	Packet header as described in Table 6.2
31:15	Type	The function to be performed by the destination agent. The function codes are application-defined
63:32		Reserved and must be 0.
127:64	return_address	Pointer to location to store the function return value(s) in
191:128	arg0	
255:192	arg1	
319:256	arg2	64-bit arguments
383:320	arg3	
447:384		Reserved and must be 0
511:448	completion_signal	HSA signaling object handle used to indicate completion of the job. Can be NULL

A kernel dispatch packet contains a complete specification of the state required to run a particular kernel, including the dimensions of the grid and work-groups, the number of dimensions, the address of the kernel object, a reference to the memory segment containing the arguments, and sizes for the private and group memory segments. Additionally, there is a handle to a completion signal that is used to report the completion of the kernel.

When the packet is ready, the type field of a kernel dispatch packet is set to HSA_PACKET_TYPE_KERNEL_DISPATCH.

- **Agent dispatch packet:**
  The ability to coordinate execution of work using HSA queues is a powerful capability. As such, HSA exposes this functionality to the application itself via soft queues and agent dispatch. Agent dispatch enables an application to launch built-in functions for a specific agent; these can be provided by the HSA implementation itself and/or by the application. Unlike kernel dispatch, there is not reference to a kernel object containing the code to execute. Instead, an integer ID is used that uniquely identifies the corresponding function with respect to a given agent. As a consequence, the set of supported functions is application-defined.[6] A small number of 64-bit arguments can be passed to an agent dispatch, and a pointer is provided for storing any return values. Table 6.4 contains details for formats of agent dispatch packets.

---

[6] The motivation for not using function pointers or objects is that it enables soft queues to expose built-in, hardened functionality that is not easily representable, in a portable manner, as pointers. It is possible to queue a soft queue for the set built-ins it provides, allowing portable code using soft queues to be developed.

Table 6.5 AQL Barrier Packets AND and OR.

Bits	Field Name	Description
15:0	Header	Packet header as described in Table 6.2
63:16		Reserved and must be 0
127:64	dep_signal0	Handles for dependent signaling objects to be evaluated by the packet processor
191:128	dep_signal1	
255:192	dep_signal2	
319:256	dep_signal3	
383:320	dep_signal4	
447:384		Reserved and must be 0
511:448	completion_signal	HSA signaling object handle used to indicate completion of the job. Can be NULL

When the packet is ready, the type field of an agent dispatch packet is set to HSA_PACKET_TYPE_AGENT_DISPATCH.

- **Barrier-AND/OR packet:**
  Barrier packets enable the application to express dependency relationships on sets of one or more signals. The number of signals for any given barrier packet is limited to a maximum of 5. Barrier packets can be made dependent on other barrier packets, and so dependencies on a larger number of signals may be specified indirectly. Two types of barrier packets currently exist, *AND* and *OR*, that enforce all signals to be signaled or just one before the barrier packet is itself considered complete, respectively.

  The barrier packet for *AND* and *OR* differs only in the *format* field of the packet and the other fields are given in Table 6.5.

  The type field of a barrier AND packet is set to HSA_PACKET_TYPE_BARRIER_AND and that of a barrier OR packet is set to HSA_PACKET_TYPE_BARRIER_OR.

6.3.2 BUILDING PACKETS

Building packets is left to the application, which manages the allocation, initialization, and submission of packets to queues. As packets are architected, the application can directly manage packet creation, without making any call to the HSA runtime. For example, the following sample C++ code[7] creates a barrier AND packet. It assumes two input signals (*signal_1* and *signal_2*) that the barrier will wait on, and a completion signal (*completion_signal*) that the packet processor will decrement when the packet completes:

---

[7] Actually the code is C++ 14 [3] as it uses binary literals.

```
unsigned char * p =
    new unsigned char *[512 / 4];
memset(p, 0, 512 / 4);
*(p + 0) = HSA_PACKET_TYPE_INVALID;
// release agent and system scope
*(p + 1) = 0b00010000;
*(((unsigned long long)p)+1) = signal_1;
*(((unsigned long long)p)+2) = signal_2;
*(((unsigned long long)p)+7) = completion_signal;
```

The packet type is stored in the first byte, and then a bit pattern is written to the second byte. This enables a release fence at scope agent and system. Finally, the three signals are stored in their respective locations.

It is important to note that we do not set the packet's type to HSA_PACKET_TYPE_BARRIER_AND and instead set it to be an invalid packet. This is necessary to avoid the packet processor reading a valid packet that has only been partially written. The actual HSA_PACKET_TYPE_BARRIER_AND value is written directly into the queue's packet buffer as the final operation to complete the packet submission.

In some cases, it is possible to generate the packet data directly into the queues packet buffer, having the advantage of avoiding having to write the invalid type at all. However, this does not allow a system to optimize barrier submission with an optimized implementation of memcpy, which is particularly used when multiple packets are submitted from a single template.

The HSA Runtime provides predefined structures, enums, and other types for easing the burden of packet creation. For example, the above barrier packet could be written as follows using the HSA runtime:

```
hsa_barrier_and_packet_t* b_packet =
    new hsa_barrier_and_packet_t;
memset(
    ((uint8_t*) b_packet),
    0,
    sizeof(hsa_barrier_packet_t));
b_packet->header =
    HSA_PACKET_TYPE_INVALID |
    HSA_FENCE_SCOPE_SYSTEM <<
        HSA_PACKET_HEADER_RELEASE_FENCE_SCOPE |
    HSA_FENCE_SCOPE_AGENT <<
        HSA_PACKET_HEADER_RELEASE_FENCE_SCOPE;
b_packet->dep_signal[0] = signal_1;
b_packet->dep_signal[1] = signal_2;
b_packet->completion_signal = completion_signal;
```

Finally, given the ability to create queues and AQL packets, we are in a position to consider the process of packet submission and scheduling. The following section outlines this process.

6.4 PACKET SUBMISSION AND SCHEDULING

The submission and scheduling of packets by the packet processor is separated into three phases: queued, active, and complete. At a high-level, this is captured by the following steps:

1. Allocate a packet slot in a queue associated with a by incrementing the *writeIndex* associated with a queue (see the following).
2. Initialize the packet, marking the packet as invalid, as previously described.
3. Copy the packet into the queue at the pre-increment *writeIndex*.
4. Modify the packet's type from invalid to the appropriate packet type.[8]
5. Notify the packet processor that a packet has been added by ringing queue's doorbell signal.[9]

In addition to the queue structure described in Table 6.1, the queue also defines two properties (*readIndex* and *writeIndex*) that reference the location of the "head" and "tail" of the queue:

• *read Index* is a 64-bit unsigned integer that specifies the packet ID of the next AQL packet to be consumed by the packet processor.
• *write Index* is a 64-bit unsigned integer that specifies the packet ID of the next AQL packet slot to be allocated.

Before detailing algorithms for adding packets to the queue, we need to take a short interlude to understand how HSA enables access to the *readIndex* and *writeIndex*. HSA has been designed in such a way to allow for multiple approaches to building conformant implementations. As such, the read and write indices are not directly exposed to the application developer. Instead, dedicated runtime APIs are provided.

As the visibility of writes to the queue indices follows the rules of the HSA memory model, as described in Chapter 5, there are sequentially consistent and relaxed variants of the operations to access the read/write indices.

The following functions load the read index for a given queue:

```
uint64_t hsa_queue_load_read_index_acquire(
    const hsa_queue_t *queue );

uint64_t hsa_queue_load_read_index_relaxed(
    const hsa_queue_t *queue );
```

The following functions store a value to the write index for a given queue:

```
uint64_t hsa_queue_store_write_index_release(
    const hsa_queue_t *queue, uint64_t value);
```

---

[8] The write must be performed as a single atomic write.
[9] If the doorbell is not rung, it is possible that the packet processor will never read the written packet. Of course, it is quite possible that the packet processor will read the packet without the doorbell being rung; it's just not guaranteed.

```
uint64_t hsa_queue_store_write_index_relaxed(
    const hsa_queue_t *queue, uint64_t value);
```

Finally, we have all the machinery needed to build algorithms capable of submitting AQL packets. As for packet allocation, the HSA runtime does not provide any implementations for packet submission. Instead it is intended that either higher-level libraries will provide common functionality, or the application will implement their requirements directly.

On allocation of a queue, the application specifies if packets will be submitted by multiple producers concurrently, for example from multiple CPU threads or multiple HSA agents, or only by a single producer. This choice has implications on the algorithm to submit packets to the queue. It also has implications on how the packet processor might consider packets for scheduling. For now we will focus on the former, as, in general, it is the job of the HSA implementation to provide a correctly working packet processor. Of course, this changes when considering soft queues that are implemented by the application itself.

When preparing for packet submission, the *writeIndex* is incremented by the producer to obtain a unique packet ID. When mod'ed (i.e., % in C) with the size of the packet buffer, this ID gives a location in the queue in which to store the corresponding packet. This is shown diagrammatically in Figure 6.3. There are two particular points of concern:

- Two units of execution might read the same value for *writeIndex* and proceed assuming they have a unique value.
- Two units of execution may try to modify, for example to increment, the *writeIndex* at the same time.

There are a number of possible (bad) consequences that might arise due to these conflicts, and here we look, in more detail, at one common issue. Consider the case when a queue's packet buffer has only a single free slot, and there are two units of execution. For example, two CPU threads what to submit a packet. If we assume that the packet processor is not going to consume any packets from the queue before these two threads race to submit their packets, then unless they coordinate this process, it is quite possible that unexpected behavior will occur. Diagrammatically we have:

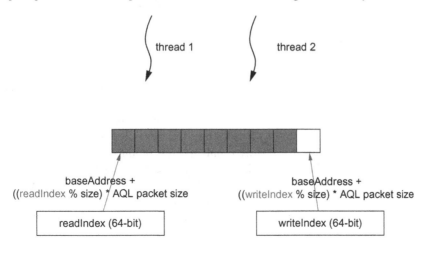

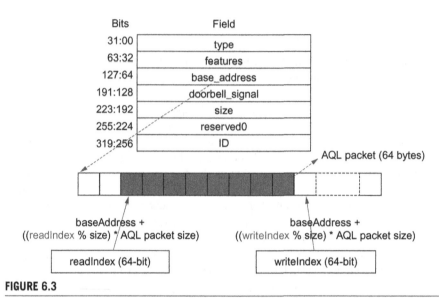

FIGURE 6.3

Queue structure and read/write access.

Consider that both threads now execute their own versions of the following code snippet:

```
// read the "write" index
uint64_t w = hsa_queue_load_write_index_acquire(queue);

// read "read" index
uint64_t r = hsa_queue_load_read_index_acquire(queue);

uint64_t size = w - r;
if ( size != queue->size ){ // queue full?
   // increment write index as queue not full
   hsa_queue_store_write_index_release(queue, w+1);
   // write packet
   queue->base_address[w % size] = packet;
   // code to set packet format and "ring" doorbell
}
```

Depending on how they are scheduled, it is possible that they read the same value for the *readIndex* and *writeIndex*, thus both successfully entering the conditional, incrementing the "same" *writeIndex*, and finally writing their own packets to the same index in the packet buffer. In general, we must assume that this is not the intended behavior.

It is important to note that if there is only a single producer, then the above code is valid, as there will be no other thread racing to access the same slot. To address these issues of multiple producers and enable the development of algorithms for concurrent packet submission, the HSA runtime provides a set of *compare-and-swap* operations for reading and writing the *write* index, with respect to a condition.

```
uint64_t hsa_queue_cas_write_index_acq_rel(
    const hsa_queue_t *queue,
    uint64_t expected,
    uint64_t value);

uint64_t hsa_queue_cas_write_index_acquire(
    const hsa_queue_t *queue,
    uint64_t expected,
    uint64_t value);

uint64_t hsa_queue_cas_write_index_relaxed(
    const hsa_queue_t *queue,
    uint64_t expected,
    uint64_t value);

uint64_t hsa_queue_cas_write_index_release(
    const hsa_queue_t *queue,
    uint64_t expected,
    uint64_t value);
```

Each variant enforces a slightly different set of memory ordering constraints, as defined by the HSA memory model (Chapter 5), but each operation performs the same underlying functionality. This behavior is captured by the following pseudocode[10]:

```
uint64_t hsa_queue_cas_write_index(
    const hsa_queue_t *queue,
    uint64_t expected,
    uint64_t value)
{
    uint64_t r;
    atomic {
        r = hsa_queue_load_write_index(queue);
        if (r = expected) {
            hsa_queue_store_write_index (queue, value);
        }
    }
    return r;
}
```

The operation reads the write index and proceeds to compare it with the *expected* value. If the values match, the operation stores *value* as the new value of *writeIndex*. In either case, it returns the value read from the write index. The key to the implementation is that the code that performs the read, test, and possible store is wrapped in an *atomic* section. This guarantees that all the contained operations execute as if they were a single indivisible instruction. HSAIL supports a set of similar

---

[10] We consider only the underlying functionality and not the memory ordering aspects, which, while important, do not add to the overall discussion at this point.

instructions for performing "compare-and-swap" on a given address in shared virtual memory (see Chapter 3). Modern CPU cores such as ARM and MIPS provide corresponding functionality.

It is this atomic test and set functionality that was missing from our earlier implementation for packet submission. Now armed with this, we can rewrite our earlier snippet:

```
// read "write" index
uint64_t w = hsa_queue_load_write_index_acquire(queue);

// read "read" index
uint64_t r = hsa_queue_load_read_index_acquire(queue);

uint64_t size = w   r;
if ( size != queue->size ){ // queue full?
    // increment write index as queue not full
    if (hsa_queue_cas_write_index_relaxed(queue, w, w+1) = w) {
        // write packet
        queue->base_address[w % queue->size] = packet;
        // code to set packet format and "ring" doorbell
    }
    else {
     // someone beat us to the punch !
    }
}
```

A complete example of a function to submit a packet to a queue, supporting multiple concurrent producers, is given in Figure 6.4. It follows the same flow as our previous example code, but now we have filled in the missing code to handle writing the packet to the buffer and "ringing" the packet processors doorbell. The function takes a queue, a packet to be submitted with the *format* set to invalid, and a format type of the final packet. Remember to avoid setting a valid format before rest of the packet is visible to other "execution" agents. We must first write the invalid packet and then perform a store of the actual format with sequentially consistent semantics, so the correct visibility ordering is guaranteed.[11]

Additionally, the function returns "true" if a packet is successfully submitted; otherwise it returns "false." In practice, a submit function might try some number of times to submit a packet, before giving up and returning to the caller.

Now that we understand how to submit AQL packets to a HSA queue, we turn to the semantics of packet consumption and execution. This is the job of the packet processor. For HSA agents and implementation-defined agents, supporting "hard"

---

[11] The function *_atomic_store_seq_cst* is a place holder for an atomic store operation that is compatible with the HSA memory model and implemented on the "executing" agent, for example the CPU. It is not possible to use the C++ 11 atomic operations in this case. In principle, the HSA packet buffer is not an array of atomic values. In practice, it is likely to work on many implementations, but should not be relied on.

```
bool submit_packet(
   hsa_queue_t * queue
   hsa_packet_t &packet
   hsa_packet_type_t type)
{
  // read "write" index
  uint64_t w =
     hsa_queue_load_write_index_acquire(queue);

  // read "read" index
  uint64_t r =
     hsa_queue_load_read_index_relaxed(queue);

  uint64_t size = w - r;
  if ( size != queue->size )
  {
    // increment write index as queue not full
    if (hsa_queue_cas_write_index_relaxed(
      queue, w, w+1) == w)
    {
      // write packet
      queue->base_address[w % queue->size] = packet;

      __atomic_store_seq_cst(
         &queue->base_address[w % queue->size],
         packet.header | type);

      hsa_signal_store_release(queue->doorbell_signal);

      return true;
    }
  }
  return false;
}
```

FIGURE 6.4

Packet submits function for multiple consumers.

queues, the packet processor is an abstract unit of execution that conforms to the HSA memory model and schedules packets on the corresponding agent. In general, it is possible for the application, via "soft" queues, to implement its own packet processor(s).

The algorithm for consuming packets is basically the same for single or multi-producer queues. However, it is possible, due to the monotonic packet ID restriction, to potentially take advantage of this in the case of single producer queues. We do not consider this case here and instead focus on the general case for the remainder of this section. Figure 6.5 provides a (pseudo) implementation of the packet processor's scheduler.[12] The function *pop* is given in Figure 6.6.

---

[12] For simplicity we only consider the single queue case. A real HSA packet processor supports queues sets, which can have one or more active queues.

```
void packet_scheduler(hsa_queue_t * queue)
{
  uint64_t write_index =
      hsa_queue_load_write_index_acquire(queue);

  while(true) { // run until...
    // wait until there is some work to consume
    hsa_signal_wait_acquire(
        queue->signal, HSA_SIGNAL_CONDITION_NE,
        write_index, UINT64_MAX,
        HSA_WAIT_STATE_ACTIVE);

    while(true) {
      hsa_packet_t * packet = pop(queue);
      if (packet != nullptr) {
        switch( packet->format ) {
          case HSA_PACKET_TYPE_VENDOR_SPECIFIC:
            // code to implement vendor packets
          case HSA_PACKET_TYPE_INVALID:
            // partially written packet
            // spin until format becomes defined
            continue;
          // other packet formats here
          case default:
            // error case, unknown packet format!!
        }
        if (packet.header |
            HSA_PACKET_HEADER_RELEASE_FENCE_SCOPE)
        {
          // code to perform release fence to given scope
        }
        packet.header.format = HSA_PACKET_TYPE_INVALID;
        if (packet->completion_signal != nullptr)
        {
          hsa_signal_add_relaxed(
              packet->completion_signal, -1);
        }

        // finally move the read index, free the packet
        hsa_queue_store_read_index_release(queue, r+1);

        if (write_index ==
            hsa_queue_load_read_index_relaxed(queue))
        {
          break;
        }
      }
      else
        break;
    } // inner while(true)
  } // outer while(true)
}
```

FIGURE 6.5

Pseudo code for packet processor scheduler.

```
hsa_packet_t * pop(hsa_queue_t * queue)
{
  uint64_t r =
    hsa_queue_load_read_index_acquire(queue);

  uint64_t w =
    hsa_queue_load_write_index_acquire(queue);

  if (r == w) {
    return nullptr; // empty
  }

  hsa_packet_t * packet =
        &queue->base_address[r % queue->size];

  return packet;
}
```

FIGURE 6.6

Helper function to "pop" an AQL packet.

The packet scheduler consists of two nested loops. The outer loop runs until the scheduler terminates, while the inner loops processes packets from the queue while some are remaining. If the queue becomes empty, the inner loop exits and the scheduler loops round to wait on the queue's doorbell, hopefully not waking again until more work is ready to be consumed.[13]

On entering the inner loop, the scheduler tries to pop a packet from the queue. If successful, this operation returns a pointer to the corresponding address in the packet buffer. Otherwise, it returns *nullptr*, and the scheduler exits the inner loop.

On success, the packet format is tested to determine the appropriate action. If the packet is valid, then control flow passes to code that handles the requested task. If the packet is marked invalid, then this implies that the particular packet is in the process of being written and the scheduler must wait for it to be complete by continuing to loop.

Once a packet has been successfully processed (executed), any release fences are applied. If the completion signal is not *nullptr*, then it is signaled by decrementing the value. Finally, the packet slot is freed by setting the packet type to invalid and incrementing the read index.[14]

---

[13] HSA signals can wake at any time, even without a corresponding signal write being performed.

[14] While we have chosen to free the packet slot after completely processing a given packet, an alternative and possibly more performant approach would be to have the packet processor (via *pop*) read a valid packet as a value, and thus free the slot at that point. This would mean pushing the check for invalid packet, i.e. one partially written, and the corresponding spin into *pop*.

6.5 CONCLUSIONS

In this chapter we have considered the process of submitting, via HSA queues, various sorts of AQL packets. HSA queues are one of the key building blocks for both application and library writers to develop low-latency asynchronous execution of parallel workloads. Queues and the corresponding packets, themselves, are necessarily low-level, with the intention that higher-level abstractions will be built on top as necessary. At the same time, they expose a "close-to-the-metal" interface for those not faint of heart, who want to control every last bit of performance.

REFERENCES

[1] OpenCL Working Group, Open Compute Language 2.0, November 2012.
[2] OpenCL Working Group, Open Compute Language 1.2, August 2010.
[3] ISO International Standard ISO/IEC 14882:2014(E) programming, Language C++, 2014.

Compiler Technology

7

W.-H. Chung*, Y.-H. Lyu[†], I-J. Sung[‡], Y.-W. Lee[§], W.-M. W. Hwu[¶]

MulticoreWare Inc., Douliou, Yunlin County, Taiwan, ROC*; MulticoreWare Inc., New Taipei, Taiwan, ROC[†]; MulticoreWare Inc., Champaign, IL, USA[‡]; National Chiao-Tung University, Hsinchu, Taiwan, ROC[§]; University of Illinois at Urbana-Champaign, Urbana, IL, USA[¶]

7.1 INTRODUCTION

Heterogeneous System Architecture (HSA) is designed to support various types of data-parallel programming models. With a standard instruction set, HSAIL, and a set of requirements provided by heterogeneous systems (such as shared virtual memory and platform atomics), HSA programs can exploit the computation power of HSA-compatible systems. These can include backend servers, desktops, or mobile devices. To help realize this goal, compilers and runtimes of high-level programming languages or domain-specific languages should target HSA for portable code generation and run-time management. By supporting HSA as the target platform, compiler writers can focus on more important, higher-level problems in language implementation. Such improved productivity can enable a proliferation of high-level programming languages such as C++, Java, and Python for programming heterogeneous computing systems.

In this chapter, we use C++ AMP, a parallel programming extension to C++, as an example to show how efficient HSAIL code can be generated from a higher level programming model. The C++ programming language provides several high-level, developer-friendly features such as object classes, class templates, lambda functions, and the C++ standard library. These high-level features support software engineering practices and improve developer productivity. It is the compiler writer's job to translate these features into HSA constructs without incurring an excessive level of overhead. We present some important implementation techniques in this translation process; these techniques can be useful for compiler writers interested in mapping other programming models to HSA.

We will start with a brief introduction of C++ AMP, and a simple vector addition "application" will serve as the running example. With the example, subsequent sections illustrate how C++ AMP features are mapped to HSA. We will then discuss how HSA-specific features such as shared virtual memory, platform atomics, and user-level queues allow for more generic C++ code on HSA systems. The actual, working implementation consists of a compiler, a set of header files, and a runtime library. This implementation is altogether publicly accessible as an open source project[1] under the University of Illinois Open Source License.

7.2 A BRIEF INTRODUCTION TO C++ AMP

C++ Accelerated Massive Parallelism (C++ AMP) is a programming model that supports expression of data-parallel algorithms in C++. In contrast to other GPU programming models such as OpenCL or CUDA C, C++ AMP encapsulates many low-level details of data movement, so the programs are more concise. Nevertheless, it still contains features to empower advanced programmers to address system intricacies for performance optimization.

Developed initially by Microsoft and released in Visual Studio 2012, C++ AMP is defined in an open specification. Based on the open source Clang and LLVM compiler infrastructure, MulticoreWare has published Kalmar, a C++ AMP implementation that targets OpenCL and HSA for GPU programs. It runs on Linux and supports all major GPU cards from vendors like AMD, Intel, and NVIDIA.

C++ AMP is an extension to the C++ 11 standard. Besides some C++ header files that define classes for modeling data-parallel algorithms, it adds two additional language-level rules to the C++ programming language. The first one specifies additional language restrictions for functions to be executed on GPUs; the second one allows cross-thread data sharing among GPU programs. This chapter does not aim to be a comprehensive introduction to C++ AMP. However, we will highlight the most important core concepts and show how a C++ AMP compiler can efficiently implement such features based on HSA. For those who are interested in a comprehensive tutorial on C++ AMP, itself, please refer to the Microsoft book on C++ AMP [1].

Let's start with a simple vector addition program in C++ AMP (Figure 7.1).

Conceptually, the C++ AMP code here computes vector addition as shown in Figure 7.2.

Line 1 includes the C++ AMP header, *amp.h*, which provides the declarations of the core features. Line 2 includes the STL class definition. The C++ AMP classes and functions are declared within the "concurrency" namespace. The "using" directive on Line 4 brings the C++ AMP names into the current scope. It is optional, but avoids the need to prefix C++ AMP names with a *concurrency::* scope specifier.

This main function in Line 5 is executed by a thread running on the host, and it contains a data-parallel computation that will be accelerated. The term "host" in C++ AMP documentation is defined as "host CPU" in HSA specification. While HSA uses the term "HSA agent" to refer to the execution environment used for accelerated execution, C++ AMP uses the term accelerator for the same purpose. One of the high level features in C++ AMP, and commonly seen in other high level languages, are lambdas. Lambdas enable the C++ AMP host and accelerator code to be colocated in the same file and even within same function. There is no separation of flow in the

---

[1] https://bitbucket.org/multicoreware/cppamp-driver-ng-35/.

```
1. #include <amp.h>
2. #include <vector>
3. #include <cstdlib>
4. using namespace concurrency;
5. int main(void) {
6.      const int N = 10;
7.      std::vector<float> a(N);
8.      std::vector<float> b(N);
9.      std::vector<float> c(N);
10.     float sum = 0.f;
11.     for (int i = 0; i < N; i++) {
12.       a[i] = 1.0f * rand() / RAND_MAX;
13.       b[i] = 1.0f * rand() / RAND_MAX;
14.     }
15.     array_view<const float, 1> av(N, a);
16.     array_view<const float, 1> bv(N, b);
17.     array_view<float, 1> cv(N, c);
18.     parallel_for_each(cv.get_extent(),
19.                     [=] (index<1> idx) restrict(amp)
20.                     {
21.                         cv[idx] = av[idx] + bv[idx];
22.                     });
23.     cv.synchronize();
24.     return 0;
25.   }
```

FIGURE 7.1

C++ AMP code example: vector addition.

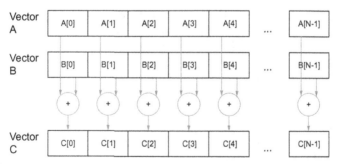

FIGURE 7.2

Vector addition, conceptual view.

source of device code and host code in C++ AMP. Later we will discuss how a C++ 11 lambda is compiled into HSAIL instructions in the context of C++ AMP.

7.2.1 C++ AMP *ARRAY_VIEW*

In C++ AMP, the primary vehicle for reading and writing large data collections is the class template *array_view*. An *array_view* provides a multi-dimensional reference to a rectangular collection of data locations. This is not a new copy of the data, but rather a new way to access the existing memory locations. The template has two parameters: the type of the elements of the source data and an integer that indicates the dimensionality of the *array_view*. Throughout C++ AMP, template parameters that indicate dimensionality are referred as the rank of the type or object. In this example, we have a 1-dimensional *array_view* (or an *array_view* of rank 1) of float values.

In Line 15 of Figure 7.1, *array_view* av(a) provides a one-dimensional reference to the C++ vector a. It tells the C++ AMP compiler that accesses to a vector through av will only use it as an input (const), treat it as a one-dimensional array (1), and assume that the size of the array is given by variable (N).

The constructor for *array_views* of rank 1, such as cv on Line 17, takes two parameters. The first is an integer value, which is the number of data elements. In the case of av, bv, and cv, the number of data elements is given by N. In general, the set of per-dimension lengths is referred to as an "extent." To represent and manipulate extents, C++ AMP provides a class template, called *extent*, with a single integer template parameter, which captures the rank. For objects with a small number of dimensions, various constructors are overloaded to allow specification of an *extent* as one or more integer values, as is done for cv. The second parameter to the cv constructor is a standard container that stores the host data.

7.2.2 C++ AMP *PARALLEL_FOR_EACH*, OR KERNEL INVOCATION

Line 18 illustrates the *parallel_for_each* construct, which is the C++ AMP code pattern for a data-parallel computation. This corresponds to the kernel dispatch in HSA. In HSA terminology, *parallel_for_each* creates a grid of work-items. In C++ AMP, the set of elements for which a computation is performed is called the compute domain and is defined by an *extent* object. Each work-item will invoke the same function for every point, and they are distinguished only by their location (work-item absolute ID) in the domain (grid).

Similar to the STL algorithm *for_each*, the *parallel_for_each* function template specifies a function to be applied to a collection of values. The first argument to a *parallel_for_each* is an *extent* object, which describes the domain over which a data-parallel computation is performed. In this example, we perform an operation over every element in an *array_view*, and so the *extent* passed into the *parallel_for_each* is the *extent* of the cv *array_view*. In the example, this is accessed through the *extent* property of the *array_view* type. This is a one-dimensional *extent*, and the domain of the computation consists of integer values $0...n-1$.

7.2.2.1 Lambdas or functors as kernels

The second argument to a *parallel_for_each* is a C++ function object (or functor). In Figure 7.1, we use the C++ 11 lambda syntax to create a functor. The core semantics of a *parallel_for_each* are to invoke the function defined by the second parameter exactly once for every element in the compute domain that is defined by the *extent* argument.

7.2.2.2 Captured variables as kernel arguments

The leading [=] indicates that variables declared inside the containing function but referenced inside the lambda are "captured" and copied into data members of the function object built for the lambda. In this case, this is the three *array_view* objects. These captured objects will be copied from host memory to the device memory on the GPU. The elements of an *array_view* may be modified, and those modifications will be reflected back to the host.

The function will then be invoked once for each thread and has a single parameter that is initialized to the location of the thread within the compute domain. This is accomplished with a class template, *index*, which represents a short vector of integer values. The dimension of an *index* is the number of elements of this vector and is the same as the dimension of the *extent*. In this example, the *index* parameter idx value is initialized to the location of the thread in the computation domain and is used to select elements in an *array_view*, as illustrated on Line 21.

7.2.2.3 The restrict(amp) modifier

A key extension to C++ is shown in this example: the *restrict(amp)* modifier. In C++ AMP, the existing C99 keyword restrict is borrowed and allowed in a new context: it may trail the formal parameter list of a function (including lambda functions). The *restrict* keyword is then followed by a parenthesized list of one or more restriction specifiers. While other uses are possible, in C++ AMP there are only two such specifiers defined: *amp* and *cpu*. They guide the compiler to generate either CPU or accelerator code out of a function definition. They also guide whether the compiler should enforce a subset of the C++ language. More details are shown in the following.

As shown in Line 19, the function object passed to *parallel_for_each* must have its declaration annotated with a *restrict(amp)* specification. Any function called from the body of that function must similarly be restricted. The *restrict(amp)* specification identifies functions that may be invoked on a hardware accelerator. Analogously, *restrict(cpu)* indicates functions that may be invoked on the host. When no restriction is specified, the default is *restrict(cpu)*. A function may have both restrictions, *restrict(cpu,amp)*, in which case it may be called from either host or accelerator contexts and must satisfy the restrictions of both contexts.

As we mentioned earlier, the restrict modifier allows a subset of C++ to be defined for use in a body of code. In the first release of C++ AMP, the restrictions reflect current common limitations of GPUs when used as accelerators of data parallel code. For example, function pointers, C++ operator *new*, recursions and, calls to virtual methods are currently prohibited. Over time, we can expect these restrictions to be lifted. The open specification for C++ AMP includes a possible roadmap of future versions, which are less restrictive. The *restrict(cpu)* specifier, of course, permits all of the capabilities of C++, but, because some functions that are part of C++ AMP are accelerator-specific, they do not have *restrict(cpu)* versions. Thus, they may only be used in *restrict(amp)* code.

Inside the body of the *restrict(amp)* lambda, there are references to the *array_view* objects declared in the containing scope. These are "captured" into the function object that is created to implement the lambda. Other variables from the function scope may also be captured by value. Each of these other values is made available to each invocation of the function executed on the accelerator. In this example, any changes to cv made inside the *parallel_for_each* will be reflected in the host data vector c.

7.3 HSA AS A COMPILER TARGET

Kalmar is an open source implementation of C++ AMP contributed by MulticoreWare; it consists of the following components:

- C++ AMP compiler: developed based on the open source Clang and LLVM projects, the compiler supports C++ AMP language extensions to C++ and generates kernel code in HSAIL, OpenCL C, or SPIR (Standard Portable Intermediate Representation) format.
- C++ AMP headers: a set of C++ header files that implement classes defined in C++ AMP specification. Some functions are simply wrappers around HSA or OpenCL built-in functions, but some require careful design and engineering.
- C++ AMP runtime: a small library acts as a bridge between host programs and kernels. Linked with built-in executables, it can load and build kernels, set kernel arguments, and launch kernels.

HSAIL is the intermediate language used in HSA programs. It is written in textual format, and BRIG is the binary representation of HSAIL. Based on the vector addition example code, the rest of the chapter will show the design of the main components of the Kalmar compiler. Some implementation details will be omitted, and we will focus on the critical aspects that allow implementing C++ AMP features on HSA. We will also show how certain C++ constructs can be mapped into HSAIL. The focus is to provide insight into the use of HSA as an implementation platform for C++ AMP.

7.4 MAPPING KEY C++ AMP CONSTRUCTS TO HSA

To map a new programming model to HSA, one can start with a mapping of the key constructs. The following table shows a mapping of the key C++ AMP constructs to their counterparts in HSA and OpenCL. As we showed in Figure 7.1, a lambda in a *parallel_for_each* construct represents a C++ functor. The instances of which should be executed in parallel. This maps naturally to HSAIL kernels, where multiple work-items execute the kernel function in parallel. As a result, we show that C++ AMP lambdas, defined in *parallel_for_each* or functors passed to *parallel_for_each*, are mapped to HSAIL kernels.

As for the names to be used for each generated HSAIL kernel, we can use the mangled names of the C++ *operator()* of the lambda/functor. C++ mangling rules will eliminate undesirable name conflicts and enforce correct scoping rules for the generated kernels.

Table 7.1 Mapping C++ AMP Key Programming Constructs to HSA and OpenCL

HSA	C++ AMP	OpenCL
Kernel	Lambda defined in *parallel_for_each*; functor passed to *parallel_for_each*	*Kernel*
Kernel name	Mangled name for the C++ *operator()* of the lambda/functor object	Kernel name
Kernel dispatch	*parallel_for_each*	Kernel enqueue
Kernel arguments	Captured variables in lambda or explicit parameters passed to non-lambda functors	Kernel arguments
Buffers in global segment	*concurrency::array_view and array*	*cl_mem buffers*

In C++ AMP, the *parallel_for_each* function is responsible for most of the host-device interactions, such as passing the kernel arguments and kernel launch. This will be implemented in the C++ AMP runtime through a sequence of HSA runtime API calls. For lambda functors such as the one shown in Figure 7.1, the arguments to be passed to the HSAIL kernels should be automatically captured according to the C++ lambda rules. On the other hand, all *array_view* instances used in the lambda should become buffers in the global segment; their pointers will be passed into HSAIL kernels.

To summarize, with this conceptual mapping (Table 7.1), we can see that the output of the C++ AMP compiler should provide the following:

1. A device HSAIL kernel compiled from the functor passing into the *parallel_for_each* construct. The kernel function parameter list is generated based on lambda capture rules, or based on the explicit parameter list of the non-lambda functor object.
2. Host code that can gather all the data needed by the kernel, pass the data to the device as kernel arguments, and then launch the kernel.

Because a C++ lambda is an anonymous functor, we can close the gap further by rewriting the lambda into a functor, as in Figure 7.3. The code makes the lambda into an explicit functor. All the captured variables, va, vb, and vc, become class members

```
1.    class vecAdd {
2.    private:
3.        array_view<const float, 1> va, vb;
4.        array_view<float, 1> vc;
5.    public:
6.        vecAdd(array_view<const float, 1> a,
7.               array_view<const float, 1> b,
8.               array_view<float, 1> c) restrict(cpu)
9.            : va(a), vb(b), vc(c) {};
10.       void operator() (index<1> idx) restrict(amp) {
11.           cv[idx] = av[idx] + bv[idx];
12.       }
13.   };
```

FIGURE 7.3

Functor version for C++ AMP vector addition (conceptual code).

of this compiler-generated functor; the body of the lambda becomes an *operator()* member function. Finally, a constructor is supplied to populate these captured variables on the host side.

However, there are still several issues that need to be addressed:

1. How are host memory buffers allocated by the array_view at the host side passed to HSAIL kernels at the device side?
2. How does one create an HSAIL kernel from this functor class, so it can be called from *parallel_ for_each*?
3. How does the C++ AMP runtime choose the right HSA kernel to execute on a particular *parallel_ for_each* call site?

To close the gaps further, we need to further augment the functor class.

With the version shown in Figure 7.4, we can see how these three remaining gaps are closed.

The *array_view* in this example provides a simplified view of the actual implementation. Because HSA allows HSA agents to directly access the HSA unified virtual memory, any pointer to host memory address space can also be used and dereferenced by HSAIL kernels. This simplifies the design of *array_view* on HSA to be merely a wrapper of a host-side pointer. This is a much simpler design than other GPGPU technology, such as OpenCL, where we need additional tricks to model memory buffers on host and device.

To ensure we have a kernel to be executed by *parallel_ for_each*, two additional functions are generated by the C++ AMP compiler automatically:

1. A class constructor is generated for the compiler-generated functor to initialize the kernel arguments. The purpose of the new constructor is to construct an almost identical copy of the lambda on the GPU side, based on the arguments received by the kernel.
2. A device function is generated that corresponds to the device kernel, which will be further compiled into HSAIL. It acts as a trampoline; it's mangled name can be queried and used by the host code at runtime. The trampoline function populates a clone of functor objects on the device side with the kernel arguments. It also populates an index object, based on the global index. Finally the cloned version of functor object is invoked in the trampoline.

Afterwards, the compiler also generates a host side member function that returns the mangled kernel name. At runtime, *parallel_ for_each* finalizes the HSA program stored in the binary executable, and obtains the address of the finalized kernel, using the name returned by this function.

7.5 C++ AMP COMPILATION FLOW

With the conceptual mapping of C++ AMP to HSA, defined previously, it's easier to understand how to compile and link a C++ AMP program (Figure 7.5). The Kalmar compiler employs a multi-step process:

```
1.    // This is to close the gap #1 (memory buffers)
2.    template <class T>
3.    class array_view {
4.         T *_host_ptr;
5.         size_t _sz;
6.    };
7.
8.    class vecAdd {
9.    private:
10.        array_view<const float, 1> va, vb;
11.        array_view<float, 1> vc;
12.
13.    public:
14.    vecAdd(array_view<const float, 1> a,
15.         array_view<const float, 1> b,
16.         array_view<float, 1> c) restrict(cpu)
17.         : va(a), vb(b), vc(c) {};
18.    void operator() (index<1> idx) restrict(amp) {
19.         cv[idx] = av[idx] + bv[idx];
20.    }
21.
22.    // This is to close the gap #2 (kernel entry point)
23.    #ifndef HOST_CODE
24.    vecAdd(float *a, size_t as, float *b, size_t bs,
25.         float *c, size_t cs) restrict(amp)
26.         : va(a, as), vb(b, bs), vc(c, cs) {};
27.
28.    void trampoline(const float *va, size_t vas,
29.                    const float *vb, size_t vbs,
30.                    float *vc, size_t vcs) {
31.        vecAdd tmp(va, vas, vb, vbs, vc, vcs);
32.        index<1> i(workitemabsid_u64(0));
33.        tmp(i);
34.    }
35.    #endif
36.
37.    // This is to close the gap #3 (kernel name)
38.    #ifdef HOST_CODE
39.    static const char * __get_kernel_name(void) {
40.         return mangled name of
41.          "void vecAdd::trampoline(const float *va, size_t vas,
42.                                   const float *vb, size_t vbs,
43.                                   float *vc, size_t vcs)"
44.    }
45.    #endif
46.
47.    };
```

FIGURE 7.4

Expanded version for C++ AMP vector addition (conceptual code).

1. As a first step, the input C++ AMP source code is compiled in a special "device mode" so that all C++ AMP-specific language rules will be checked and applied. The Kalmar compiler will produce HSA kernels (based on AMP-restricted functions called from the *parallel_for_each* function) into a LLVM bitcode file. All function calls within the kernels are inlined to simplify and optimize the codes generated.

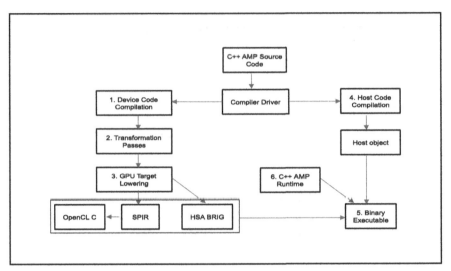

FIGURE 7.5

The Kalmar compiler compilation process.

2. The LLVM bitcode file will then go through some transformation passes to ensure that it can be lowered into a correct HSAIL program. All host code will be pruned first, then all pointers in the kernels and instructions that use them will be declared with the correct memory segment (*global*, *readonly*, *group*, or *private*) per HSA specification. It is worth noting that there is a fundamental difference between HSA and C++ AMP on the address spaces. In HSA, address space is part of the pointer type; whereas in C++ AMP, it is part of the pointer value. Hence a static compiler analysis is necessary to infer the address space of pointers from how they are assigned and used. Additional metadata will also be provided by the transformation, so the resulting LLVM bitcode can be lowered to HSAIL format.

3. The transformed LLVM bitcode is lowered into HSAIL and BRIG format by the LLVM compiler, targeting the HSAIL architecture.[2] It is saved as an object file, which is linked against host programs. The same bitcode is also lowered to OpenCL C or SPIR format, so the resultant kernel can be used on any OpenCL platforms that don't support HSA.

4. The input C++ AMP source code is then compiled again in "host mode" to emit host code. C++ AMP headers are designed so that none of the kernel code are directly used in host mode. Instead, calls to C++ AMP runtime API functions are used to launch kernels.

5. Host code and device code are linked to produce the final executable file.

6. Different C++ AMP runtime implementations can be loaded at runtime, so one executable can be used in HSA or OpenCL systems.

---

[2] https://github.com/HSAFoundation/HLC-HSAIL-Development-LLVM.

7.6 COMPILED C++ AMP CODE

Let's revisit the C++ AMP lambda in the vector addition sample (Line 21 of Figure 7.1), shown again in Figure 7.6 for easy reference.

After being compiled by the Kalmar compiler, the resultant HSAIL kernel code is shown in Figure 7.7. Please notice that the pragma section is omitted for brevity:

The compiled code may seem daunting at first, but it's actually not hard to understand with the following mapping:

- Line 1: common header of an HSAIL program
- Line 2: name of trampoline, mangled
- Line 3-10: serialized *array_view va*
- Line 11-18: serialized *array_view vb*
- Line 19-26: serialized *array_view vc*
- Line 30-31: get absolute work-item index, `idx` in C++ AMP lambda
- Line 43: obtain pointer to `va`
- Line 46: obtain pointer to `vb`
- Line 47: obtain pointer to `vc`
- Line 48-49: obtain address of `va[idx]`
- Line 50: load `va[idx]`
- Line 55-56: obtain address of `vb[idx]`
- Line 57: load `vb[idx]`
- Line 58: calculate `va[idx]` + `vb[idx]`
- Line 63-64: obtain address of `vc[idx]`
- Line 65: store the result of `va[idx]` + `vb[idx]` to `vc[idx]`

In Figure 7.7 there are some other kernarg load instructions, as well as some type conversion and addition instructions. Those instructions are code, which represent implementation details in *array_view*. In this example, those values are all zero and don't affect the calculation.

7.7 COMPILER SUPPORT FOR TILING IN C++AMP

Tiling is one of the most important techniques in optimizing GPU programs. Depending on the level of abstraction, a programming model can either provide implicit or explicit support for tiling. An implicit approach may involve automatically deducing the part of memory accesses to be tiled from a given kernel, and generating appropriate code to either transparently or semi-transparently tile the memory access pattern. This is done to achieve better memory locality and usually better performance. Conversely, an explicit

```
[=] (index<1> idx) restrict(amp) { cv[idx] = av[idx] + bv[idx]; }
```

FIGURE 7.6

C++ AMP lambda: vector addition.

```
1. version 0:20140528:$full:$large;
2. prog kernel
   &ZZ4mainEN3_EC__019__trampolineEPfiiiiiiiiS0_iiiiiiiS0_iiiiiii(
3.    kernarg_u64 %__arg_p3,
4.    kernarg_u32 %__arg_p4,
5.    kernarg_u32 %__arg_p5,
6.    kernarg_u32 %__arg_p6,
7.    kernarg_u32 %__arg_p7,
8.    kernarg_u32 %__arg_p8,
9.    kernarg_u32 %__arg_p9,
10.   kernarg_u32 %__arg_p10,
11.   kernarg_u64 %__arg_p11,
12.   kernarg_u32 %__arg_p12,
13.   kornarg_u32 %__arg_p13,
14.   kernarg_u32 %__arg_p14,
15.   kernarg_u32 %__arg_p15,
16.   kernarg_u32 %__arg_p16,
17.   kernarg_u32 %__arg_p17,
18.   kernarg_u32 %__arg_p18,
19.   kernarg_u64 %__arg_p19,
20.   kernarg_u32 %__arg_p20,
21.   kernarg_u32 %__arg_p21,
22.   kernarg_u32 %__arg_p22,
23.   kernarg_u32 %__arg_p23,
24.   kernarg_u32 %__arg_p24,
25.   kernarg_u32 %__arg_p25,
26.   kernarg_u32 %__arg_p26)
27.   {
28.   @ZZ4mainEN3_EC__019__cxxamp_trampolineEPfiiiiiiiiS0_iiiiiiiS0_iii
   iiii_entry:
29.   // BB#0:
30.   workitemabsid_u32      $s0, 0;
31.   cvt_u64_u32       $d0, $s0;
32.   ld_kernarg_align(8)_width(all)_u64      $d1, [%__global_offset_0];
33.   add_u64 $d0, $d0, $d1;
34.   cvt_u32_u64       $s0, $d0;
35.   ld_kernarg_align(4)_width(all)_u32      $s1, [%__arg_p24];
36.   add_u32 $s1, $s0, $s1;
37.   cvt_s64_s32       $d0, $s1;
38.   ld_kernarg_align(4)_width(all)_u32      $s1, [%__arg_p26];
39.   cvt_s64_s32       $d1, $s1;
40.   ld_kernarg_align(4)_width(all)_u32      $s1, [%__arg_p16];
41.   add_u32 $s1, $s0, $s1;
42.   add_u64 $d2, $d0, $d1;
43.   ld_kernarg_align(8)_width(all)_u64      $d3, [%__arg_p19];
44.   ld_kernarg_align(4)_width(all)_u32      $s2, [%__arg_p8];
45.   add_u32 $s0, $s0, $s2;
46.   ld_kernarg_align(8)_width(all)_u64      $d1, [%__arg_p11];
47.   ld_kernarg_align(8)_width(all)_u64      $d0, [%__arg_p3];
48.   shl_u64 $d2, $d2, 2;
```

FIGURE 7.7

Compiled HSAIL code: vector addition kernel.

```
49.   add_u64 $d2, $d3, $d2;
50.   ld_global_align(4)_f32  $s2, [$d2];
51.   cvt_s64_s32     $d2, $s1;
52.   ld_kernarg_align(4)_width(all)_u32    $s1, [%__arg_p18];
53.   cvt_s64_s32     $d3, $s1;
54.   add_u64 $d2, $d2, $d3;
55.   shl_u64 $d2, $d2, 2;
56.   add_u64 $d1, $d1, $d2;
57.   ld_global_align(4)_f32  $s1, [$d1];
58.   add_ftz_f32     $s1, $s1, $s2;
59.   cvt_s64_s32     $d1, $s0;
60.   ld_kernarg_align(4)_width(all)_u32    $s0, [%__arg_p10];
61.   cvt_s64_s32     $d2, $s0;
62.   add_u64 $d1, $d1, $d2;
63.   shl_u64 $d1, $d1, 2;
64.   add_u64 $d0, $d0, $d1;
65.   st_global_align(4)_f32  $s1, [$d0];
66.   ret;
67.   };
```

FIGURE 7.7, CONT'D

approach relies on the user to explicitly define memory objects in different address spaces that corresponds to on-chip and off-chip memory, and also the data movement between them. C++ AMP, HSA, CUDA, and OpenCL are all examples of such explicit programming models. The rest of this section deals with supporting explicit tiling in C++ AMP from a compiler writer's perspective.

For programming models that explicitly support tiling, one can usually find the following traits:

- A way to divide compute domain into fixed-sized chunks.
- A way to explicitly specify the address space where a data buffer resides, which is usually on-chip, off-chip, or thread-private. In HSA nomenclature, these address spaces are called memory segments; they map to *group*, *global*, and *private*, respectively.
- A way to provide synchronization barriers within these fixed-sized chunks of computation (i.e., work-items in a work-group).

We first review some background knowledge for readers who are not familiar with tiling in C++ AMP. In C++ AMP, an *extent* describes the size and the dimension of the compute domain. In addition, *tiled_extent* describes how to divide the compute domain. The division is analogous to how HSA work-group sizes divide the HSA work-item dimensions.

7.7.1 DIVIDING COMPUTE DOMAIN

In C++ AMP, a template method, "tile," is used in the class extent to compute a *tile_extent*. Its template parameters indicate the tiling size. Tiling in C++ AMP is

```
1. void mxm_amp_tiled(int M, int N, int W,
2.                    const std::vector<float>& va,
3.                    const std::vector<float>& vb,
4.                    std::vector<float>& result) {
5.    extent<2> e_a(M, N), e_b(N, W), e_c(M, W);
6.
7.    array_view<const float, 2> av_a(e_a, va);
8.    array_view<const float, 2> av_b(e_b, vb);
9.    array_view<float, 2> av_c(e_c, vresult);
10.
11.   extent<2> compute_domain(e_c);
12.   parallel_for_each(compute_domain.tile<TILE_SIZE, TILE_SIZE>(),
13.     [=] (tiled_index<TILE_SIZE, TILE_SIZE> tidx) restrict(amp)
14.       { mxm_amp_kernel(tidx, av_a, av_b, av_c); });
15.   }
```

FIGURE 7.8

A simple tiling example.

parameterized statically. To notify the library and compiler about tiling, we use a lambda kernel that has a slightly different signature (Line 13 in Figure 7.8) that, in turn, uses *tiled_index*. A *tiled_index* is analogous to a tuple that represents values retrieved from HSAIL instructions such as *workitemabsid*, *workitemid*, and *workgroupid*.

7.7.2 SPECIFYING ADDRESS SPACE AND BARRIERS

In a C++ AMP kernel function, *tile_static* qualifier is used to declare a memory object that resides in on-chip memory (*group* memory segment in HSA terms). And to force synchronization across threads in a C++ AMP tile, *tidx.barrier.wait* method can be used. As in HSA, work-items in the same tiling group will stop at the same program point where wait is called.

An interesting difference between HSA and C++ AMP lies in how the address space information is carried in pointers. In HSAIL memory instructions, memory segments must be specified in each memory operation. For example, to dereference a pointer in host memory and read value from it (*global* memory segment in HSA terms), *ld_global* instructions would be used. And to dereference a pointer in on-chip memory and store value to it (*group* memory segment in HSA terms), *st_group* instructions would be used. In C++ AMP, however, the address space information is part of the pointer's value. One could have a general pointer like:

```
float *foo
```

The pointer foo can point to a buffer declared using *tile_static* (which is equivalent to a *group* memory segment in HSA), and, with certain limitations, the same pointer can point to a value in global memory.

One could attempt to define C++ AMP *tile_static* as a macro that expands to Clang/LLVM's *__attribute__((address_space()))* qualifier, which is an extension made for Embedded C that goes to part of the pointer and memory object type.

However, the approach would fail to generate the correct address space information for pointer `foo` in following code snippet:

```
tile_static float bar;
float *foo = &bar;
```

In other words, we cannot embed the address space qualifier as part of the pointer type, but we need to be able to carry that information as part of variable definitions. The template approach does not allow proper differentiation between these values within the compiler.

An alternative approach is to specify address space as variable attributes, which are special markers that go with a particular variable, but are not part of its type. An example of such an attribute would be a compiler extension that specifies in which section of the object file a variable is defined. These kinds of attributes go with the variable's definition, but not its type. One can have two integers of the same type that stay in different sections; a pointer can be pointing to either of these two without type errors. We follow simple mapping approach that allows a data flow analysis to annotate address space information. The resultant code still looks largely like legitimate C++:

- Define C++ AMP *tile_static* as a variable attribute
- All pointers are initially without address spaces
- An SSA-based analysis is introduced to annotate the point-to variable attributes

The analysis only aims at an essentially easy subset of the much harder pointer analysis problems, which are generally undecidable. The next section describes in detail how the address space annotation is done.

7.8 MEMORY SEGMENT ANNOTATION

As we stated in the previous section, in HSAIL kernels, each memory operation must be associated with a memory segment. This indicates which memory region that a memory operation will commence. The notion of memory segments is a fundamental feature of HSA. This feature, however, is typically missing from high-level language such as C++ AMP. High-level languages put data into a single generic address space, and there is no need to indicate address space explicitly. To resolve this discrepancy, a special transformation is required to append correct memory segment designation for each memory operation.

In LLVM terminology, "address space" has the same meaning as "memory segment" in HSA. In the Kalmar compiler, after LLVM bitcode is generated, the generated code goes through a LLVM transformation pass to decide and promote (i.e., add type qualifiers to) declaration to the right address space. In theory, it is almost impossible to conclusively deduce address space for each declaration, because the analyzer lacks the global view that identifies how the kernels interact with each other. However, there are clues we can use to deduce correct address space in practical programs.

The implementation of *array* and *array_view* provides a hint to deduce correct address space. In C++ AMP, the only way to pass bulk data to kernels is to wrap them by *array* and *array_view*. C++ AMP runtime will register the underlying pointer with HSA runtime. Those data will be used in kernel by accessing the corresponding pointer on the argument of kernel function. Those pointers, as a result, should be qualified as in a global segment, because the data pointed to by them reside in host memory and are visible among all work-items in the grid. The pass will iterate through all the arguments of the kernel function, promote pointers to a *global* memory segment, and update all the memory operations associated with that pointer.

The *tile_static* data declarations cannot be deduced simply by data flow analysis, so they need to be preserved from the Kalmar compiler front end. In the current implementation, declarations with *tile_static* are placed into a special section in the generated bitcode. The LLVM transformation will identify it and mark all the memory operations with the correct address space.

Let us use a tiny C++ AMP code example to illustrate this annotation process (Figure 7.9).

After the Kalmar compiler front end, the code is transformed to pure LLVM IR (shown in Figure 7.10). There is no address space annotation in this version,

```
1.    void mm_kernel(int *p, int n)
2.    {
3.        tile_static int tmp[30];
4.        int id = amp_get_global_id(0);   // get work-item ID
5.        tmp[id] = 5566;
6.        amp_barrier(0);   // wait on all work-items to enter barrier
7.        p[id] = tmp[id];
8.    }
```

FIGURE 7.9

C++ AMP code to demonstrate memory segment annotation.

```
1. @mm_kernel.tmp  =  internal  unnamed_addr  global  [30  x  i32]
   zeroinitializer, align 16, section "clamp_opencl_local"
2. define void @mm_kernel(i32* nocapture %p, i32 %n) {
3.    %1 = tail call i32 bitcast (i32 (...)* @amp_get_global_id to i32
   (i32)*)(i32 0)
4.    %2 = sext i32 %1 to i64
5.    %3 = getelementptr inbounds [30 x i32]* @mm_kernel.tmp, i64 0,
   i64 %2
6.    store i32 5566, i32* %3, align 4, !tbaa !1
7.    %4 = tail call i32 bitcast (i32 (...)* @amp_barrier to i32
   (i32)*)(i32 0) #2
8.    %5 = load i32* %3, align 4, !tbaa !1
9.    %6 = getelementptr inbounds i32* %p, i64 %2
10.   store i32 %5, i32* %6, align 4, !tbaa !1
11.   ret void
12.   }
```

FIGURE 7.10

LLVM IR produced for the kernel in Figure 7.9, before memory segment annotation.

```
1. @mm_kernel.tmp = internal addrspace(3) unnamed_addr global [30 x
   i32] zeroinitializer, align 4
2. define void @mm_kernel(i32 addrspace(1)* nocapture %p, i32 %n) {
3.    %1 = tail call i32 bitcast (i32 (...)* @amp_get_global_id to i32
   (i32)*)(i32 0)
4.    %2 = getelementptr inbounds [30 x i32] addrspace(3)*
   @mm_kernel.tmp, i32 0, i32 %1
5.    store i32 5566, i32 addrspace(3)* %2, align 4, !tbaa !2
6.    %3 = tail call i32 bitcast (i32 (...)* @amp_barrier to i32
   (i32)*)(i32 0)
7.    %4 = load i32 addrspace(3)* %2, align 4, !tbaa !2
8.    %5 = getelementptr inbounds i32 addrspace(1)* %p, i32 %1
9.    store i32 %4, i32 addrspace(1)* %5, align 4, !tbaa !2
10.   ret void
11.   }
```

FIGURE 7.11

LLVM IR produced for the kernel in Figure 7.9, after memory segment annotation.

and it will produce incorrect results. Notice that at the top of Figure 7.10, variable tmp is placed into a special ELF section (clamp_opencl_local). This section name is inherited from an original implementation of C++ AMP based on OpenCL from MulticoreWare. The section is shared between the OpenCL-based and HSAIL-based C++ AMP implementations, as the nature of the variables placed in this section are compatible between these two implementations.

Note that Line 6 in Figure 7.10 corresponds to the assignment "tmp[id] = 5566" in Figure 7.9. However, there is no annotation that this store instruction is directed to the address space of tmp[id]. Similarly, Line 8 corresponds to the part of the statement "p[id] = tmp[id]" that reads tmp[id]. There is also no indication that this load accesses the address space of tmp[id].

After processing by a special LLVM pass, the correct address spaces are deduced and appended to the associated memory operations. The store instruction to and load instruction from tmp[id] are annotated with *addrspace(3)*, which is mapped to the group memory segment of HSA. The generated code can now be executed correctly, as illustrated in the following refined LLVM IR (Figure 7.11).

After all address space qualifiers are specified, HSAIL compiler can take this LLVM bitcode and emit HSAIL memory instructions with correct memory segments.

7.9 TOWARDS GENERIC C++ FOR HSA

Until now, we have used code examples to illustrate the important aspects of compiling C++ AMP programs into host code and HSAIL kernels. In previous sections, the power of shared virtual memory was briefly mentioned in the conceptual implementation of *array_view*. On HSA, it is just a wrapper of a pointer to a memory buffer on host memory. On other GPU computing platforms without shared virtual memory support, special attention must be carried out to correctly model and move memory buffers between host memory and device memory.

C++ AMP was developed prior to HSA, thus it imposes rather strict rules on the kind of host objects that can be captured by kernels in C++ AMP. Essentially, to let C++ AMP kernels access large memory buffers and perform computations, buffers must be encapsulated in instances of *array* or *array_view*, so they can be captured and used within C++ AMP kernels.

On HSA systems, such restrictions can be lifted. With shared virtual memory, it is actually possible to capture all kinds of data structures on host memory and access them in HSAIL kernels. In the Kalmar compiler, a special compilation flag (*-Xclang -fhsa-ext*) is created to enable this feature. For example, to do vector addition on HSA, we can write codes like the one shown in Figure 7.12.

Compare the new vector addition example (Figure 7.12) with the original C++ AMP version (Figure 7.1). It is obvious that all instances of *array_view* are gone. Instead, pointers to arrays are captured by copy (*[=]* in C++ 11 syntax) within the C++ AMP kernel, and calculations are carried out via these pointers. Before HSA, such kind of variable capturing was not supported by hardware and not allowed in C++ AMP specification.

The ability to capture generic C++ pointer variables by the Kalmar compiler is enabled by three important features of HSA:

1. Same machine model on host CPU and HSA agents: widths of scalar and pointer types are consistent among computing devices in an HSA system. Compilers can use the same code generation logic for both host code and HSAIL kernels, especially for instructions that dereference memory via pointers.

```
1. #include <amp.h>
2. #include <cstdlib>
3. using namespace concurrency;
4. int main(void) {
5.      const int N = 10;
6.      float a[N];
7.      float b[N];
8.      float c[N];
9.      float sum = 0.f;
10.     for (int i = 0; i < N; i++) {
11.       a[i] = 1.0f * rand() / RAND_MAX;
12.       b[i] = 1.0f * rand() / RAND_MAX;
13.     }
14.     float *p_a = &a[0];
15.     float *p_b = &b[0];
16.     float *p_c = &c[0];
17.     extent<1> e(N);
18.     parallel_for_each(e,
19.                 [=] (index<1> idx) restrict(amp)
20.                 {
21.                     p_c[idx[0]] = p_a[idx[0]] + p_b[idx[0]];
22.                 });
23.     return 0;
24. }
```

FIGURE 7.12

More generic C++ code example: vector addition in HSA (first version).

2. Shared virtual memory: host memory (*global* memory segment) is visible among all HSA agents. This means that as long as the value of a host pointer is obtained in HSAIL kernels, it can be used to load and store host memory.
3. Cache coherency domains: data access to global memory from all HSA agents is coherent without the need for explicit cache maintenance actions. This means that no special care is required in HSAIL kernels with respect to CPU caches.

More detailed information of these three features can be found in the *HSA platform system architecture specification* [2]. Based on these features of HSA, the Kalmar compiler literally reuses existing code generation logic and memory segment annotation logic to generate correct code. This code correctly dereferences host pointers, and is thus captured when compiled with the appropriate compiler flag settings for HSA.

The previously shown code can be further simplified by capturing host data structures by reference (*[&]* in C++ 11 syntax). For example, vector addition on HSA can be implemented in Figure 7.13.

The mechanism to capture host objects by reference is a bit more complicated than capturing host pointers by copy. The compiler needs to provide special logic to create pointers to host data structures, append them as HSAIL kernel arguments, and use them in the calculations within kernels.

Note that currently there are still some limitations in the Kalmar compiler with respect to shared virtual memory. For example, virtual member functions cannot be used within C++ AMP kernels as of now, because all functions used by HSAIL kernels are currently inlined at compile time; also, addresses of virtual member

```
1. #include <amp.h>
2. #include <cstdlib>
3. using namespace concurrency;
4. int main(void) {
5.      const int N = 10;
6.      float a[N];
7.      float b[N];
8.      float c[N];
9.      float sum = 0.f;
10.     for (int i = 0; i < N; i++) {
11.       a[i] = 1.0f * rand() / RAND_MAX;
12.       b[i] = 1.0f * rand() / RAND_MAX;
13.     }
14.     extent<1> e(N);
15.     parallel_for_each(e,
16.                       [&] (index<1> idx) restrict(amp)
17.                       {
18.                         c[idx[0]] = a[idx[0]] + b[idx[0]];
19.                       });
20.     return 0;
21. }
```

FIGURE 7.13

C++ AMP code example: vector addition in HSA (second version).

functions can only be determined at runtime via C++ virtual tables. However, this limitation is expected to be removed in the future by supporting indirect function calls in HSA kernels.

7.10 COMPILER SUPPORT FOR PLATFORM ATOMICS

With shared virtual memory, it is possible to create programs that allow host code and HSAIL kernels to process the very same data structure in host memory. In this section, we show how to map C++ 11 *<atomic>* operations into HSAIL instructions, and how we can create HSA programs where host code and HSAIL kernels cooperate with each other through atomic operations.

HSA provides several features to ensure operations from host code and HSAIL kernels are well synchronized:

- Atomic memory operations
- Memory consistency model
- Signal and synchronization instructions

The first two features are also standardized in C++ 11, and can be found in *<atomic>* header. However, C++ 11 specification only defines the behavior for CPUs and doesn't take heterogeneous systems into consideration. On the other hand, HSA specifies instructions for atomic memory operations but doesn't specify how high-level programming languages should use them. Therefore there is a gap to be filled by the compiler.

In the C++ 11 *<atomic>* header, there are class templates that create classes with atomic operations. Specializations of these class templates provide classes that could instantiate atomic objects for common data types, such as integer or floating point numbers. Almost all atomic objects also support the following atomic operations: load from memory, store to memory, read-modify-write, exchange memory location, and compare-and-swap. The atomic store and atomic load operations are stores and loads that can have memory ordering actions associated with them.

The implementation of libc++, the C++ library used in the Kalmar compiler, translates classes and functions defined in the *<atomic>* header into the following LLVM IR instructions: *cmpxchg*, *atomicrmw*, *atomic load*, and *atomic store*. Basically, they all take the following operands:

- Data type and length
- Pointer to the memory location to be accessed
- Memory order: to specify synchronization between memory operations among different CPU threads. Possible values are: *monotonic, acquire, release, acq_rel, seq_cst*.

For more detailed information about atomic operations in C++ 11, please refer to Chapter 29 of *Working Draft, Standard for Programming Language C++* [3]. For implementation details of *<atomic>*, please refer to the source code of libc++ and *LLVM Language Reference Manual* [4].

HSA requires the following standard atomic memory operations to be supported: load from memory, store to memory, read-modify-write, exchange memory location, and compare-and-swap. Each atomic memory operation must specify the following properties:

- Data type and length
- Address of the memory location to be accessed
- Memory segment: which memory segment (e.g., global segment or group segment) does the operation take place
- Memory order: memory ordering model used to synchronize between memory operations among different work-items. Possible values are: `rlx` (relaxed), `scacq` (sequentially consistent acquire), `screl` (sequentially consistent release), `scar` (sequentially consistent acquire and release)
- Memory scope: the scope of an atomic operation and memory fence. It determines the set of work-items that are affected by atomicity and memory order of an operation. Possible values are: `wi` (work-item), `wv` (wavefront), `wg` (work-group), `cmp` (HSA component), and `sys` (HSA system).
- Equivalence class: an optional field used to provide alias information to the HSA finalizer. The HSA finalizer will assume that any two memory operations in different classes do not overlap and can be reordered.

For more detailed information about memory operations on HSA, please refer to Chapter 6 of *HSA Programmer's Reference Manual* [5].

Based on the observations above, we can understand how the C++ 11 *<atomic>* header can be translated into atomic operations in LLVM IR. And to correctly further lower the LLVM IR into HSAIL instructions, we need to build a mapping table between them, as shown in Table 7.2.

Based on Table 7.2, we can make the following observations:

- The list of supported atomic instructions and their semantics have 1-1 mapping between LLVM IR and HSAIL.
- Thanks to shared virtual memory and the consistent machine model between HSA agent and the host CPU, a valid pointer on the host is also used as valid in HSAIL kernels.
- The list of memory order and their semantics could almost be 1-1 mapped.
- The notion of memory segment, memory scope, and equivalence class in HSAIL is absent in LLVM IR.

Therefore, once we resolve the gap and fill in the information of memory segment, memory scope, and equivalence class into the LLVM IR, we can compile atomic operations defined in the C++ 11 *<atomic>* header into HSAIL instructions.

In Section 7.8, we demonstrated that by using an SSA analysis pass, we can deduce the memory segment for memory operations within HSAIL kernels. We can further extend this analysis pass to specify the memory scope for atomic memory operations. This is done by appending a metadata for each atomic operation. Due to the status of currently available HSA implementations, we will always use `sys` memory scope for

Table 7.2 Mapping of Atomic Operations Between LLVM IR and HSAIL

Concepts	LLVM IR	HSAIL
Atomic instructions	*atomic load*	*atomic_ld*
	atomic store	*atomicnoret_st*
	atomicrmw	*atomic_and, atomic_or, atomic_xor, atomic_add, atomic_sub, atomic_exch, atomic_max, atomic_min, atomicnoret_ and, atomicnoret_and, atomicnoret_or, atomicnoret_xor, atomicnoret_add, atomicnoret_sub, atomicnoret_max, atominoret_min* depending on the operation operand of *atomicrmw*
	cmpxchg	*atomic_cas, atomicnoret_cas*
Memory location	Must be specified	Must be specified
Data type and length	Must be specified ·	Must be specified
Memory segment	N/A	Must be specified
Memory order	*monotonic*	`rlx`
	acquire	`scacq`
	release	`screl`
	acq_rel	`scar`
	seq_cst	For *atomicrmw* and *cmpxchg*, use `scar`
		For *atomic load* and *atomic store*, use `screl` or `scacq`, plus a corresponding *memfence* HSAIL instruction
Memory scope	N/A	Must be specified. Possible values: `wi`, `wv`, `wg`, `cmp`, `sys`.
Equivalence class	N/A	Optional

now. Equivalence class could be omitted, because it's an optional field in HSAIL. To our knowledge, no HSA implementation uses this field for optimization yet.

7.10.1 ONE SIMPLE EXAMPLE OF PLATFORM ATOMICS

With the mapping defined in Table 7.2, let's use a simple example to illustrate how platform atomics are compiled into LLVM IR and HSAIL instructions (Figure 7.14).

In the example above, we prepare three arrays of atomic integers, and capture them via shared virtual memory in the kernel. Assume `tid` is the work-item index of the grid; various atomic instructions are carried out for each element in those arrays:

- Line 27: `a[tid]` is atomically increased by 1. Note that no memory ordering model is specified in the atomic operation. The default in C++ is sequential consistency (*std::memory_order_seq_cst*), which will be assumed by the Kalmar compiler.
- Line 28: `b[tid]` is atomically decreased by 1.
- Line 29: `c[tid]` is atomically stored as 0.

```
1.    #include <random>
2.    #include <atomic>
3.    #include <amp.h>
4.    int main () {
5.       // define inputs and output
6.       const int vecSize = 2048;
7.       std::atomic_int table_a[vecSize];
8.       std::atomic_int table_b[vecSize];
9.       std::atomic_int table_c[vecSize];
10.      auto ptr_a = &table_a[0];
11.      auto ptr_b = &table_b[0];
12.      auto ptr_c = &table_c[0];
13.
14.      // initialize test data
15.      std::random_device rd;
16.      std::uniform_int_distribution<int32_t> int_dist;
17.      for (int i = 0; i < vecSize; ++i) {
18.        table_a[i].store(int_dist(rd));
19.        table_b[i].store(int_dist(rd));
20.      }
21.      // launch kernel
22.      Concurrency::extent<1> e(vecSize);
23.      parallel_for_each(
24.        e,
25.        [=](Concurrency::index<1> idx) restrict(amp) {
26.          int tid = idx[0];
27.          (ptr_a + tid)->fetch_add(1);
28.          (ptr_b + tid)->fetch_sub(1);
29.          (ptr_c + tid)->store(0);
30.          (ptr_c + tid)->fetch_add(
31.            (ptr_a + tid)->load(std::memory_order_acquire),
32.            std::memory_order_release);
33.          (ptr_c + tid)->fetch_add(
34.            (ptr_b + tid)->load(std::memory_order_seq_cst),
35.            std::memory_order_acq_rel);
36.      });
37.      return 0;
38.    }
```

FIGURE 7.14

C++ AMP code example: atomic integer arithmetic in HSAIL kernel.

- Line 30: Atomically load the value of a[tid] with memory order *std::memory_order_acquire*. And atomically add the value to c[tid] with memory order *std::memory_order_release*.
- Line 31: Atomically load the value of b[tid] with memory order *std::memory_seq_cst*. And atomically add the value to c[tid] with memory order *std::memory_order_acq_rel*.

The net effect of the kernel would be:

- Each element in a[] would be increased by 1.
- Each element in b[] would be decreased by 1.
- Each element in c[] would become the sum of the elements in a[] and b[] with the same index number.

The Kalmar compiler would emit the following LLVM IR for the kernel, after the SSA analysis pass. This would deduce the memory segment and assign the memory scope for atomic memory operations (Figure 7.15).

It can be observed atomic instructions in C++ are now mapped to LLVM IR. They are:

- Line 2-4: compute `tid`, work-item index within the grid
- Line 5: get address of `a[tid]`
- Line 6: *atomicrmw* add 1 to `a[tid]`, with memory order *seq_cst*, memory scope specified in metadata !6. Line 5-6 corresponds to Line 27 in Figure 7.14. Note that *seq_cst* is the default memory order for C++ atomic operations.
- Line 7: get address of `b[tid]`
- Line 8: *atomicrmw* subtract 1 from `b[tid]`, with memory order *seq_cst*, memory scope specified in metadata !6. Line 7-8 corresponds to Line 28 in Figure 7.14.
- Line 9: get address of `c[tid]`

```
1.   define                    cc76                    void
     @ZZ4mainEN3_EC__019__cxxamp_trampolineEPNSt3__16atomicIiEES3_S3_({
     { { i32 } } } addrspace(1)*, { { { i32 } } } addrspace(1)*,
     { { { i32 } } } addrspace(1)*) {
2.   %4 = tail call spir_func i64 @amp_get_global_id(i32 0)
3.   %sext = shl i64 %4, 32
4.   %5 = ashr exact i64 %sext, 32
5.   %6 = getelementptr inbounds { { { i32 } } } addrspace(1)* %0,
     i64 %5, i32 0, i32 0, i32 0
6.   %7 = atomicrmw add i32 addrspace(1)* %6, i32 1 seq_cst, !
     mem.scope !6
7.   %8 = getelementptr inbounds { { { i32 } } } addrspace(1)* %1,
     i64 %5, i32 0, i32 0, i32 0
8.   %9 = atomicrmw sub i32 addrspace(1)* %8, i32 1 seq_cst, !
     mem.scope !6
9.   %10 = getelementptr inbounds { { { i32 } } } addrspace(1)* %2,
     i64 %5, i32 0, i32 0, i32 0
10.  store atomic i32 0, i32 addrspace(1)* %10 seq_cst, align 4, !
     mem.scope !6
11.  %11 = load atomic i32 addrspace(1)* %6 acquire, align 4, !
     mem.scope !6
12.  %12 = atomicrmw add i32 addrspace(1)* %10, i32 %11 release, !
     mem.scope !6
13.  %13 = load atomic i32 addrspace(1)* %8 seq_cst, align 4, !
     mem.scope !6
14.  %14 = atomicrmw add i32 addrspace(1)* %10, i32 %13 acq_rel, !
     mem.scope !6
15.  ret void
16.  }
17.
18.  !6 = metadata !{i32 5}
```

FIGURE 7.15

Compiled LLVM IR for code in Figure 7.14.

- Line 10: *store atomic* 0 to c[tid], with memory order *seq_cst*, memory scope specified in metadata !6. Line 9-10 corresponds to Line 29 in Figure 7.14.
- Line 11: *load atomic* from a[tid], with memory order *acquire*, memory scope specified in metadata !6.
- Line 12: *atomicrmw* add a[tid] to c[tid], with memory order *release*, memory scope specified in metadata !6. Line 11-12 corresponds to Line 30 in Figure 7.14.
- Line 13: *load atomic* from b[tid], with memory order *seq_cst*, memory scope specified in metadata !6.
- Line 14: *atomicrmw* add b[tid] to c[tid], with memory order *acq_rel*, memory scope specified in metadata !6. Line 13-14 corresponds to Line 31 in Figure 7.14.
- Line 18: metadata !6 is defined to be an integer value 5, which corresponds to sys memory scope in HSAIL.

LLVM IR produced in the previous step would then be lowered to HSAIL format.

Atomic statements written in C++ in Figure 7.14 are now compiled to LLVM IR in Figure 7.15, and lowered to HSAIL in Figure 7.16. The following is a brief explanation of the HSAIL codes:

- Line 11-17: compute tid, work-item index within the grid
- Line 22-23: get address of a[tid]
- Line 25-26: use *atomicnoret_add_global_scar_sys* to atomically add 1 to a[tid], which is in *global* memory segment, with memory order scar, memory scope sys. This corresponds to Line 5-6 in Figure 7.15, and Line 17 in Figure 7.14.
- Line 18, Line 21: get address of b[tid]
- Line 25, Line 27: use *atomicnoret_sub_global_scar_sys* to atomically subtract 1 from b[tid], which is in *global* memory segment, with memory order scar, memory scope sys. This corresponds to Line 7-8 in Figure 7.15, and Line 28 in Figure 7.14.
- Line 19-20: get address of c[tid]
- Line 24, Line 28: use *atomicnoret_st_global_screl* to atomically store 0 to c[tid], with memory order screl, memory scope sys. This corresponds to Line 9-10 in Figure 7.15, and Line 29 in Figure 7.14. Also because *seq_cst* memory order is used in LLVM IR, one *memfence_scacq_global(sys)* instruction is inserted in Line 29 to ensure results of all memory access in previous instructions are visible to work-items.
- Line 30: use *atomic_ld_global_scacq_sys* to atomically load a[tid], which is in *global* memory segment, with memory order scacq, memory scope sys.
- Line 31: use *atomicnoret_add_global_screl_sys* to atomically add a[tid] to c[tid], with memory order screl, memory scope sys. Line 29-Line 31 corresponds to Line 11-12 in Figure 7.15, and Line 30 in Figure 7.14.

```
1.   prog                                                          kernel
  &ZZ4mainEN3_EC__019__trampolineEPNSt3__16atomicIiEES3_S3_(
2.        kernarg_u64 %__qlobal_offset_0,
3.        kernarg_u64 %__global_offset_1,
4.        kernarg_u64 %__global_offset_2,
5.        kernarg_u64 %__arg_p3,
6.        kernarg_u64 %__arg_p4,
7.        kernarg_u64 %__arg_p5)
8.   {
9.   @ZZ4mainEN3_EC__019__cxxamp_trampolineEPNSt3__16atomicIiEES3_S3
  __entry:
10.       // BB#0:
11.       workitemabsid_u32     $s0, 0;
12.       cvt_u64_u32     $d0, $s0;
13.       ld_kernarg_align(8)_width(all)_u64     $d1,
  [%__global_offset_0];
14.       add_u64 $d0, $d0, $d1;
15.       shl_u64 $d0, $d0, 32;
16.       shr_s64 $d0, $d0, 32;
17.       shl_u64 $d2, $d0, 2;
18.       ld_kernarg_align(8)_width(all)_u64     $d1, [%__arg_p4];
19.       ld_kernarg_align(8)_width(all)_u64     $d0, [%__arg_p5];
20.       add_u64 $d0, $d0, $d2;
21.       add_u64 $d1, $d1, $d2;
22.       ld_kernarg_align(8)_width(all)_u64     $d3, [%__arg_p3];
23.       add_u64 $d2, $d3, $d2;
24.       mov_b32 $s0, 0;
25.       mov_b32 $s1, 1;
26.       atomicnoret_add_global_scar_sys_s32     [$d2], $s1;
27.       atomicnoret_sub_global_scar_sys_s32     [$d1], $s1;
28.       atomicnoret_st_global_screl_sys_b32     [$d0], $s0;
29.       memfence_scacq_global(sys);
30.       atomic_ld_global_scacq_sys_b32 $s0, [$d2];
31.       atomicnoret_add_global_screl_sys_s32   [$d0], $s0;
32.       memfence_screl_global(sys);\
33.       atomic_ld_global_scacq_sys_b32 $s0, [$d1];
34.       atomicnoret_add_global_scar_sys_s32   [$d0], $s0;
35.       ret;
36.   };
```

FIGURE 7.16

Compiled HSAIL instructions.

- Because *seq_cst* memory order is used in the next instruction in LLVM IR, one *memfence_screl_global(sys)* instruction is inserted in Line 32 to ensure results of all memory access in previous instructions are visible to work-items.
- Line 33: use *atomic_ld_global_scacq_sys* to atomically load b[tid], which is in *global* memory segment, with memory order scacq, memory scope sys.
- Line 34: use *atomicnoret_add_global_scar_sys* to atomically add b[tid] to c[tid], with memory order scar, memory scope sys. This corresponds to Line 13-14 in Figure 7.15, and Line 31 in Figure 7.14.

The reader is encouraged to check the mapping between C++, LLVM IR, and HSAIL, along with Table 7.2, to get a more clear understanding of how these HSAIL atomic instructions are produced.

7.11 COMPILER SUPPORT FOR NEW/DELETE OPERATORS

In the programs seen in previous sections, all memory allocations were determined statically before program execution. But there are cases where the memory used by a program can only be determined at runtime. C++ programming language provides the operators new and delete, so programs can dynamically allocate memory. According to the original C++ AMP specification, dynamic memory allocation is not allowed in functions with the *restrict(amp)* restriction specifier. In this section, we show how we can lift this restriction in the Kalmar compiler, and use HSA-specific features such as shared virtual memory, platform atomics, and signal to implement the operators *new* and *delete* in HSA kernels. This is a small step to make the Kalmar compiler to become a generic C++ 11 compiler for HSA systems.

Figure 7.17 shows a simple memory allocation application in C++ AMP.

To support memory allocation/deallocation operators such as *new*, *new[]*, *delete*, and *delete[]*, additional library functions must be provided. Take Figure 7.17 as an example:

1. The call to operator *new* in Line 7 is compiled into a LLVM IR *call* instruction, which references to a symbol called *@_Znwm*. *@_Znwm* is an built-in function that contains the actual algorithm for dynamic memory allocation, and is expected to be supplied by the runtime library.
2. The promoted LLVM IR goes through the HSAIL back end. The LLVM *call* instruction would be lowered to an HSAIL *call* instruction.
3. The dynamic memory allocation logic is implemented in handwritten HSAIL assembly, embedded in the HSAIL function *&_Znwm* function, which is placed into the HSAIL built-in library. The Kalmar compiler completes the process by concatenating the HSAIL generated from C++ AMP source code and HSAIL built-in library.

```
1.    array_view<unsigned long int, 1> sum(vecSize, sumCPP);
2.    const int vecSize = 16;
3.    unsigned long int sumCPP[vecSize];
4.    parallel_for_each(
5.        extent<1>(vecSize),
6.        [=](index<1> idx) restrict(amp) {
7.        sum[idx[0]] = (unsigned long int)new unsigned int(idx[0]);
8.    });
```

FIGURE 7.17

C++ AMP code example: operator *new*.

Table 7.3 Mapping Between C++ Dynamic Memory Operators, LLVM and HSAIL Functions

C++ Dynamic Memory Operators	LLVM Function	HSAIL Function
void* operator new (std::size_t);	@_Znwm	&_Znwm
void* operator new[] (std::size_t);	@_Znam	&_Znam
void operator delete (void*) noexcept;	@_ZdlPv	&_ZdlPv
void operator delete[] (void*) noexcept;	@_ZdaPv	&_ZdaPv

The table above summarizes these operators and their corresponding LLVM function symbols (Table 7.3).

7.11.1 IMPLEMENTING NEW/DELETE OPERATORS WITH PLATFORM ATOMICS

The simplest way to implement dynamic allocation/deallocation is to statically allocate a block of memory in the HSAIL built-in library first. All of the allocation and deallocation calls then just manipulate that memory block. But under such a paradigm, the total allocation memory size needs to be determined at the beginning of the application execution and cannot be extended at runtime. To avoid the limitation, we can leverage HSA platform atomics to implement a scheme based on CPU-GPU communication.

In this scheme, GPU threads send their memory allocation/deallocation requests to one CPU thread. Then the CPU thread invokes *malloc()/free()* in C standard library and sends the result back to the GPU threads. Figure 7.18 shows the conceptual implementation of *&_Znwm* (operator *new*) *&_Znam* (operator *new[]*):

```
1.   int index = idx[0];
2.   // store the parameter
3.   (ptr_param + index)->store(n, std::memory_order_release);
4.   // store the flag value
5.   (ptr_flag + index)->store(1, std::memory_order_release);
6.   // wait until syscall returns
7.   while ((ptr_flag + index)->load(std::memory_order_acquire));
8.   // load result from CPU thread
9.   long address =
10.      (ptr_param + index)->load(std::memory_order_acquire);
11.  return address;
```

FIGURE 7.18

Implementation of *&_Znwm* (*new*) and *&_Znam* (*new[]*) (conceptual code).

- In Line 1, `ptr_param` is a pointer that points to `param`, where `param[index]` stores the parameter for the GPU work-item of *index* to communicate with the CPU thread that provides memory allocation service. The `ptr_flag` is a pointer that points to `flag`, which is an array, as well. The `flag[index]` is dedicated to store the synchronization flag for CPU-GPU communication.
- In Line 3, a work-item stores `n`, which is the requested size of memory allocation, into `param[index]`.
- In Line 5, 1 is stored in `flag` (which means *malloc()*). The flag would be set to 0 by the CPU thread after the memory allocation request is handled.
- In Line 7, the GPU work-item waits for the flag. When the flag is set to 0 by the CPU, the `param[index]` would contain the address returned by the *malloc()* executed by CPU.

Let's take a look of the conceptual implementation of *&_ZdlPv* (operator *delete*) and *&_ZdaPv* (operator *delete[]*) (Figure 7.19).

The basic idea of operator *delete/delete[]* is almost the same as operator *new/new[]*. One difference is that in Line 3, we store 2 (it means *free()*) rather than 1 (it means *malloc()*) in `flag`. The other difference is that the result from the CPU thread is ignored.

We also need to create a CPU thread to handle the memory allocation/deallocation request from GPU threads. A simple implementation is shown in Figure 7.20:

- `ptr_param` and `ptr_flag` are the same as those of Figures 7.18 and 7.19.
- `max_vec_size` is the largest possible grid size.
- The loop of Line 2 is a polling operation.
- In Line 4, the value of `flag` is atomically loaded and saved into `syscall` variable. The store operation with *std::memory_order_release* in the implementation of operator new/delete, and the load operation here in Line 4 with *std::memory_order_acquire* would establish proper release-acquire memory ordering.
- In Line 7, the parameter `param`, stored by the GPU thread, is loaded.
- If `syscall` equals to 1, the memory allocation request would be redirected to *malloc()* in Line 13.
- If `syscall` equals to 2, the memory deallocation request would be redirected to *free()* in Line 16.
- In Line 20, the return address of *malloc()* is stored into `param`.
- In Line 23, `flag` is reset, and the loop (i.e., Line 7 of Figures 7.18 and 7.19) of operator *new/delete* implementation stops.

```
1.    int index = idx[0];
2.    // store the parameter
3.    (ptr_param + index)->store(address, std::memory_order_release);
4.    // store the flag value
5.    (ptr_flag + index)->store(2, std::memory_order_release);
6.    // wait until syscall returns
7.    while ((ptr_flag + index)->load(std::memory_order_acquire));
```

FIGURE 7.19

Implementation of *&_ZdlPv* (*delete*) and *&_ZdaPv* (*delete[]*) (conceptual code).

```
1.    while (true) {
2.      for (int i = 0; i < max_vec_size; ++i) {
3.        // load the flag value
4.        syscall = (ptr_flag + i)->load(std::memory_order_acquire);
5.        if (syscall) {
6.          // load parameter
7.          long param =
8.              (ptr_param + i)->load(std::memory_order_acquire);
9.          // do actual stuff
10.         long result;
11.         switch (syscall) {
12.           case 1: // new, new[]
13.             result = (long)malloc(param);
14.           break;
15.           case 2: // delete, delete[]
16.             free ((void *)param);
17.           break;
18.         }
19.         // store result
20.         (ptr_param + i)->store(result,
21.                               std::memory_order_release);
22.         // reset flag
23.         (ptr_flag + i)->store(0,
24.                               std::memory_order_release);
25.      }
26.    }
27.  }
```

FIGURE 7.20

C++ AMP runtime: a CPU thread to handle memory allocation/deallocation requests from GPU threads.

7.11.2 PROMOTING NEW/DELETE RETURNED ADDRESS TO GLOBAL MEMORY SEGMENT

In our scheme, GPU work-items leverage a CPU thread to allocate memory. The memory allocated is in the global segment, so the HSAIL load and store instructions accessing the allocated memory should be annotated as accesses to the global segment. The Kalmar compiler implements an LLVM pass to identify all memory accesses (e.g., "store i32, i32*," "load i32*," ...) that use the address returned by &_Znwm and &_Znam and transform them into memory access of global memory (e.g., "store i32, i32 addrspace(1)*," "load i32 addrspace(1)*," ...).

7.11.3 IMPROVE NEW/DELETE OPERATORS BASED ON WAIT API/SIGNAL HSAIL INSTRUCTION

We have so far presented a working implementation of the *new/delete* operators. However, the busy waiting (polling) by the GPU work-items on the CPU thread and vice versa can result in significant performance degradation. We use the HSA runtime wait API [6] and the HSAIL signal instruction to resolve this issue. Signals are used for communication between HSA agents. Wait API (e.g., *hsa:signal_wait_acquire*) is used to wait until a signal value satisfies a specified condition, or a certain amount of time has elapsed. The HSAIL signal instruction (*signal*) is intended for notification between agents. We want the CPU thread to block until GPU threads enter operator *new/delete*. The CPU thread then begins polling when GPU threads are in operator *new/delete*. Therefore, we rewrite the possible implementation of the CPU thread in Figure 7.21.

The main change is in Line 3 of Figure 7.21. The purpose of Line 3 is to wait until *signalHandle* becomes a nonzero number. This version takes advantage of the HSA wait API to put the CPU thread to sleep until it receives a signal. To prevent the CPU thread from waiting endlessly after the application terminates, the *hsa:signal_wait_acquire* returns with a return value of −1 when the application terminates. In this case, Line 4 will be true and the loop is terminated.

The conceptual device code of the *new/delete* operators should be revised, as shown in Figures 7.22 and 7.23.

```
1.    while (true) {
2.      hsa_signal_value_t ret;
3.      while ((ret = hsa_signal_wait_acquire(signalHandle, HSA_NE,
            0, UINT64_MAX, HSA_WAIT_EXPECTANCY_UNKNOWN)) == 0);
4.      if (ret == -1)
5.          break;
6.      for (int i = 0; i < max_vec_size; ++i) {
7.        // load the flag value
8.        syscall = (ptr_flag + i)->load(std::memory_order_acquire);
9.        if (syscall) {
10.           // load parameter
11.           long param =
12.               (ptr_param + i)->load(std::memory_order_acquire);
13.           // do actual stuff
14.           long result;
15.           switch (syscall) {
16.             case 1: // new, new[]
17.                result = (long)malloc(param);
18.             break;
19.             case 2: // delete, delete[]
20.                free ((void *)param);
21.             break;
22.           }
23.           // store result
24.           (ptr_param + i)->store(result,
25.                                   std::memory_order_release);
26.           // reset flag
27.           (ptr_flag + i)->store(0,
28.                                   std::memory_order_release);
29.      }
30.    }
31.  }
```

FIGURE 7.21

C++ AMP runtime: rewrite of Figure 7.20 with HSA runtime wait API.

```
1.    signalnoret_add_screl_s64_sig64 signalHandle, 1;
2.    int index = idx[0];
3.    // store the parameter
4.    (ptr_param + index)->store(n, std::memory_order_release);
5.    // store the flag value
6.    (ptr_flag + index)->store(1, std::memory_order_release);
7.    // wait until syscall returns
8.    while ((ptr_flag + index)->load(std::memory_order_acquire));
9.    // load result from CPU thread
10.   long address =
11.       (ptr_param + index)->load(std::memory_order_acquire);
12.   return address;
13.   signalnoret_sub_screl_s64_sig64 signalHandle, 1;
```

FIGURE 7.22

Implementation of &_Znwm (*new*) and &_Znam (*new[]*) (conceptual code): rewrite of Figure 7.18 with HSAIL signal instruction.

```
1.    signalnoret_add_screl_s64_sig64 signalHandle, 1;
2.    int index = idx[0];
3.    // store the parameter
4.    (ptr_param + index)->store(address,
5.                               std::memory_order_release);
6.    // store the flag value
7.    (ptr_flag + index)->store(2, std::memory_order_release);
8.    // wait until syscall returns
9.    while ((ptr_flag + index)->load(std::memory_order_acquire));
10.   signalnoret_sub_screl_s64_sig64 signalHandle, 1;
```

FIGURE 7.23

Implementation of &_ZdlPv (*delete*) and &_ZdaPv (*delete[]*) (conceptional code): rewrite of Figure 7.19 with HSAIL signal instruction.

Figures 7.22 and 7.23 depict how HSAIL signal instructions are used in the implementation of the operators *new/delete* in the device code. Line 1 is used to increase *signalHandle*, and thus activate the CPU thread. Line 13 of Figure 7.22 and Line 10 of Figure 7.23 is used to decrease *signalHandle*, and thus deactivate the CPU thread.

7.12 CONCLUSION

In this chapter, we presented a case study of implementing C++ AMP on the HSA platform. Key transformations for compiling high-level, object-oriented C++ code into HSAIL instructions were demonstrated. With data flow analysis, we can compile tiled C++ AMP application into device code with properly formed work-groups that take advantage of the HSA group memory. We have also demonstrated how to enable and use HSA-specific features, such as shared virtual memory and platform atomics.

As we show in this chapter, the HSA features have allowed us to support more generic C++ AMP code than what the current C++ AMP standard allows. For example, we show that with the HSA shared virtual memory feature, we can support capture of array references without requiring *array_view*. For another example, with the HSA wait API and HSAIL signal instructions, we can efficiently support dynamic memory allocation within device code, which is not allowed in the current HSA standard. This illustrates that HSA features will enable more mainstream languages with little or no special restrictions to program heterogeneous computing systems.

There are still quite a few HSA features yet to be exploited by the Kalmar compiler. For example, user-level command queues on HSA agents could be used to enable dynamic parallelism, where one kernel can invoke other kernels at runtime. C++ virtual member functions could be supported, if C++ virtual tables could be accessed via shared virtual memory. As HSA platforms become more mature, we expect even more C++ constructs to be made available within HSAIL kernels.

REFERENCES

[1] K. Gregory, A. Miller, C++ AMP: Accelerated Massive Parallelism with Microsoft Visual C++ – Microsoft, ISBN: 9780735664739, 2012. 326 pages.
[2] HSA Platform System Architecture Specification 1.0 Final – HSA Foundation, 2015 – 69 pages – http://www.hsafoundation.com/?ddownload=4944.
[3] Working Draft, Standard for Programming Language C++ – ISO/IEC, 2012 – 1324 pages – http://www.open-std.org/jtc1/sc22/wg21/docs/papers/2012/n3376.pdf.
[4] LLVM Language Reference Manual – LLVM Project, 2015 – http://llvm.org/docs/LangRef.html.
[5] HSA Programmer's Reference Manual Specification 1.0.1 – HSA Foundation, 2015 – 391 pages – http://www.hsafoundation.com/?ddownload=4945.
[6] HSA Runtime Programmer's Reference Manual 1.00 Provisional Ratified – HSA Foundation, 2014 – 130 pages – http://www.hsafoundation.com/?ddownload=4946.

Application Use Cases
Platform Atomics

J. Gómez-Luna*, I.-J. Sung†, A.J. Lázaro-Muñoz‡, W.-H. Chung§,
J.M. González-Linares‡, N. Guil‡

University of Córdoba, Córdoba, Spain*; MulticoreWare Inc., Champaign, IL, USA†;
University of Málaga, Málaga, Spain‡; MulticoreWare Inc., Douliou, Yunlin County, Taiwan, ROC§

8.1 INTRODUCTION

Platform atomics provide memory consistency and atomicity between the host code and the compute kernel. They allow both to simultaneously access the same memory locations without losing any of the results. They are intended to implement producer-consumer mechanisms or lock/wait-free data structures, enabling fine-grained synchronization between latency compute units (i.e., CPU cores) and throughput compute units (i.e., GPU compute units). Thus, kernel relaunch or rough memory-fence-based synchronization mechanisms between CPU and GPU threads are no longer necessary, as platform atomics provide a new, efficient way for the host and the devices to communicate and collaborate. In addition, in terms of programmability, they may facilitate a more intuitive and natural way of coding, saving many lines of code for many types of parallel algorithm patterns.

This chapter describes three application examples, each of which is devoted to a case study of algorithm patterns that benefit from platform atomics.

The first case study corresponds to a pattern that appears in many applications where the work to be processed by the GPU is dynamically identified by the CPU. It is a dynamic task queue system, where the host produces tasks that are processed by the device. The applicability of this task queue system is illustrated by a real-world kernel, a histogram calculation of frames from a video sequence.

The second case study illustrates a frequently used pattern for an application to use both the CPU and the GPU to process the tasks that are dynamically identified as more appropriate for one or the other to execute. It implements a widely used graph algorithm, breadth-first search (BFS), as an example of coordinated execution between CPU cores and GPU compute units. Thus, program execution can occasionally swap between the CPU and the GPU, depending on workload characteristics, such as the input queue size.

The third case study represents a pattern that uses the CPU and the GPU to collaborate closely to process a pool of fine-grained tasks. It is an elementary transposition,

131

which belongs to a data layout conversion system [1]. Data layout conversion is needed in heterogeneous systems to reshape data, so that memory parallelism and locality can be exploited by both latency-oriented and throughput-oriented compute units. The presented elementary transposition implements a load-balanced algorithm that transforms a Structure of Array (SoA) to an intermediate representation called Array of Structure of Tiled Arrays (ASTA), which ensures high-throughput memory accesses across diverse architectures and low-cost marshaling from/to SoA and AoS (Array of Structures). The HSA implementation of this elementary transposition carries out the simultaneous execution of CPU and GPU to attain a performance improvement.

In these case studies, legacy implementations that lack platform atomics are compared to new HSA implementations, which take advantage of platform atomics and memory coherency between CPU and GPU. These features allow efficient synchronization, data sharing, and concurrent data accesses across the entire heterogeneous system. In summary, thanks to the HSA features, the three case studies of this chapter show:

- Task queue system: Efficient concurrent access to task queues, with simpler coding. It uses persistent work-groups to avoid kernel relaunch and to ensure load balancing.
- Breadth-first search: Low-cost CPU-GPU switching mechanism that chooses the most appropriate compute units depending on the workload size.
- Data layout conversion: Collaborative scheme where CPU threads and GPU work-groups are coordinated to simultaneously shift elements of the same array in place.

This chapter is organized as follows. Section 8.2 introduces HSA platform atomics using C++ AMP. In Section 8.3, we present our first case study, a task queue system committed to achieving load balancing on the GPU side. Section 8.4 compares a legacy implementation of BFS for heterogeneous platforms to an HSA implementation. Section 8.5 describes the HSA implementation of an elementary transposition that transforms the layout of an array. Finally, the conclusions are stated in Section 8.6.

8.2 ATOMICS IN HSA

The C++ interface of HSA atomics has been implemented as an extension of the C++ AMP 1.2 specification. The compiler and runtime is freely available.[1] The interface is modeled after C++11 atomics, and allows direct use of C++11 atomics inside C++ AMP kernels.

Figure 8.1 shows an example code using atomic operations inside a C++ AMP kernel. The computation itself is straightforward, in order to focus attention on the

---

[1] https://bitbucket.org/multicoreware/cppamp-driver-ng/wiki/Home.

```
1  int main ()
2  {
3      // define inputs and output
4      const int vecSize = 2048;
5
6      std::atomic_int table_a[vecSize];
7      std::atomic_int table_b[vecSize];
8      std::atomic_int table_c[vecSize];
9      auto ptr_a = &table_a[0];
10     auto ptr_b = &table_b[0];
11     auto ptr_c = &table_c[0];
12
13     // initialize test data
14     std::random_device rd;
15     std::uniform_int_distribution<int32_t> int_dist;
16     for (int i = 0; i < vecSize; ++i) {
17         table_a[i].store(int_dist(rd));
18         table_b[i].store(int_dist(rd));
19     }
20
21     // Launch kernel. Variables referenced in the kernel are captured
           in the lambda
22     Concurrency::extent<1> e(vecSize);
23     parallel_for_each(
24         e, [=](Concurrency::index<1> idx) restrict(amp) {
25
26             int tid = idx[0];
27             (ptr_a + tid)->fetch_add(1); // std::atomic member functions
                   can be used
28             (ptr_b + tid)->fetch_sub(1); // in GPU kernels
29             (ptr_c + tid)->store(0);
30             (ptr_c + tid)->fetch_add(
31                         (ptr_a + tid)->load(std::memory_order_acquire),
                             std::memory_order_release);
32             (ptr_c + tid)->fetch_add(
33                         (ptr_b + tid)->load(std::memory_order_seq_cst),
                             std::memory-order-acq-rel);
34
35     });
36
37     // Verify the results. They should agree.
38     int error = 0;
39     for(unsigned i = 0; i < vecSize; i++) {
40         error += table_c[i] - (table_a[i] + table_b[i]);
41     }
42     if (error == 0) {
43         std::cout << "Verify success!\n";
44     } else {
45         std::cout << "Verify failed!\n";
46     }
47
48     return error != 0;
49 }
```

FIGURE 8.1

Example code using C++11 atomic operations inside a C++AMP kernel.

syntax and semantics of the atomic operations. We refer the reader to C++11 speci-fication for any further details.

As can be seen, the std::atomic_int tables are declared in host code and are di-rectly used inside kernels. While the kernel executes, the host code can also atomi-cally operate on these tables. This is informally called platform atomics, because it allows both CPU and GPU to atomically operate on the same data structure.

These are a sample of the C++11 `std:: atomic<>` member functions, which are supported in C++AMP kernels. In line 27,`fetch_add` increments atomically every element in input vector `table_a`. `fetch_sub` in line 28 decrements atomically every element in input vector `table_b`. Line 29 presents atomic store, which initializes every element in output vector `table_c`. Then, lines 30-33 show a vector addition, `table c[i] = table_a[i] + table_b[i]`, where the addition is done through atomic operations. Atomic load operations read input elements from `table_a` and `table_b`. `fetch_add` operations add the loaded values to output elements in `table_c`. As shown, these atomic operations can specify memory ordering constraints:

- `memory_order_acquire`: A load operation with this memory order performs the acquire operation on the affected memory location: no memory accesses in the current thread can be reordered before this load. This ensures that all writes in other threads that release the same atomic variable are visible in the current thread.
- `memory_order_release`: A store operation with this memory order performs the release operation: no memory accesses in the current thread can be reordered after this store. This ensures that all writes in the current thread are visible in other threads that acquire; it also ensures that the same atomic variable and writes that carry a dependency into the atomic variable become visible in other threads that consume the same atomic.
- `memory_order_acq_rel`: A read-modify-write operation with this memory order is both an acquire operation and a release operation. No memory accesses in the current thread can be reordered before this load, and no memory accesses in the current thread can be reordered after this store. It ensures that all writes in other threads that release the same atomic variable are visible before the modification, and the modification is visible in other threads that acquire the same atomic variable.
- `memory_order_seq_cst`: Same as `memory_order_acq_rel`, plus a single total order exists in which all threads observe all modifications in the same order.

8.3 TASK QUEUE SYSTEM

Load balancing is a well-known concern on throughput-oriented architectures. Applications exposing workload-dependent computations might be burdened by the fact that some compute units carry out more intensive computations than others. Such a load imbalance can significantly increase the total execution time and reduce the benefit of parallel computation.

Several works have tried to deal with load balancing on GPU, using work-stealing [2,3] and task queues [4]. Introduced by Lamport [5], concurrent lock-free queues are recommendable for that goal. Chen et al. [6] propose a GPU task queue system that allows the host to enqueue tasks on several queues residing in the device memory. By using asynchronous data transfers, zero-copies, and events, they are able to compose task enqueue and dequeue routines.

With the advent of HSA and platform atomics, such a task queue system can be implemented with fewer lines of code.

In the following sections, we describe three approaches to processing a pool of tasks with possible load imbalance. The first one consists of a static execution queueing scheme in which the kernel is relaunched as many times as necessary until the task pool is empty. Tasks are statically assigned to work-groups. The second one dynamically assigns tasks to work-groups using atomic updates to a global counter. The third one is the HSA task queue system. Note that the last two approaches launch persistent work-groups, which fetch tasks enqueued by the host. The HSA version also uses a persistent kernel, which does not need to be relaunched every time the host enqueues tasks.

8.3.1 STATIC EXECUTION

Consider a pool of tasks residing in the host memory. A host thread will be in charge of copying a chunk of these tasks into the device memory. The kernel is then launched. Because the kernel is not launched until the chunk of tasks has been copied, the host does not need to use any atomic operation to coordinate with the device. As many work-groups as tasks in the chunk are launched, so each work-group executes one task. When the kernel finishes, the results are copied back to the host memory. These steps should be repeated as many times as necessary to process the entire pool of tasks, as it can be seen in Algorithm 8.1.

The static approach may suffer from load imbalance, due to the fact that the tasks are statically assigned to the work-groups, which are mapped onto the compute units. Depending on the distribution of these tasks, some compute units might fetch very time-consuming tasks, while others would fetch more lightweight tasks. This situation would delay the end of the kernel; some compute units might be still busy, while others are already idle.

8.3.2 DYNAMIC EXECUTION

In order to avoid the load imbalance in the static approach, the work-groups executing on the compute units can fetch tasks dynamically, as shown in the dynamic kernel of Algorithm 8.1. These work-groups are persistent, meaning that they run during the entire lifetime of the kernel. A work-group atomically increments a global counter that indicates the next task to fetch. Despite the cost of an atomic increment, better performance can be expected, because load balancing is ensured.

ALGORITHM 8.1 STATIC AND DYNAMIC APPROACHES TO PROCESSING A TASK POOL

Arrays in host memory: Task pool of size *task_pool_size*, associated input data, and results

Arrays in device memory: Chunk of tasks of size *CHUNK_SIZE*, associated input data, and results. Each task will be performed by a work-group

Atomic variables in device memory (dynamic execution only): Global counter *counter*

Pseudo-code:

Host thread:

1: **do**
2:　　Copy *CHUNK_SIZE* tasks (and associated input data) from task pool to device memory
3:　　*task_pool_size* −= *CHUNK_SIZE*
4:　　**GPU_kernel (Static or Dynamic)**
5:　　Copy results from device memory to host memory
6: **while** (*task_pool_size* > 0)

GPU kernel (Static):

1: Fetch *task* (statically assigned)
2: Perform computation on data associated to *task*

GPU kernel (Dynamic):

1: **if** (*thread_id* = 0) **then**
2:　　*task* = *atomic_add*(*counter*, 1)
3: **endif**
4: **local barrier**
5: **do**
6:　　Perform computation on data associated to *task*
7:　　**if** (*thread_id* = 0) **then**
8:　　　　*task* = *atomic_add*(*counter*, 1)
9:　　**endif**
10:　　**local barrier**
11: **while** (*task* < *CHUNK_SIZE*)

8.3.3 HSA TASK QUEUE SYSTEM

This section first describes a legacy task queue system for GPUs. Then, it shows the drawbacks of this legacy approach, and demonstrates a new system based on HSA features.

8.3.3.1 A legacy task queue system on GPU

A task queue system on GPU is proposed in Chen et al. [6]. This scheme uses a number of persistent work-groups that is equal to the maximum number of work-groups that can concurrently run on the GPU. The work-groups have access to several queues located in device memory. A host thread enqueues tasks into these queues, and the work-groups dequeue tasks (using atomic operations on device memory), and execute them. Figure 8.2 illustrates the entire process.

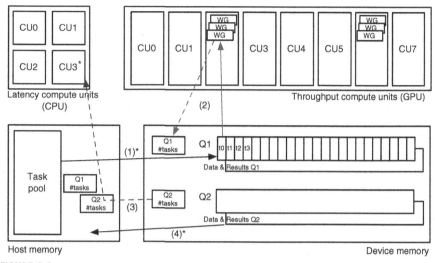

FIGURE 8.2

Scheme of a legacy implementation of a task queue system on an heterogeneous platform.
In (1), a host thread transfers tasks and associated data to device memory (* indicates
host thread action). Then, persistent work-groups in the compute units dequeue tasks
from the queue, and atomically update a counter variable (2). When a queue becomes
empty, the host detects the completion of the tasks via polling using a zero-copy operation
(3). Results are asynchronously transferred (4) before the host enqueues new tasks.

Compared to the static and the dynamic execution queueing schemes outlined
above, this scheme has the inherent advantage that the kernel does not need to be
relaunched. Moreover, it ensures load balancing across work-groups, as those work-
groups that were assigned a quick task do not need to wait for others to finish before
starting a new computation. They can just dequeue a new task.

The host thread carries out asynchronous transfers of tasks and associated data
between host memory and device memory. With each of these transfers, it populates
a queue. Once all the tasks in a queue have been consumed, the host becomes aware
that the queue is empty by reading or polling a mapped memory variable that is
updated by a zero-copy operation. Then, an asynchronous transfer copies the results
from device memory to host memory. The host can next enqueue new tasks into that
queue.

8.3.3.2 A simpler, more intuitive implementation with HSA features

That legacy task queue system was developed in NVIDIA's CUDA programming
language [7]. It represents a commendable attempt to achieve load balancing on
GPUs. However, its implementation is fairly complicated. It relies on asynchronous
transfers between host and device that require the programmer to explicitly control
all coordination aspects. It also uses implicit zero-copy operations, but these have

the disadvantage that the exact latency needed to get completed is not guaranteed. Moreover, duplicated atomic variables and pointers are necessary.

Simpler coding would be obtained by using new CUDA features, such as CUDA unified memory [7]. For instance, it would not be necessary to have a double declaration and allocation of pointers and atomic variables, and data transfers would be transparent to the programmer. However, such a task queue system is not implementable with CUDA unified memory, because it is not possible to use a persistent kernel. This is because data transfers in CUDA unified memory are not guaranteed to be completed until the execution of a queue synchronization after kernel termination.

Thanks to the new features of HSA, such as host coherent memory and platform atomics, we can propose an HSA implementation of a task queue system, which is inspired by the one presented in Chen et al. [6]. It can be implemented in a more natural way, saving many lines of code. For instance, there is no need of double declaration and allocation. Data transfers are not necessary, as the GPU work-groups can access host memory. A scheme is depicted in Figure 8.3.

A detailed pseudo-code can be found in Algorithm 8.2. Several queues are allocated in host coherent memory. Host and device access them by atomically updating three variables per queue that represent the number of enqueued tasks, the number of consumed tasks, and the current number of tasks in queue.

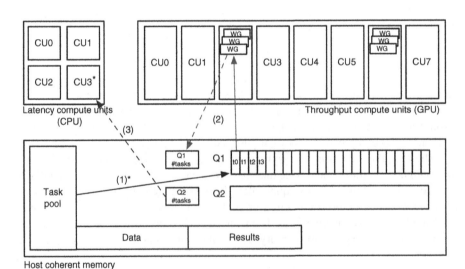

FIGURE 8.3

Scheme of an HSA implementation of a task queue system on an integrated heterogeneous platform. In (1), a host thread copies tasks to one queue (* indicates host thread action). Then, persistent work-groups in the compute units dequeue tasks from the queue, and update a counter variable using platform atomics (2). When a queue becomes empty, the host detects that by reading the counter (3). Input data/results are read/written from/to host memory.

ALGORITHM 8.2 HSA IMPLEMENTATION OF A TASK QUEUE SYSTEM

Arrays in host coherent memory: *NUM_QUEUES* task queues *queues[ ]* of size *QUEUE_SIZE*
Atomic variables in host coherent memory: Number of tasks enqueued in each queue *num_written_tasks[ ]*, number of tasks consumed from each queue *num_consumed_tasks[ ]*, current number of tasks in queue *num_tasks_in_queue[ ]*

Pseudo-code:

Host thread:

```
 1: do
 2:     Host_tasks_enqueue(task_pool, queues, num_written_tasks, num_consumed_tasks, num_tasks_in_queue)

 3:     task_pool_size -= QUEUE_SIZE
 4: while(task_pool_size > 0)
 5: Host_tasks_enqueue(stop_tasks, queues)
```

GPU kernel:

```
 1: do
 2:     GPU_tasks_dequeue(task, queues, num_written_tasks, num_consumed_tasks, num_tasks_in_queue)

 3:     if (task ≠ stop_task) then
 4:         Perform computation on data associated to task
 5:     else
 6:         break
 7:     endif
 8: while(true)
```

Host_tasks_enqueue:

```
 1: do
 2:     if (num_written_tasks[i].load() = num_consumed_tasks[i].load()) then
 3:         Copy tasks from task_pool to queues[i]
 4:         num_written_tasks[i].fetch_add(QUEUE_SIZE)
 5:         num_tasks_in_queue[i].store(QUEUE_SIZE)
 6:         break
 7:     else
 8:         i = (i + 1)%NUM_QUEUES
 9:     endif
10: while(true)
```

GPU_task_dequeue:

```
 1: if (thread_id = 0) then
 2:     do
 3:         if (num_written_tasks[i].load() = num_consumed_tasks[i].load()) then
 4:             i = (i + 1)%NUM_QUEUES
 5:         else
 6:             if (num_tasks_in_queue[i].load() > 0) then
 7:                 num_consumed_tasks[i].fetch_add(1)
 8:                 num_tasks_in_queue[i].fetch_sub(1)
 9:                 Copy task from queues[i] to task
10:                 break
11:             endif
12:         endif
13:     while(true)
14: endif
15: local barrier
```

8.3.4 EVALUATION

This section includes some experimental results that compare the static and the dynamic execution queueing schemes to the HSA implementation of the task queue system. The code has been developed in C++AMP.

The experiments have been run on an AMD Kaveri A10-7850 K APU with Radeon R7 Graphics. This APU contains four CPU cores and eight GPU compute units. It supports HSA features such as pageable shared virtual memory, full memory coherency between CPU and GPU, user mode queuing, and signaling.

The first results were obtained with synthetic input data. Then, we experimented with a real-world kernel: histogram computation of the frames of a video sequence.

8.3.4.1 An experiment with synthetic input data

We have performed a synthetic experiment where 320,000 tasks are executed on the GPU. This number is a multiple of the maximum number of residing wavefronts in the GPU of the Kaveri A10-7850 K. It contains eight GPU compute units, each of which can concurrently hold up to 40 wavefronts [8].

In the case of the HSA implementation, 320 work-groups of size 1 wavefront (64 work-items), and two queues of size 320 are employed. Each time the host enqueues tasks, it fills up one queue. The dynamic execution queueing scheme also launches 320 work-groups per kernel call. In the case of the static scheme, we ran tests for 640, 1600, and 3200 work-groups per kernel call. For the static and the dynamic schemes, each kernel call processes 640, 1600, or 3200 tasks. In the HSA implementation, the kernel is persistent, and all the tasks in the task pool are continuously processed.

The task pool of 320,000 tasks contains two types of tasks. One of them is time-consuming, while the other is very lightweight. The amount of time-consuming tasks has been changed: 0%, 10%, 25%, 50%, 75%, and 100% of the 320,000 tasks. For each of these, 100 random patterns have been tested.

Figure 8.4 shows a code segment for this synthetic experiment. All work-items of a work-group are assumed to collaboratively work on the same task. Once a task

```
1  if(t.op == SIGNAL_HEAVY_KERNEL){
2    for(int i=0; i < iterations; i++)
3      data[t.id * wg_size + tid] += value;
4    data[t.id * wg_size + tid] += t.id;
5  }
6  if(t.op == SIGNAL_LIGHT_KERNEL){
7    for(int i=0; i < 1; i++)
8      data[t.id * wg_size + tid] += value;
9    data[t.id * wg_size + tid] += t.id;
10 }
```

FIGURE 8.4

Code segment of a synthetic experiment for an HSA task queue system. `t.id` and `t.op` are the identifier and the type of task. Tasks can be time-consuming (`HEAVY`) or lightweight (`LIGHT`). tid is the work-item ID, and `wg_size` is the work-group size. For heavyweight tasks, `iterations + 1` additions are performed (`iterations=50` in our experiment). For lightweight tasks, two additions are carried out.

has been fetched by the work-group, the work-items have to carry out some arithmetic additions on input data elements. Each work-item updates one input element. Depending on the type of task, the number of additions is high or low (51 or 2, respectively, in our experiment).

Average execution times are shown in Figure 8.5. Moreover, Figure 8.6 shows the speedup of the HSA implementation to the static and the dynamic schemes, and

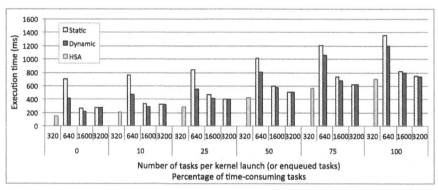

FIGURE 8.5

Average execution time (ms) for the comparison between an HSA implementation of a task queue system, and static and dynamic execution queueing schemes. Each kernel call for the static and the dynamic schemes processes 640, 1600, or 3200 tasks. In the HSA implementation, the host enqueues 320 tasks each time. 320,000 synthetic tasks are executed. 0%, 10%, 25%, 50%, 75%, or 100% of them are time-consuming. For each value of distribution, 100 random patterns have been used.

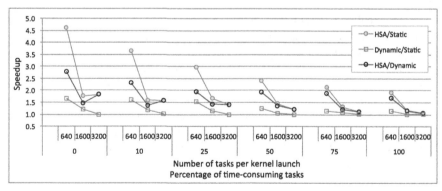

FIGURE 8.6

Speedup of the HSA implementation of a task queue system to static and dynamic execution queueing schemes. Each kernel call for the static and the dynamic schemes processes 640, 1600, or 3200 tasks. In the HSA implementation, the host enqueues 320 tasks each time. Speedup of the dynamic scheme to the static scheme is also shown. 320,000 synthetic tasks are executed with a variable percentage of time-consuming tasks.

the speedup of the dynamic to the static version. As can be observed, the dynamic execution always outperforms the static one when the number of tasks per kernel call is 640 and 1600. This is due to the better load balancing that the dynamic scheme attains. When this number is 3200, the execution time is similar. This means that such a number is sufficiently large for the compute units to process a similar amount of heavyweight and lightweight tasks, even though a static assignment is carried out.

Compared to the dynamic scheme, the HSA implementation entails the additional advantage that the kernel does not need to be relaunched. In addition, the static and the dynamic schemes need to copy input tasks and data from the pool to a memory space accessible by the GPU work-groups, and results in the opposite direction. In the HSA implementation, the task queue system is able to overlap the tasks copy with the kernel execution, while input data and results are directly accessed on host memory. The overlap is enabled by the platform atomic operation, which allows correct simultaneous insertion and deletion activities by the host and the device.

8.3.4.2 A real-world application experiment: histogram computation

The HSA task queue system can be used in many applications where there are workload-dependent computations. As an illustrative example, in this section we use a real-world kernel that calculates a histogram on each frame in a video sequence. Each histogram reflects the brightness distribution of the pixels of each frame. Due to the fact that histogramming needs atomic additions by concurrently executing work-items, the execution time for each frame can vary significantly.

In our implementation, the histogram of one frame is computed by one GPU work-group. We prepare static execution, dynamic execution, and HSA versions, following the three schemes explained above. Our tests use four video sequences of 3200 frames from the MPEG-7 Content Set. For the static and the dynamic schemes, the kernel is called several times. Frames are processed in chunks of 640, 1600 or 3200. In the HSA version, the kernel is only launched once. It uses two queues of 320-frame chunks. This allows the host thread to enqueue a chunk of frames in one queue, while the GPU work-groups fetch frames from the other queue.

Figure 8.7 shows the execution times of the three versions. Histograms of 32, 64, 128, or 256 bins are calculated. In the case of the static and the dynamic versions, the figure displays the results for chunks of 640 frames. This gives better results than the other two (1600 or 3200 frames). The dynamic version minimally outperforms the static version in all cases. The HSA implementation performs significantly better across all video sequences. A better load balancing is attained than both the static and dynamic implementations, thanks to the HSA task queue system.

8.4 BREADTH-FIRST SEARCH

BFS is an algorithm for searching in a graph. It begins in a source node, and expands the frontier in successive iterations. In each iteration, the algorithm

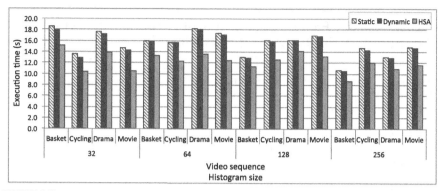

FIGURE 8.7

Execution times (s) for the comparison between an HSA implementation of histogram calculation of a video sequence to static and dynamic queueing schemes. Each kernel call for the static and the dynamic schemes processes 640 frames. Each video sequence contains 3200 frames.

visits the current frontier nodes to gain access to their neighboring nodes that have not yet been accessed and collects them as the next frontier nodes. A typical application is finding the shortest path between the source node and every node in the graph.

As presented in Algorithm 8.3, a sequential implementation of BFS takes every node in the current frontier (from an input queue) and enqueues all unvisited neighboring nodes to the next frontier (in an output queue). It is an iterative process until the input queue is empty. Inherently, BFS has irregular memory accesses, as the order in which nodes are visited is dependent on the topology of the graph and the starting node of the search. Moreover, the number of neighboring nodes for each visited node can be variable.

Several parallel implementations on GPU have been presented in the last few years [9–12]. The implementation by Luo et al. [13] is one of the benchmarks in the Parboil suite [14]. In this implementation, a thread dequeues a node in the current frontier, and visits all its neighbors. A number of unvisited ones are enqueued to the next frontier. As this number is variable, a dynamic queue with atomic updates is needed. In order to reduce the amount of contention on a single centralized output queue in global memory, privatization is applied to define a hierarchical queue system. Local output queues residing in on-chip memory are updated by work-groups. When all the nodes of the current frontier have been visited, the local output queues are merged into a centralized one, which will become the input queue of the next frontier. Contention is reduced in the sense that the tails of the local queues are atomically updated in on-chip memory. Later, only one atomic update by the leader thread (thread 0) of each work-group is performed on the global tail when the local queues are merged.

ALGORITHM 8.3 PSEUDO-CODE OF A SEQUENTIAL IMPLEMENTATION OF THE BREADTH-FIRST SEARCH ALGORITHM

Input: A graph G with *num_nodes* nodes and *num_edges* edges, and a source node s
Output: The complete list of nodes N with the frontier f in which they have been discovered (i.e, f indicates the steps it takes to go from s to n). Each node n is represented by a tuple (n, f)

Pseudo-code:
```
 1: Allocate an input queue Qin and an output queue Qout
 2: Frontier f = 0
 3: Enqueue s into Qin
 4: while Qin not empty do
 5:    for all nodes n in Qin do
 6:       Dequeue node n from Qin
 7:       Insert (n, f) into N
 8:       for all edges e connected to n do
 9:          if node m connected to e is not in N then
10:             Enqueue m into Qout
11:          end if
12:       end for
13:    end for
14:    Swap Qin and Qout
15:    f = f + 1
16: end while
```

In the baseline implementation [13], the kernel is launched for every frontier. This entails an inherent overhead due to kernel relaunch. A more efficient version of the kernel assumes every frontier fits in the combined local memories of the entire GPU. A number of work-groups equal to the number of compute units is created. Thus, all on-chip resources are utilized. When the current frontier has been explored, the concurrently executing work-groups perform a global barrier synchronization (see code segment in Figure 8.8).

```
1  if(tid == 0){
2     atomic_add(&count, 1);
3     while(count < num_wg){
4        ;
5     }
6  }
7  // Synchronization
8  barrier();
```

FIGURE 8.8

Code segment of global barrier synchronization on GPU. In each work-group, thread with thread ID `tid = 0` updates a global counter `count`, and waits until all work-groups have reached that point (`num_wg` is the number of work-groups). The `barrier()` synchronization is the OpenCL work-group barrier synchronization and ensures that the other threads of the work-group wait until they are enabled to continue execution. It can be removed if the work-group size is a wavefront.

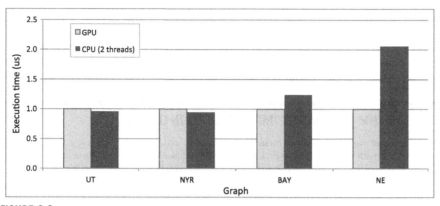

FIGURE 8.9

Execution time in microseconds of BFS on CPU (using 2 threads) and GPU. Results are normalized to execution time on GPU. The CPU version uses 2 threads, and the GPU version uses 8 work-groups of 64 threads.

With a similar approach, we have implemented a C++AMP version to run on GPU cores. We have compared it to a C++ version of BFS that runs on CPU cores. Figure 8.9 shows the execution results on a Kaveri A10-7850 K for four graphs [14,15]. Note that the algorithm runs faster on CPU for some graphs, and on GPU for others. Actually, this is related to the average number of nodes per frontier. For instance, the median of nodes per frontier in NYR is 388, which is less than the number of GPU threads, and 1283 in NE. If the execution time per iteration is analyzed, it is noticeable that very short frontiers are processed faster on CPU cores. As the number of nodes increases, the GPU cores become a better alternative. Then, it is only worthwhile to run on GPU when the number of nodes per frontier is large.

Following this observation, it can be profitable to run each iteration of BFS on the most appropriate cores, depending on the number of nodes per frontier. In the following sections, a legacy implementation and an HSA implementation are explained, and later compared.

8.4.1 LEGACY IMPLEMENTATION

The legacy implementation does not use HSA features such as host coherent memory and platform atomics. It carries out a coordinated execution of CPU and GPU that switches between them according to the number of nodes per frontier. A threshold is established for the number of nodes to visit next. If the number of nodes is smaller than the threshold, CPU threads explore the next frontier. Otherwise, the GPU kernel is launched. The only possible way to synchronize

CPU and GPU, when switching is necessary, is finishing the GPU kernel or the CPU threads. When switching is not necessary, the CPU threads or the GPU kernel continue to generate and process consecutive frontiers, as the number of nodes remains under or over the threshold. Algorithm 8.4 presents a pseudo-code of the legacy implementation.

ALGORITHM 8.4 LEGACY IMPLEMENTATION OF BFS

Arrays and variables in host memory: A graph G with nodes and edges, a list of nodes N with the frontier f in which they have been discovered, an input queue Q_input, an output queue Q_output, and the number of nodes in the current frontier $nodes\_in\_queue$

Arrays and variables in device memory: A copy of each of the above arrays and variables

Pseudo-code:

```
 1: Copy G from host memory to device memory
 2: nodes_in_queue = 1
 3: do
 4:    if nodes_in_queue < THRESHOLD then
 5:       Create CPU threads
 6:       Join CPU threads
 7:    else
 8:       Copy Q_input from host memory to device memory
 9:       Copy N from host memory to device memory
10:       Copy nodes_in_queue from host memory to device memory
11:       Copy current frontier f from host memory to device memory
12:       GPU_kernel
13:       Copy Q_input from device memory to host memory
14:       Copy N from device memory to host memory
15:       Copy nodes_in_queue from device memory to host memory
16:       Copy next frontier f from device memory to host memory
17:    endif
18: while (nodes_in_queue > 0)
```

CPU threads:

```
1: do
2:    Visit nodes in Q_input and enqueue unvisited neighboring nodes into Q_output
3:    Synchronize CPU threads
4:    Swap Q_input and Q_output
5: while (nodes_in_queue < THRESHOLD & nodes_in_queue > 0)
```

GPU kernel:

```
1: do
2:    Visit nodes in Q_input and enqueue unvisited neighboring nodes into local
       output queue
3:    Merge local output queues into Q_output
4:    Synchronize GPU work-groups
5:    Swap Q_input and Q_output
6: while (nodes_in_queue ≥ THRESHOLD & nodes_in_queue > 0)
```

As can be seen, the GPU kernel is launched every time the number of nodes per frontier exceeds a threshold. The frontier nodes are copied from the host memory to the device memory before launching the kernel. It is a persistent kernel where work-groups synchronize at the end of the iterations, using the global synchronization in Figure 8.8. The kernel continues running, if the number of nodes of the next frontier is still higher than the threshold. As in the efficient version presented by Luo et al. [13], it assumes the frontiers fit in the combined local memories, so there is no need to relaunch the kernel for every iteration. Only when this threshold is not exceeded, the kernel finishes, the frontier nodes are copied from the device memory to the host memory, and the CPU threads process the next frontier.

Similarly, the CPU threads are created when the number of nodes is under the threshold. If more than one CPU thread is used, it is necessary to synchronize when all the nodes in the frontier have been visited. Then, the number of nodes is compared to the threshold, and consequently the threads either continue the execution of the next frontier, or finish.

Both CPU threads and GPU threads fetch nodes from an input queue *Q_input*, and insert unvisited nodes to an output queue *Q_output*. Dynamic input assignment can be implemented for both, in order to ensure load balancing when the number of neighbors of a given node is very variable. The CPU threads use C++11 atomic *fetch_and_add* on a variable in host memory to index the next node to dequeue from *Q_input*. The GPU threads perform similarly using a global atomic addition on a variable in device-accessible memory. In the case of the output queue, the CPU threads update the associated tail variable with *fetch_and_add* as well. The GPU threads use local output queues that are merged at the end of the iteration, as explained above.

8.4.2 HSA IMPLEMENTATION

Thanks to the HSA features, it is possible to implement a scheme with persistent CPU threads and GPU kernels. Thus, the overheads due to kernel launch and CPU thread creation are avoided. Moreover, CPU and GPU threads can share global queues in host coherent memory, as well as atomic variables to coordinate the execution. This saves memory space and copy times between host and device memories. This scheme is depicted in Algorithm 8.5.

As can be seen, it is necessary to implement a global synchronization across CPU and GPU. This is possible with platform atomics on host coherent memory. Figure 8.10 shows a code segment to implement it. On the CPU side, one leading thread waits until all CPU threads and GPU work-groups have reached the synchronization point (i.e., they have increased the atomic variable pointed by ptr end). Then, the leading thread updates the atomic variable pointed by ptr_ run, and consequently the rest of CPU threads and GPU work-groups are freed to continue the execution.

ALGORITHM 8.5 HSA IMPLEMENTATION OF BFS

Arrays in host memory: A graph G with nodes and edges
Arrays in device memory: A copy of the graph G with nodes and edges
Arrays and variables in host coherent memory: A list of nodes N with the frontier f in which they have been discovered, an input queue Q_input, an output queue Q_output, and the number of nodes in the current frontier $nodes\_in\_queue$

Pseudo-code:

1: Copy G from host memory to device memory
2: $nodes\_in\_queue = 1$
3: Create CPU threads
4: **GPU_kernel**
5: Join CPU threads

CPU threads:

1: **do**
2:    **if** $nodes\_in\_queue$ < THRESHOLD **then**
3:       Visit nodes in Q_input and enqueue unvisited neighboring nodes into Q_output
4:       Swap Q_input and Q_output
5:    **endif**
6:    Synchronize CPU threads and GPU work-groups
7: **while** ($nodes\_in\_queue$ > 0)

GPU kernel:

1: **do**
2:    **if** $nodes\_in\_queue$ ≥ THRESHOLD **then**
3:       Visit nodes in Q_input and enqueue unvisited neighboring nodes into local output queue
4:       Merge local output queues into Q_output
5:       Swap Q_input and Q_output
6:    **endif**
7:    Synchronize CPU threads and GPU work-groups
8: **while** ($nodes\_in\_queue$ > 0)

8.4.3 EVALUATION

This section compares the legacy and the HSA implementations of BFS. The experiments have been run on an AMD Kaveri A10-7850 K APU with Radeon R7 Graphics. The code has been developed in C++AMP. 14 different graphs are used in these experiments. Two of them come from the Parboil datasets [14]. The rest can be found in the DIMACS challenge site [15].

On the GPU side, both implementations use the same number of work-groups as the number of compute units, that is, 8 in this Kaveri APU. The size of each work-group is one wavefront. We tested other execution configurations (e.g., up to 4 wavefronts per work-group, and up to 16 work-groups per GPU), but the performance results were similar. In the case of the CPU side, we experimented with 1, 2, and 4 CPU threads. The highest performance is always obtained with 2 CPU threads sharing the L2 cache. The CPU side of Kaveri has an L2 cache for each two CPU cores. The two running CPU threads are scheduled to share the L2 cache, so that the memory coherence traffic across L2 caches is avoided. In the case of running 4 CPU threads, the coherence traffic burdens the performance.

```
1  // CPU side
2  f++;
3  (ptr_end)->fetch_add(1);
4  if(CPUtid == 0){
5    while((ptr_end)->load() < num_wg + num_CPUthreads){
6      ;
7    }
8    (ptr_end)->store(0);
9    (ptr_run)->fetch_add(1);
10 }
11 else{
12   while((ptr_run)->load() < f){
13     ;
14   }
15 }
16
17 // GPU side
18 f++;
19 if(tid == 0){
20   (ptr_end)->fetch_add(1);
21   while((ptr_run)->load() < f){
22     ;
23   }
24 }
25 barrier(); // Synchronization
```

FIGURE 8.10

Code segment of global barrier synchronization across CPU and GPU. It uses platform atomics on two atomic variables in host coherent memory that are pointed by ptr_end and ptr_run. A CPU thread with ID CPUtid = 0 waits until all CPU threads and GPU work-groups have updated the variable pointed by ptr_end. Next, this CPU thread increases the variable pointed by ptr_run, which counts the number of frontiers f. Then, all CPU threads and GPU work-groups can continue running.

Both legacy and HSA implementations alternatively execute one iteration, that is, visit the nodes of one frontier, on CPU or on GPU. This depends on the number of nodes of the frontier compared to a certain threshold. We have tested with different threshold values: 64, 128, 256, and 512. Pure CPU and pure GPU implementations are also executed for comparison purposes.

Figure 8.11 shows the execution results for the legacy implementation. It is compared to a pure CPU implementation using 2 threads. Together with the execution time, for each of the tests (threshold value and graph), the number of GPU kernel calls is represented. The clear relation between the number of GPU kernel calls and the execution time is noticeable. As can be seen, the main drawback of this legacy implementation is that the GPU kernel should be relaunched, or the CPU threads should be created, each time the number of nodes of the next frontier changes with respect to the threshold. There is significant overhead due to kernel relaunch, or CPU thread creation, and data transfers, as seen in Algorithm 8.4. This makes the switching execution on CPU and GPU completely unpractical, as it is always outperformed by the pure CPU version with 2 threads.

The HSA implementation benefits from the dynamic swapping between CPU and GPU, as can be observed in Figure 8.12. There is a sweet spot threshold of 64 or 128

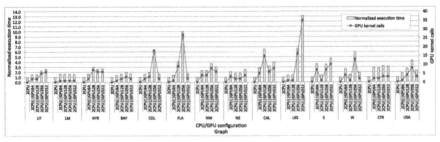

FIGURE 8.11

Execution results for a legacy implementation of BFS on CPU (using 2 threads) and GPU. Results are normalized to execution time on 2 CPU threads. Thus, columns taller than 1.0 represent the slowdown with respect to the 2 CPU threads version. Each combined CPU||GPU version has a threshold of 64, 128, 256, and 512 nodes per frontier.

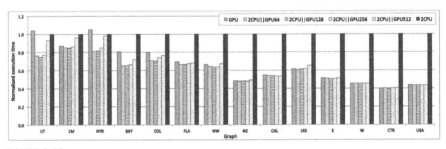

FIGURE 8.12

Execution results for an HSA implementation of BFS on CPU (using 2 threads) and GPU. Results are normalized to execution time on 2 CPU threads. Each combined CPU||GPU version has a threshold of 64, 128, 256, and 512 nodes per frontier.

(i.e., one fourth or one half of the launched GPU threads), which typically gives the best performance. In the figure, the input graphs are sorted by the total number of nodes. The right-most ones usually have large frontiers, so that the pure GPU version clearly outperforms the pure CPU version. In these cases, the coordinated HSA implementation chooses the GPU side for most of the frontiers. Particularly interesting are the left-most graphs, where the HSA implementation significantly beats both pure CPU and pure GPU versions. For instance, on the sweet spot for graph UT, the HSA implementation is 39% faster than pure GPU and 34% faster than pure CPU. The average number of nodes per frontier, and the percentage of frontiers that are visited on CPU and GPU are presented in Figure 8.13. Both show a similar trend, and can be compared to the execution time results.

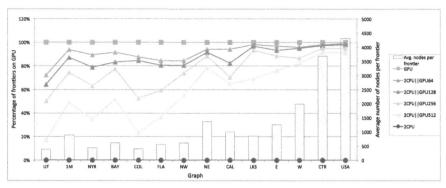

FIGURE 8.13

Percentage of frontiers visited on GPU, and average number of nodes per frontier for 14 graphs. Each combined CPU||GPU version has a threshold of 64, 128, 256, and 512 nodes per frontier.

8.5 DATA LAYOUT CONVERSION

Data layout transformation routines can be of great help in heterogeneous systems, as they are able to reshape data according to the memory access preferences of latency-oriented and throughput-oriented compute units.

Traditionally, latency-oriented CPUs have large on-chip cache memories. As long as a data set fits into the cache, the achievable memory bandwidth is fairly insensitive to the access patterns. Thus, CPU data sets tend to assume layouts that follow the natural organization used in external data files. For example, if each element of the data set consists of several values, such as the RGB values of a color pixel, the values for each data element are laid out in consecutive memory locations, which is consistent with most natural file formats of video cameras. Such layout is commonly referred to as the Array-of-Structure (AoS) layout.

However, throughput-oriented GPUs tend to have much smaller on-chip cache memories. Thus, efficient off-chip memory access is crucial for performance. Towards this aim, the most common optimization is having coalesced memory accesses, that is, making adjacent threads access adjacent memory locations. This way, memory transactions are more efficiently exploited, because strided accesses are avoided. In the pixel example, GPUs tend to prefer a data layout where all the R values of the pixels processed by concurrently executing threads are in consecutive locations, followed by G values, and then followed by B values. Such layout is commonly referred to as the SoA layout, or the related Discrete Arrays (DA) layout.

In order to illustrate these differences, we have tested a simple code on an AMD Kaveri where the elements of an input array are loaded, updated (adding a constant value), and stored into an output array. We have prepared CPU and GPU versions. In both versions, each CPU or GPU thread is in charge of a power-of-two (from 1 to 1024) number of consecutive elements. Each of these groups of consecutive elements

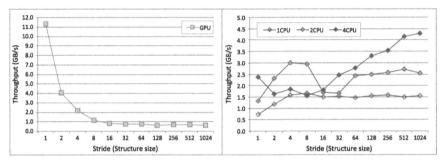

FIGURE 8.14

Throughput results on GPU (using 128 work-groups of 256 work-items) and CPU (1, 2, and 4 threads) for a code that reads input elements, updates them, and stores in an output array. A number from 1 to 1024 consecutive elements (structure size) is assigned to each CPU or GPU thread.

can be seen as a structure. The size of this structure is the stride between memory accesses of consecutive threads. Figure 8.14 shows the throughput results. The GPU suffers a dramatic slowdown when the structure size increases: AoS layout is not a good election for GPUs. In the case of the CPU, the AoS layout can be beneficial, as it can be noticed in the graph. Together with caching, these kind of accesses can also take advantage of hardware prefetching.

Sung et al. [1] presented a data layout conversion system. It consists of a set of elementary transformations that convert SoA and AoS from/to an intermediate representation called ASTA. A key feature of these elementary transformations is that they work in-place, that is, the output lies on the same physical locations as the input. This entails a great saving of memory space, as the memory overhead is zero or very negligible (only some auxiliary bits for coordination). Figure 8.15 shows the three layouts SoA, AoS, and ASTA.

The ASTA layout demonstrated high-bandwidth memory accesses across different architectures. Moreover, the elementary transformations achieve a high fraction of peak memory bandwidth, so that SoA-ASTA and AoS-ASTA conversions can be performed at low cost. Recently, these elementary transformations have been successfully used to implement full in-place transposition of general matrices on NVIDIA and AMD GPUs [16]. Among them, the particular case of transposition of skinny matrices is equivalent to SoA-AoS or AoS-SoA conversion. This means that it can be tackled by sequences such as SoA-ASTA plus ASTA-AoS transformations, or AoS-ASTA plus ASTA-SoA transformations.

In this section, we focus on the SoA-ASTA transformation, as it is based on an algorithm that uses atomic operations on GPU memory to coordinate the execution. By replacing these GPU atomic operations with platform atomics, it is possible to design a cooperative HSA implementation where the workload is shared by CPU threads and GPU work-groups. Thus, higher throughput than a pure GPU version can be attained.

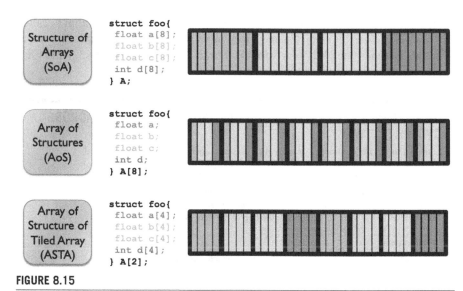

FIGURE 8.15

Three possible layouts of an array: Structure-of-Arrays (SoA), Array-of-Structures (AoS), and Array-of-Structure-of-Tiled-Arrays (ASTA).

8.5.1 IN-PLACE SoA-ASTA CONVERSION WITH PTTWAC ALGORITHM

A SoA is a two-dimensional organization $M \times N$. In a row-major layout, M is the number of arrays, and N is the size of each array. Typically, $M \ll N$. In order to convert to the ASTA layout, N can be factorized as $N' \times n$, so that the SoA can be seen as a three-dimensional organization $M \times N' \times n$. Each n element can be considered as a super-element or a tile.

Essentially, the SoA-ASTA conversion performs the transposition of a matrix $M \times N'$ where each element is a super-element of size n. In this way, the SoA-ASTA conversion transforms from $M \times N' \times n$ to $N' \times M \times n$. According to the definition of matrix transposition, each super-element in position (i, j) will be moved to position (j, i). In a linearized row-major layout, the super-element in position (i, j) is in address $k = i \times N' + j$. After transposing, that super-element will be in address $k' = j \times M + i$. The expression that maps from k to k' is in Equation 8.1.

$$k' = \begin{cases} k \times M \quad \mathrm{mod} \left(M \times N' - 1 \right), & \text{if } 0 \le k < M \times N' - 1 \\ M \times N' - 1, & \text{if } k = M \times N' - 1 \end{cases} \tag{8.1}$$

Equation 8.1 calculates the destination a matrix element is moved to. Because the super-elements are moving in place, each super-element has to be saved and further shifted to the next location. This generates cycles or chains of shifting. For instance, for a 5×3 row-majored matrix, the cycles are (0)(1 5 11 13 9 3)(7)(2 10 8 12 4 6)(14).

A straightforward parallel implementation of this transposition assigns each of these cycles to a GPU work-group or a CPU thread. They just need to follow the cycle that is generated with Equation 8.1. This cycle-following algorithm is called IPT [17]. However, this algorithm has a load imbalance problem, because the number of cycles and their length is very variable. For instance, the above 5×3 matrix has cycles of length 6 and cycles of length 1.

ALGORITHM 8.6 PARALLEL-TILE-TRANSPOSE-WITHIN-AND-ACROSS-CYCLES (PTTWAC)

Arrays in device memory: An array A of n-sized super-elements (it is reshaped from $M \times N'$ to $N' \times M$). An auxiliary array *finished* with $M \times N'$ flags to mark whether a super-element has been shifted.

Arrays and variables in on-chip memory: Temporary storage (registers or local memory) for super-elements: *data* and *backup*. A variable *done* visible to all work-items in the work-group to store the flag of the current super-element.

Pseudo-code:

```
1: Launch num_wg work-groups with ID wg_id, which contain wg_size work-items
     with ID tid
 2: gid = wg_id
 3: while gid < M × N' − 1 do
 4:     next = gid × M mod (M × N' − 1)
 5:     if next = gid then
 6:         Continue // No need to shift
 7:     end if
 8:     Save super-element A[gid] into data
 9:     if tid = 0 then
10:         done = atomic_or(finished[gid]; 0)
11:     endif
12:     Local barrier synchronization
13:     while done = 0 do
14:         Save super-element A[next] in to backup
15:         if tid = 0 then
16:             done = atomic_or(finished[next], 1)
17:         end if
18:         Local barrier synchronization
19:         if done = 0 then
20:             Move super-element in data to A[next]
21:         end if
22:         Move super-element in backup to data
23:         next = next × M mod (M × N' − 1)
24:     end while
25:     gid = gid + num_wg
26: end while
```

To solve this load imbalance problem, Sung et al. [1] proposed a new algorithm called Parallel-Tile-Transpose-Within-and-Across-Cycles (PTTWAC). The gist of this algorithm is having multiple work-groups working on the same cycle, and coordinating them by employing atomic operations. An $M \times N'$-bit auxiliary storage is used to mark when a super-element has already been shifted. Algorithm 8.6 describes the algorithm.

8.5.2 AN HSA IMPLEMENTATION OF PTTWAC

It is possible to implement an HSA version of PTTWAC by allocating the array A and the auxiliary array *finished* in host coherent memory. The flags in auxiliary array *finished* can be read with platform atomic *load*() (line 10 of Algorithm 8.6), and updated with platform atomic *exchange*(1) (line 16). In this way, CPU threads can collaborate with GPU work-groups to shift super-elements across the cycles.

Instead of statically assigning super-elements to work-groups (lines 2 and 25), we deploy a dynamic assignment. An atomic variable in host coherent memory is updated with platform atomic *fetch_add*(1). The return value is the index of the super-element to shift.

8.5.3 EVALUATION

This section evaluates the HSA version of PTTWAC and compares it to pure CPU and pure GPU versions. The experiments have been run on an AMD Kaveri A10-7850K APU with Radeon R7 Graphics. The code has been developed in C++AMP.

First, we have run more than 300 experiments with different array sizes. M is a power-of-two in the range 2 to 256. N is a power-of-two in the range 16,384-131,072. The super-element size n is a power-of-two between 2 and 1024. For each combination of M, N and n, we run a pure GPU version, a pure CPU version (with 1, 2 and 4 CPU threads), and collaborative HSA versions (1, 2, and 4 CPU threads plus GPU). The GPU launches 128 work-groups of 256 work-items.

The goal of these experiments is finding some trends that define which configuration is more profitable for each array. In this way, in Figure 8.16, we have normalized the execution results, and sorted them by the super-element size n. As can be seen, the pure CPU version with 1 thread gives the best results for most of the cases with $n \leq 32$. It is very likely that the coherence protocol invalidates cache lines due to false sharing on L2, when more than one CPU thread is used. This would burden the CPU version with 2 and 4 threads. It can also be observed that the pure GPU

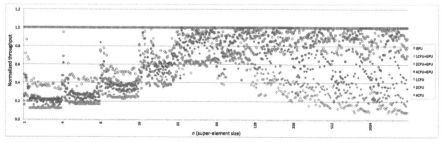

FIGURE 8.16

Normalized throughput for pure CPU, pure GPU, and collaborative HSA versions of PTTWAC. The results are sorted by the super-element size n from 2 to 1024. The number of CPU threads is 1, 2, or 4.

version usually gets the lowest throughput in these cases. Assuming that memory transactions from GPU should be optimized for entire wavefronts, the fact that the super-elements are so small makes the work-groups use only part of each memory transaction.

When $n > 32$, we detect that the performance of each configuration is related to the number of super-elements $M \times N'$. Figure 8.17 shows the normalized throughput for 160 experiments with n between 64 and 1024. We have sorted the results by the number of super-elements. It can be seen that the pure GPU version generally outperforms the collaborative versions when the number of super-elements is 512 or less. Once the number of super-elements increases, it can be noticed that the execution benefits from the help of 1, 2, or 4 CPU threads.

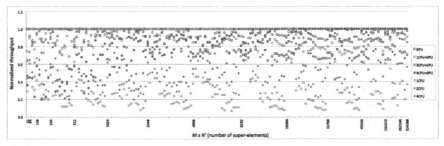

FIGURE 8.17

Normalized throughput for pure CPU, pure GPU, and collaborative HSA versions of PTTWAC. The results are sorted by the number of super-elements $M \times N'$. The number of CPU threads is 1, 2, or 4.

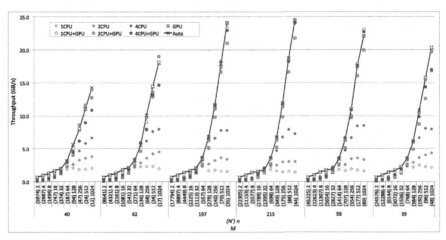

FIGURE 8.18

Execution results for an HSA implementation of in-place SoA-ASTA conversion. Six input arrays are tested. Abscissas represent $M \times N' \times n$.

With these observations, it is possible to automatically choose the most appropriate configuration, given the array dimensionality. In Figure 8.18 we have tested six real-world arrays that were used by Sung et al. [1]. The black thin line represents the auto configuration results. It can be observed that it matches very well the best performing version in each case.

8.6 CONCLUSIONS

This chapter has presented three case studies of the use of HSA platform atomics and coherent shared memory across host and devices. For each case study, we show experimental results based on real hardware and demonstrate that implementations that use HSA features clearly outperform legacy implementations.

The HSA task queue system obtains better load balancing and avoids kernel relaunch. The heterogeneous implementation of BFS can advantageously select to explore a graph frontier on CPU or on GPU at low cost. The elementary transposition can achieve a performance improvement from the simultaneous execution of CPU and GPU compute units.

These case studies indicate that HSA can support real-world applications to efficiently make fine-grained decisions using CPUs and/or GPUs on the application phases that better match the capabilities of one or the other. We are at the beginning of an era where the heterogeneous compute engines can closely collaborate and contribute to improving the performance and energy efficiency of demanding applications.

ACKNOWLEDGMENT

We would like to thank Francisco Hurtado Berlanga for technical support.

REFERENCES

[1] I.-J. Sung, G. Liu, W.-M. Hwu, DL: a data layout transformation system for heterogeneous computing, in: Innovative Parallel Computing, InPar, 2012, pp. 1–11, http://dx.doi.org/10.1109/InPar.2012.6339606.

[2] D. Cederman, P. Tsigas, Dynamic load balancing using work-stealing, in: GPU Computing Gems Jade Edition, 2011, pp. 485–499.

[3] S. Chatterjee, M. Grossman, A. Sbrlea, V. Sarkar, Dynamic task parallelism with a GPU work-stealing runtime system, in: S. Rajopadhye, M. Mills Strout (Eds.), Languages and Compilers for Parallel Computing, Lecture Notes in Computer Science, vol. 7146, Springer, Berlin, Heidelberg, 2013, pp. 203–217, http://dx.doi.org/10.1007/978-3-642-36036-7_14. http://dx.doi.org/10.1007/978-3-642-36036-7_14.

[4] D. Cederman, P. Tsigas, On dynamic load balancing on graphics processors, in: Proceedings of the 23rd ACM SIGGRAPH/EUROGRAPHICS Symposium on Graphics Hardware, GH '08, Eurographics Association, Aire-la-Ville, Switzerland, 2008, pp. 57–64. http://dl.acm.org/citation.cfm?id=1413957.1413967.

[5] L. Lamport, Specifying concurrent program modules, ACM Trans. Program. Lang. Syst. 5 (2) (1983) 190–222, http://dx.doi.org/10.1145/69624.357207. http://doi.acm.org/10.1145/69624.357207.

[6] L. Chen, O. Villa, S. Krishnamoorthy, G. Gao, Dynamic load balancing on single- and multi-GPU systems, in: Parallel Distributed Processing (IPDPS), 2010 IEEE International Symposium, 2010, pp. 1–12, http://dx.doi.org/10.1109/IPDPS.2010.5470413.

[7] NVIDIA Corporation, NVIDIA CUDA C Programming Guide 6.5, 2014.

[8] AMD, AMD Accelerated Parallel Processing. OpenCL User Guide, 2014.

[9] P. Harish, P.J. Narayanan, Accelerating large graph algorithms on the GPU using CUDA, in: Proceedings of the 14th International Conference on High Performance Computing, HiPC'07, Springer-Verlag, Berlin, Heidelberg, 2007, pp. 197–208. http://dl.acm.org/citation.cfm?id=1782174.1782200.

[10] Y. Deng, B. Wang, S. Mu, Taming irregular EDA applications on GPUs, in: IEEE/ACM International Conference on Computer-Aided Design – Digest of Technical Papers, ICCAD 2009, 2009, pp. 539–546.

[11] C. Lauterbach, M. Garland, S. Sengupta, D. Luebke, D. Manocha, Fast BVH construction on GPUs. Comput. Graph. Forum. 28 (2) (2009) 375–384, http://dx.doi.org/10.1111/j.1467-8659.2009.01377.x. http://dx.doi.org/10.1111/j.1467-8659.2009.01377.x.

[12] D. Merrill, M. Garland, A. Grimshaw, Scalable GPU graph traversal, in: Proceedings of the 17th ACM SIGPLAN Symposium on Principles and Practice of Parallel Programming, PPoPP '12, ACM, New York, NY, USA, 2012, pp. 117–128, http://dx.doi.org/10.1145/2145816.2145832. http://doi.acm.org/10.1145/2145816.2145832.

[13] L. Luo, M. Wong, W.-M. Hwu, An effective GPU implementation of breadth-first search, in: Proceedings of the 47th Design Automation Conference, DAC '10, ACM, New York, NY, USA, 2010, pp. 52–55, http://dx.doi.org/10.1145/1837274.1837289. http://doi.acm.org/10.1145/1837274.1837289.

[14] J.A. Stratton, C. Rodrigues, I.-J. Sung, N. Obeid, L. Chang, G. Liu, W.-M.W. Hwu, Parboil: a revised benchmark suite for scientific and commercial throughput computing, Tech. Rep. IMPACT-12-01, University of Illinois at Urbana-Champaign, 2012.

[15] University of Rome "La Sapienza", 9th DIMACS Implementation Challenge, http://www.dis.uniroma1.it/challenge9/index.shtml, 2014.

[16] I.-J. Sung, J. Gómez-Luna, J.M. González-Linares, N. Guil, W.-M.W. Hwu, In-place transposition of rectangular matrices on accelerators, in: Proceedings of the 19th ACM SIGPLAN Symposium on Principles and Practice of Parallel Programming, PPoPP '14, 2014, http://dx.doi.org/10.1145/2555243.2555266.

[17] F. Gustavson, L. Karlsson, B. Kågström, Parallel and cache-efficient inplace matrix storage format conversion, ACM. T. Math. Software. 38 (3) (2012) 17:1–17:32. http://doi.acm.org/10.1145/2168773.2168775.

HSA Simulators

Y.-C. Chung*, W.-C. Hsu**, S.-H. Hung**, T.B. Jablin†, D. Kaeli‡, Y. Sun‡, R. Ubal‡

National Tsing Hua University, Hsinchu City, Taiwan, ROC*; National Taiwan University, Taipei, Taiwan, ROC**; University of Illinois at Urbana-Champaign, Urbana, IL, USA and MulticoreWare Inc., Champaign, IL, USA†; Northeastern University, Boston, MA, USA‡

9.1 SIMULATING HSA IN MULTI2SIM

9.1.1 INTRODUCTION

Heterogeneous computing combines CPUs, GPUs and other types of accelerators such as digital signal processors (DSPs) and field programmable gate arrays (FPGAs) into a single computing fabric. These multi-device, many-core systems are attractive in terms of both performance and power. Heterogeneous systems have become the norm for low power devices such as tablet and smart phones, integrating the GPU and other accelerators such as systems on a chip (SOCs). As the CPU and GPU devices are integrated into a single chip, the cooperation and scheduling between the CPU and GPU devices has become a growing issue in order to obtain good performance and reduce power consumption.

The heterogeneous system architecture (HSA) is an architectural specification targeted at defining coordination between devices that seeks to overcome challenges on the path of integration of multiple devices. To better understand how different types of devices can work together effectively, we have developed an HSA-compliant simulation infrastructure. The simulator can support computer architecture research, software tuning, and compiler and finalizer optimization. We have developed Multi2Sim [1] to serve many needs as a heterogeneous computer architecture simulator.

Multi2Sim [1] is an open source toolset for heterogeneous computer architecture simulation. It provides simulation of several different popular CPU instruction set architectures (ISAs) including x86, ARM, and MIPS and GPU ISAs such as AMD's Evergreen and Southern Islands and NVIDIA's Fermi and Kepler. The developers of Multi2Sim have allowed for the interaction between computing devices, even if they are running different ISAs. For example, Multi2Sim can simulate an OpenCL program, which is composed of a host program that is running on a CPU device and a parallel execution kernel targeting a GPU device. The simulated CPU device executes the host program and launches NDRanges on a Southern Islands target. Moreover, Multi2Sim supports simulation of the entire memory hierarchy on the

GPU. The key feature of Multi2Sim is the ability to provide timing simulation results for heterogeneous systems on a cycle-by-cycle basis.

The Multi2Sim simulator uses an application-only simulation scheme, emulating interaction with the underlying operating systems. This choice is in contrast to either a full-system simulator or an instruction-based simulator. A full system simulator implements the whole ISA specification and simulates all connected devices, including disk and networking. This class of simulator attempts to provide the same user experience running an unmodified operating system as running on a native machine.

Alternatively, an instruction level simulator faithfully emulates instruction execution of an executable program. It implements a subset of the ISA specification, but simply emulates memory and registers. An instruction level simulator is a great tool for verification and debugging purposes. However, to deliver a robust simulation environment that supports heterogeneous execution, we have elected to follow the middle road.

Multi2Sim is implemented as an application-only simulation methodology. The simulator core implements a subset of ISA specification that is associated with a set of instructions present in the application. Multi2Sim virtualizes system calls, faithfully executing OpenCL programs out of the box, but only proving detailed simulation of the application code. By removing the overhead of interacting with the operating system, simulation can be faster and simpler.

The Multi2Sim simulator is composed of dependent components, as shown in Figure 9.1, which include: (1) a disassembler, (2) an emulator, (3) a timing simulator, and (4) a visual tool. Each component relies on the component(s) on its left, but can be used as a standalone tool without the component(s) on its right. For example, the emulator can be used to verify the execution output without knowing any result produced from the timing simulator, but it requires the disassembler to parse the binary executable files. The disassembler takes in binary files and produces the exact same assembly code as popular disassemblers for any supported architecture. In addition, the disassembler provides a rich application program interface (API) to parse the instruction

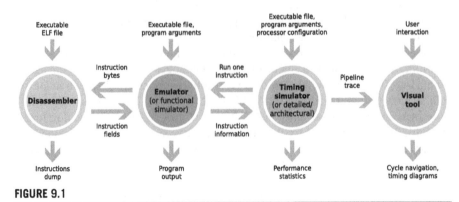

FIGURE 9.1

The four components of the Multi2Sim simulator.

fields for other components in Multi2Sim. The purpose of the emulator is to produce the same result, step by step, as if the program was run on the native machine.

The Multi2Sim emulator virtualizes the register files and the memory system and maintains the internal state of an execution (such as the program counter) of the running program. The timing simulation can accurately estimate the execution time of the guest program, according to the machine description provided by the user. The timing simulator is cycle-based and, if fairly detailed, provides high relative fidelity to performance of the targeted device. Finally, the visual tool provides interactive visualization for the processor pipelines. At the present time, Multi2Sim's HSA support includes the disassembler and the emulator components, though the other two components are under development presently.

9.1.2 **MULTI2SIM-HSA**

The idea of building Multi2Sim is to support heterogeneous computing simulation, particularly for CPU and GPU devices. Therefore, Multi2Sim is one of the best candidate simulation frameworks to perform HSA simulation. Recently, Multi2Sim started to support functional simulation HSA at the intermediate language level. To be specific, HSA simulation in Multi2Sim is platform-independent and the simulation does not require finalization of the code into an ISA. The platform-independent design guarantees that the simulation result is universal and not influenced by the hardware or the finalizer design. Moreover, the Multi2Sim simulator provides detailed logging functionalities of the internal execution state, including work-item formation, register storage, and the memory hierarchy. Therefore, Multi2Sim can be a very useful tool for debugging serial and parallel programs. In this section, we will give a brief walkthrough on how to use Multi2Sim to simulate HSA program execution and discuss its underlying simulation engine. We assume the user has properly installed and compiled Multi2Sim. For installation instructions, please refer to Section 9.1.8.

We start our discussion with a simple "helloworld" program sample, as an overview of how to simulate the execution of an HSA program with Multi2Sim. The following Heterogeneous System Architecture Intermediate Language (HSAIL) [2] code is provided for the helloworld HSA program, which only has one function. The program simply adds number 1 and number 2 in order to output the summation.

```
function &m2s_print_u32 () (arg_u32 %integer) {};
kernel &main ()
{
    mov_u32 $s0, 1;
    mov_u32 $s1, 2;
    add_u32 $s2, $s0, $s1;
    {
        arg_u32 %num;
        st_arg_u32 $s2, [%num];
        call &m2s_print_u32 () (%num);
    }
};
```

Once you have typed in the source code, save it as `helloworld.hsail` and assemble it with HSAILTools [3]. The HSAILTool can compile HSAIL code to its equivalent binary format, namely BRIG. Assuming that the output file of the HSAILTools is `helloworld.brig`, then you can issue the following command:

```
m2s helloworld.brig
```

As Multi2Sim is provided as a Linux command line tool, it follows the standard command line format. The first token is `m2s` (name of the simulator), and the second is the name of the executable that you want to simulate. Multi2Sim accepts arguments to modify its default options. All arguments passed to Multi2Sim should be added between the `m2s` command and the executable file name. If the simulated program also needs some command-line argument, you can always add one after the executable file. For example, command passes two arguments to Multi2Sim, enabling logging the binary-level execution, which is stored in the log file `isa.debug`. It also passes the argument "`abc`" to the guest program, although our particular guest program in this example ignores this argument.

```
m2s --hsa-debug-isa isa.debug helloworld.brig abc
```

If you see the output number 3, you have successfully simulated your first HSA program in Multi2Sim. The sample HSAIL program is very simple. It sets the value in registers $s1 and $s2 to be 1 and 2, respectively, and then calculates their sum. However, you may experience two major differences if you run the HSA code on a native machine. First, you do not need a host program to launch the kernel in Multi2Sim. Second, generally speaking, a kernel cannot perform I/O operations by itself, but Multi2Sim provides some I/O functions for users to easily read or print data.

One of the design principles of Multi2Sim-HSA is to allow users to test their code as easily as possible. Users are not supposed to write long and repetitive host code in order to test simple kernels. For this reason, we added support to standalone HSA programs, supporting HSAIL execution and allowing a program to be entered from the main kernel. In addition, users should be able to debug their code and produce output in this environment. Therefore, Multi2Sim allows users to read from and write to the console, providing some basic input/output functionality.

9.1.3 HSAIL HOST HSA

To remove the need for the host code, Multi2Sim allows users to launch HSA execution directly from an HSAIL program. This allows users to focus on learning HSAIL and enables them to debug an HSA program without the overhead of writing the host code, which can take longer than just writing the simple kernel itself. Multi2Sim implements a kernel launch and execution. First, it launches the kernel automatically as soon as the simulator starts. Second, the whole HSA runtime system [4] is supported by Multi2Sim in HSAIL via a set of runtime functions and a set of virtual device drivers. Although the HSA Foundation provides Okra [5], which is a lightweight interface to launch kernels on a simulator, Multi2Sim simulates the system runtime, allowing the user to capture the interaction between devices and provide more information about the runtime execution.

9.1.3.1 Program entry

The main kernel is defined as:

```
kernel &main (kernarg_u32 %argc, kernarg_u64 %argv)
```

Execution starts with a kernel named &main. Main has two arguments: %argc and %argv. This standard C style program interface is utilized. In detail, the %argc is an unsigned 32-bit long integer and stores the number of arguments, while the %argv is the flat address pointing to an array of argument strings (starting at the first character). These kernel arguments can be omitted if a developer decides not to use command-line arguments. When the simulation starts, the simulator would first create an architected queuing language (AQL) queue for the hosting CPU device. This automatically injects an AQL packet into the queue to launch the &main kernel. This kernel launch forms a grid on the main CPU device with only a single work-item on the grid. The execution of the main grid is serialized. However, by using runtime functions, the user can easily discover other devices running in the simulated machine and launch parallel kernels.

9.1.3.2 HSA runtime interception

The runtime system is defined as a set of functions. Users may need to call those runtime functions to add queues, dispatch kernels, or do other runtime-related tasks. There is a one-to-one mapping between the official runtime functions and Multi2Sim HSAIL runtime functions. The mapping is simple. To utilize runtime functions in Multi2Sim directly, we need to know the associated official runtime function. For example, if the official runtime function in c is:

```
uint64_t hsa_queue_add_write_index_relaxed
    (hsa_queue_t * queue, uint64_t value);
```

then the corresponding Multi2Sim HSAIL function would be:

```
function &hsa_queue_add_write_index_relaxed
    (arg_u64 %ret) (arg_u64 %queue, arg_u64 %value) {};
```

The basic rules are as follows:

- The name of the function is identical, except for the & added in front of the function name, which is required by the HSAIL specification.
- Input and output arguments keep the same type. The name of the argument can be any valid HSAIL variable name.
- Pointers are all represented by 64-bit integer addresses, regardless of the machine type. Users have to cast the type if they are using a narrower (e.g., 32-bit) machine.
- Users do not need to implement the function. Even if they write in the function body, the instructions will be ignored by the simulator.

Internally, the simulator does not actually execute the runtime functions. Instead, it intercepts their invocations and converts them into application binary interface (ABI) calls that are passed to the HSA virtual device driver. The driver performs the designated action and returns the result via memory. A special case occurs when the runtime function uses a callback function. The driver builds a stack frame for the callback function and returns to the emulation environment. After the callback function returns, the driver intercepts execution again and returns to the place where the runtime function was called.

9.1.3.3 Basic I/O support

Because Multi2Sim-HSA supports running a standalone HSA program, we needed to provide the capability to effectively interact with the program. We have provided limited I/O support for HSAIL in Multi2Sim-HSA. In real hardware, if the kernel wants to perform an I/O operation, it has to build an AQL packet and send it to the CPU. Simulators commonly handle I/O commands using system calls, as has been implemented in the SPIM MIPS simulator. However, a system call interface is not presently available in the current HSAIL specification. Therefore, Multi2Sim supports a customized set of library-like functions for I/O. The general format is as follows:

```
function &m2s_action_TypeLength
    (arg_TypeLength %input)
    (arg_TypeLength %output)
```

where the action can be either print or read. The type and length can be an integer, unsigned integer, bit string, or float type, and is supported by HSAIL. For input functions, only the argument in the first set of parentheses would appear, while the argument is only used for output functions. The argument type and length must be identical to the type and length in the function name.

9.1.4 HSA RUNTIME

Although it is very convenient to launch kernels from an HSAIL program, users may want to simulate some unmodified HSA programs, which are composed of a host program running on CPU ISA and BRIG files for the parallel execution kernels. Moreover, writing a host program in a high level language can be much easier than in HSAIL. Therefore, the developers decided to let Multi2Sim supports simulate the execution of a host program by the x86 component of Multi2Sim.

An HSA runtime implementation is provided in the Multi2Sim directory. However, it is not part of the Multi2Sim simulator. When compiling the host program, users would have to link with the Multi2Sim provided runtime library. If the runtime library is linked statically, it will become part of the guest program to be simulated in Multi2Sim. When the runtime library is simulated, it uses ioctl system calls to communicate with Multi2Sim HSA device drivers and can perform various actions, such as device capability query, queue creating, kernel dispatching, and atomic signal operations on devices.

9.1.5 EMULATOR DESIGN

9.1.5.1 Emulator hierarchy

The Multi2Sim-HSA emulator has been designed hierarchically, as shown in Figure 9.2, where each level is expressed at a finer granularity as we move down the hierarchy. The emulator is composed of a number of HSA kernel agents. In HSA terminology, a kernel agent is a device that supports the HSA specification and runs HSA kernels. It both creates and consumes AQL kernel dispatch packets. When a kernel is dispatched, it forms a one-dimensional, two-dimensional, or three-dimensional grid. Depending on the capabilities of the device, an agent can run one or more grids simultaneously. If other kernels are dispatched while the device is busy, they wait in the AQL queue. A grid can be divided into work-groups and can be further divided into wavefronts and work-items. A work-item is the lowest-level unit of computational work; all computation occurs in terms of work-item units. The dispatch of work-items is performed in a round-robin fashion. For example, if a work-group has 4 wavefronts, the second wavefront would start its execution after the first one finishes. During the execution of the first wavefront, all of the work-items that belong to the wavefront will emulate one instruction in turn.

Each work-item holds a standalone function call stack. According to the HSA specification, registers are bound to functions and arguments cannot be passed through registers. In addition, variables are allocated to specific memory segments and have discrete addresses. Thus, a standard stack frame addressed as a memory region at the end of the program stack would not be suitable for HSAIL simulation. We need a mechanism that can manage the register file and work with variables stored in several different places. In Multi2Sim-HSA, we have provided a stack frame that is different from a traditional stack frame. In our simulator, each stack frame captures a snapshot of the state of simulation. The stack frame holds the current status of registers, arguments, and variables. For registers, the stack frame maintains variable names and values. A traditional stack frame would have to keep track of its addresses in memory.

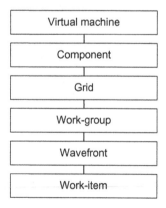

FIGURE 9.2

Hierarchical design of the Multi2Sim-HSA simulator.

When a work-item is created, the first stack frame is also created in the stack. The simulator sets the program counter to point to the first entry in the code section of the BRIG file. According to the BRIG specification, the instructions and the directives are mixed in the code section, and so the program counter can be pointing at either a directive or an instruction. Multi2Sim treats directives the same as instructions, consuming an emulator cycle to execute them. A pragma or variable declaration are examples of a directive. Once the execution of an instruction or directive is finished, the program counter is updated to point to the next entry in the hsa_code section. By repeating this action, the simulator executes instructions/directives, until all the work-items finish execution and there are no more kernels waiting in the queue.

9.1.5.2 Memory systems

Multi2Sim-HSA strictly follows the memory hierarchy defined in the HSA specification [6], but also creates its own memory system, as shown in Figure 9.3. There is a single memory object that requests memory from the host environment and manages the guest memory space. The memory object is managed as a flat memory address space. Memory allocation and deallocations is delegated to a memory manager, which runs a best-fit algorithm. The memory manager is also responsible for allocating the memory for global variables.

The segmented memory space requires an address translation between the inner-segment address and the flat address. Therefore, the segment memory manager is created to delegate operations involving non-global segments. When a memory segment is requested, the corresponding memory segment manager is invoked and the requested amount of memory is allocated via the global memory manager. For example, when a kernel is launched, the AQL packet explicitly requests an amount of memory required to hold the group segment and the private segment. Whenever a work-group or a work-item is initiated, the memory is allocated from the global segment and is marked to denote the specific type of segment. After completing these

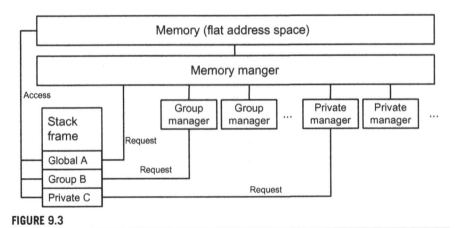

FIGURE 9.3

The segment management system.

steps for each variable, all variables that are declared in the segment have an address defined relative to the beginning of the segment. When accessing those variables, the segment manager first translates the inner-segment address to a flat address, such that a work-item can then issue loads or stores to memory directly.

9.1.6 LOGGING AND DEBUGGING

In addition to supporting HSAIL program output, the Multi2Sim-HSA simulator provides a rich set of logging tools to capture and log the internal state of the simulator. For example, by issuing:

```
m2s --hsa-debug-isa isa.debug hello_world.brig
```

users can record detailed information about the execution of each instruction in the log file isa.debug.

The following log excerpt corresponds to the execution of one line of the helloworld sample.

```
Executing: st_arg_u32 $s2, [%num] ;
***** Stack frame *****
    Function: &main,
    Program counter (offset in code section): 0xe4, call &m2s_print_u32
    () (%num) ;

    ***** Registers *****
      $s0: 1, 1, 0.000000, 0x00000001
      $s1: 2, 2, 0.000000, 0x00000002
      $s2: 3, 3, 0.000000, 0x00000003
    ***** ********* *****

    ***** Function arguments *****
    ***** ******** ********* *****

    ***** Argument scope *****
      u32 %num(0x4) = 3 ( 0x00000003 )
    ***** ******** ***** *****

    ***** Variables *****
    ***** ********* *****
    ***** Backtrace *****
      #1 &main ()
    ***** ********* *****
***** ***** ***** *****
```

From this log, we can see that the simulator just finished executing the st_arg_u32 instruction and shows the internal state of the Stack Frame section. The information captured includes the function associated with the current context, the program counter value, registers/values of interest, calling parameters and their values, calling argument scope details, local variables and their values, and finally a stack backtrace. When debugging an HSA program, a programmer can easily trace back to the instruction where the error first started and fix the problem accordingly.

Besides ISA logging, we provide additional logging options. For example, `--hsadebug-aql` can trace the AQL queue creation and removal, AQL packet reads and writes, and grid formation. Option `--hsa-debug-driver` records details on how driver functions were invoked. For detailed information and description of the entire debug selections, the user can run command `m2s --help`.

9.1.7 MULTI2SIM-HSA ROAD MAP

In the future, Multi2Sim will provide a detailed timing simulation of the HSA architecture. An HSAIL program cannot run a timing simulation directly, as HSAIL is an intermediate language and not intended to run directly on hardware. However, equipped with the finalizer for a specific device, we can translate HSA kernels to target a device-specific ISA and perform detailed timing simulation. Fortunately, Multi2Sim provides several timing simulation modules, including both CPU and GPU devices. Invoking the HSA runtime provided in Multi2Sim and connecting it to different devices can easily achieve the desired timing simulation.

9.1.8 INSTALLATION AND SUPPORT

All updated information on the Multi2Sim project can be found at

```
https://www.multi2sim.org/
```

The technical support is hosted by Top of Trees and is available at

```
https://topoftrees.com/Multi2Sim/Multi2Sim/
```

Multi2Sim is an actively managed open source project, and provides a number of help facilities and complete bug tracking and resolution.

At the time of this writing, the latest stable version of Multi2Sim is 4.2. As Multi2Sim-HSA is an active and ongoing development, users should check back often to see the latest features being released. Therefore, the user can download the developing version of the Multi2Sim and check the options through the `m2s -help` command. Users can retrieve the source code via the SVN server with command

```
svn co
http://www.multi2sim.org/svn/multi2sim/branches/multi2sim-hsa
[local_dir]
```

To become a Multi2Sim developer/contributor and receive write permission to the public repository, please refer to

```
https://www.multi2sim.org/development/
```

After downloading the code from the repository server, you can enter the newly created directory and use the following command to compile Multi2Sim:

```
libtoolize
aclocal
```

```
autoconf
automake --add-missing
./configure
make
```

During the configuration and compilation steps, you may be required to install some other software packages. Please follow the instruction to install those required packages. After compilation is complete, users can set the system path to include `multi2sim-hsa/bin` directory. If Multi2Sim is installed, command `m2s` should be able to be used in any directory. For more samples related to simulating HSA in Multi2Sim, please refer to samples in `multi2sim-hsa/sample/hsa/`. The current version of Multi2Sim is tested on `Linux Ubuntu 14.04 LTS` with `GCC` and `G++` 4.8.

9.2 EMULATING HSA WITH HSAᴇᴍᴜ
9.2.1 INTRODUCTION

For application developers and system architects to exploit the design space with HSA, full system emulators are necessary to execute parallel programs written in high level languages, such as OpenCL [7], C++ Aparapi [8], etc., via the HSA runtime. During an early development stage, functional emulation would be suitable for the purposes of basic debugging and simple profiling by allowing the user to observe coarse-grain hardware-software interactions. For example, QEMU [9] is a functional full-system emulator, which was adopted by Google and third parties to develop the Android OS and Android applications before Android smartphones were available on the market. For more accurate profiling and performance evaluation, application developers and architects would switch from functional emulators to more detailed cycle-accurate or cycle-approximate simulators. However, cycle-accurate simulators are very slow and would take days to finish a parallel application that runs for seconds. As a trade-off, cycle-approximate simulators are used in between the early development stage and the final verification stage to obtain performance metrics by modeling parts of the system with less detail.

This chapter presents a full system HSA emulator/simulator framework, called "HSAemu" [10], which has been developed according to the HSA specifications to support application and architecture development on HSA. As a framework, HSAemu enables the user to establish a full-system emulator/simulator by mixing existing functional emulators and cycle simulators. As a result, HSAemu can execute OpenCL applications over the HSA runtime with functional models of HSA user mode queue and HSA uniform memory access on emulated CPU and GPU cores. For more accurate results, the user can plug in cycle simulators for the CPU caches, GPUs and/or other components, using tools such as GEMS [11] or Multi2Sim [1], etc.

The rest of this chapter is structured as follows. In Section 9.2.2, we describe the major hardware/software features of HSA that HSAemu models after. Section 9.2.3 introduces an overall architecture design and implementation of HSAemu. Finally, we discuss the emulation of HSA-compliant GPU devices with HSAemu in Section 9.2.4.

9.2.2 MODELED HSA COMPONENTS

An HSA-compliant full system emulator should be able to support the following hardware/software features, based on the current draft of HSA Specifications [6]:

- **Shared virtual memory**: This shared virtual memory model, known as hUMA in the earlier draft, allows heterogeneous processors in a system to exchange data by sending pointers. hUMA also supports a relaxed memory consistency model with memory paging and various coherent memory scopes to enable different scales of collaborations and efficient implementations on global, grouped, and private data accesses. The reader is referred to Chapter 5 for more details of the HSA memory model. Unlike traditional GPGPU computing kernels, which have separate, limited memory space, hUMA enables computing kernels to access large, sparse data structures without copying them from the host memory in advance.

- **Hardware queue and user mode queue**: Each GPU computing component contains hardware queues, known as hQ in the earlier draft, for receiving and scheduling tasks. Used in conjunction with the user mode queuing mechanism provided by the HSA runtime, HSA aims to shorten work dispatching latency and communication delay between CPU and GPU. One processor may directly dispatch tasks onto a ring buffer (user mode queue), which are mapped to a hardware queue attached to another processor, without the need to invoke the operating system and device drivers. The tasks are encapsulated as "packets" defined by AQL. The reader is referred to Chapter 6 for more details of AQL. The structure of AQL is known to the application, but also to the hardware, which is a key HSA feature that enables applications to launch a packet in a specific agent by simply placing it in one of its queues.

- **HSA agent and packet processor**: The HSA API uses opaque handles of type `hsa_agent_t` to represent agents and kernel agents. An application may directly access the packet buffer of any queue and setup a kernel dispatch by simply filling all the fields mandated by the kernel dispatch packet format. On the receiving end, an entity called "HSA packet processor" is responsible for managing the hardware queue and decoding the AQL packet. This can also be done by hardware and is tightly bound to one or more HSA agents to provide the user mode queue functionality for the HSA agents [4]. The GPU emulator in HSAemu models the user mode queues and contains a module to emulate the packet processor.

- **Heterogeneous system architecture intermediate language (HSAIL)**: To maintain portability, HSA defines this virtual instruction set and allows the processor vendors to implement their own native instruction set and translation schemes. The current HSAIL defines 120 instructions, performing arithmetic, memory, branch, image-related, parallel synchronization, device function operations, and vector operations. In HSAemu, we provide a functional emulator to execute HSAIL programs. To simulate a specific computing device, a finalizer is needed to translate HSAIL instructions into native instructions. A cycle simulator is then used to execute the translated instruction streams. The reader is referred to Chapter 3 for more details on HSAIL and its execution model.

- **HSA agent and topology table**: An HSA agent is a hardware or software component that can be a target of the AQL queries and has the ability to access the shared virtual memory model of the HSA. The HSA agent may have many ALU units for computation. An HSA component, which is responsible for executing the kernel function, may be a GPU, FPGA, DSP, or ASIC. An HSA-compliant system should maintain a topology table that shows the available HSA agents in the current system and connections between them. The information on this table, which contains the system-wide topological relation and the limitation of relevant system resources like memory and caches, is important for applications and system software to discover and characterize the available HSA agents.

9.2.3 DESIGN OF HSAᴇᴍᴜ

This section discusses the design of HSAemu, a framework that aims to support application and architecture development on HSA by enabling the user to emulate a basic HSA platform and add their own cycle-based simulation models. From an application developer's point of view, the emulated HSA platform provides the basic features of the HSA and enables HSA-compliant applications to be executed on virtually any Linux-based machine. For architectural studies, HSAemu provides interfaces for users to plug in their own cycle simulators. For example, those who are interested in designing a GPU for HSA may add a detailed cycle simulator, such as the GPU simulator provided by Multi2Sim, to HSAemu or collect traces for post-mortem performance evaluation, as illustrated Figure 9.4.

If an emulated HSA system contains a large number of processor cores, the emulator will be very slow in real time, especially if the emulation process is "sequential" (i.e., the emulator is executed by a single thread on the host). Some recent works started to parallelize an emulator so that the emulation process can be performed by multiple threads simultaneously to take advantage of a multicore host machine. HSAemu adopts PQEMU [12], a multithreaded full-system emulator based on QEMU, to emulate the main system, including CPU cores and I/O devices. To speed up the emulation of GPU, HSAemu contains a multithreaded HSA GPU Emulator (HGE). Thus, the emulation process can be significantly accelerated if the host machine has many CPU cores.

Internally, HSAemu uses a command buffer for the main system emulator, that is, PQEMU, to control the plug-in simulators. For example, if the user wish to plug in a GPU simulator, code modifications in PQEMU and the GPU simulator are needed for the main system emulator to set up the HSA agent and the user mode queue. The user may use the command buffer to exchange information between QEMU the GPU simulator. As a case study, we have taken the GPU simulator from Multi2Sim and plugged it into HSAemu with an adapter. The implementation requires thirteen commands (opcodes) for HSAemu to communicate with the cycle-accurate microarchitectural simulator. The format of the command is shown in Figure 9.5,

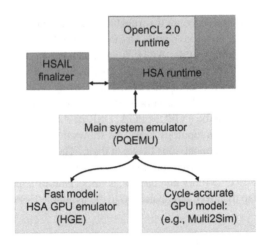

FIGURE 9.4

The HSAemu framework.

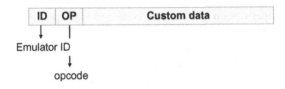

FIGURE 9.5

The format of the command between the main system and the plug-in simulator.

where the first two bytes in a command specify which emulator/simulator to receive this command, the next two bytes specify the operation code for it to execute, and the remaining bytes are optional for the arguments of the opcode.

As shown in Figure 9.6, when the HSA runtime executed on the main system emulator stores some critical information in its data section (e.g., the pointer of user mode queue, size of the native object, size of kernel arguments, etc.), the main system emulator issues a corresponding command to the HGE or a plug-in emulation engine (e.g., Multi2Sim), via the command buffer. The user may employ MMIO (memory-mapped I/O), system call, or software interrupt for the HSA runtime to deliver commands to a plug-in emulation engine. For HGE, we use software interrupt to implement the command delivery. When the adapter on the destination emulation engine receives a command, it decodes the opcode along with the data section and has the emulation engine execute the command accordingly.

While the command buffer and adapters allows the main system emulator to successfully control the emulation engines, this does not mean that the emulation engine can be plugged unmodified. To plug in the GPU simulator from Multi2Sim, we needed to modify its source code to meet the requirements of the HSA specifications, such as shared memory accesses, memory-based synchronization, and timing calculations.

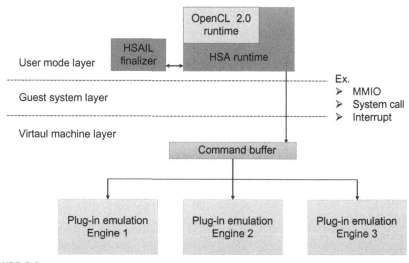

FIGURE 9.6

Communications between HSA runtime and plug-in emulation engines.

For example, the following pseudo code of demonstrates the use of command buffer for the HSA runtime on the main simulator to communicate with an HSA kernel agent. The `hsa_enqueue_cmd` function fetches the command from the memory of PQEMU and then forwards the command to either HGE or Multi2Sim according to the `dev` field of the command.

```
int hsa_enqueue_cmd(void *env, guest_vaddr addr)
{
hsa_copy_from_guest(&cmd, addr, sizeof(hsa_cmd_t)); //Fetch command
switch(cmd.dev) {
case HGE:
  hsa_device_hge(env, &cmd); //Send command to HGE
  break;
case Multi2Sim:
  hsa_device_m2s(env, &cmd); //Send command to Multi2Sim
  break;
}
}
```

The following is the pseudo code of our adapter for Multi2Sim. For creating a kernel, the adapter first allocates the memory space from the shared virtual memory for the kernel, and then calls textttclCreateKernel to generate the kernel code for the ISA modeled by Multi2Sim. Finally, the adapter needs to push the function pointer of the kernel onto the stack of Multi2Sim, so that Multi2Sim will be able to execute kernel code. Similarly, the adapter is responsible for setting up the arguments and NDrange for OpenCL/HSA runtime for Multi2Sim.

```
int hsa_device_m2s(void *env, hsa_cmd_t *cmd)
{
switch(cmd->op) {
case Kernel_Create:
  Set_up_virtual_shared_memory_for_kernel;
  clCreateKernel;
  Push_kernel_to_Multi2Sim;
  break;
case Kernel_Set_Arg_Value:
  Set_up_value_for_the_arguments_of_the_kernel_in_Multi2Sim;
  break;
case NDrange_Initialize
  Initialize_NDrange_for_Multi2Sim;
  break;
case …
  .
  .
  .
}
}
```

9.2.4 MULTITHREADED HSA GPU EMULATOR

As mentioned in the previous section, HSAemu provides a fast, multithreaded functional HGE to enable generic HSA application development. At the moment, HGE models after the graphics core next (GCN) ISA defined by AMD. The GCN architecture was launched in 2011 and has been used widely for recent GPU products by AMD, including the Kaveri chip, the first implementation of HSA.

Following the HSA specifications, HGE implements an AQL queue, an HSA kernel agent, and an AQL packet processor for each compute unit. The emulation of a compute unit is parallelized with the POSIX Threads to run on multiple processor cores on the host machine. The threads in each compute unit may access the shared virtual memory via its own soft-memory management unit (MMU), which translates addresses based on the page table maintained by the OS on the CPU side. The major components of HGE are illustrated in Figure 9.7 and discussed in detail in the following.

9.2.4.1 HSA agent and packet processor

HGE emulates an HSA kernel agent in handling HSA signals, hQ, and HSA packet processing. When the HSA agent receives an HSA signal, it copies the AQL packet from the user mode queue to hQ and wakes up the HSA packet processor. The HSA packet processor decodes the AQL packets in hQ one by one in the FIFO (first-in, first-out) order. To execute a kernel code, the HSA packet processor copies the kernel code and kernel arguments onto the shared virtual memory, links the kernel code to HGE, puts the kernel code into the code cache, and dispatches kernel jobs to the destination compute units.

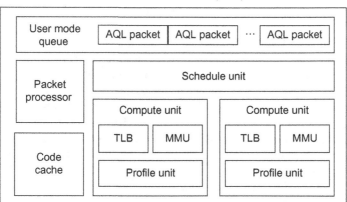

FIGURE 9.7

An overview of HSA GPU emulator.

9.2.4.2 Code cache

HGE implements a code cache to speed up the execution by saving the overhead required to repeatedly copy the same kernel code into HGE. The first time HGE receives a kernel code, the HSA packet processor generates a hashed key for the kernel code as it puts the code into the code cache. Later, when the same kernel function is executed again, the HSA packet processor will use the hashed key to find the kernel code in the code cache to avoid the overhead of copying and linking the kernel code.

9.2.4.3 HSA kernel agent and work scheduling

HGE models an HSA kernel agent with one schedule unit and multiple compute units. The schedule unit is responsible for managing a centralized pool of work items generated by a kernel function, and each compute unit in an HSA agent is carried out by a thread. A kernel function can be divided into work-groups, which are then assigned to compute units by the schedule unit. The assignment is dynamic, that is, the scheduler assigns work-items to a compute unit when the computer unit finishes its previous work. The maximum number of threads is limited by the host operating system. The schedule unit notifies the user application when all the work items in the pool are completed.

9.2.4.4 Compute unit

HGE uses one emulation thread to model a computer unit and executes the work items specified by a work-group. There is little point of executing a work-group on multiple CPU threads, as the group barrier synchronization overhead across multiple CPU threads may slow down the emulation. It is more efficient for HGE to handle group synchronization operations if a work-group is executed by a thread in a time-sharing fashion. When a group barrier instruction occurs in a work-item, the emulation thread simply records the state of the work-item and switches to another work-item. If the host machine provide more than one processor core to run HGE, then HGE will be configured with multiple compute units.

9.2.4.5 Soft-MMU and soft-TLB

To support the shared virtual memory features specified by HSA, HGE implements an MMU in software (soft-MMU) for each compute unit to translate memory addresses for the emulated GPU. To speed up the address translation, HGE implements an address translation cache, called soft-TLB, similarly to the concept of a translation lookaside buffer (TLB) in modern processors. The results of frequent and recent translations can be quickly retrieved instead of walking through levels of page tables. If an address is not found in the soft-TLB, then the address is handled by the soft-MMU with a page table walker. The soft-MMU also checks if the address is valid and if the GPU has the right permission to access the address. If not, the compute unite will jump to an exception handler and notifying HSA agent, which usually results in an abortion of the current kernel execution. For performance reasons, each compute unit maintains its own copy of soft-TLB, which raises a coherence issue. Thus, when HGE caches a mapping in a soft-TLB, it puts a mark in the page table. Whenever any cached translation is changed in the page table, HGE is notified to flush the contents of soft-TLB's.

9.2.5 PROFILING, DEBUGGING AND PERFORMANCE MODELS

HSAemu allows the users to add their own profiling support and performance models. For performance analysis, one can use the high-speed CPU/GPU emulators included in HSAemu to quickly obtain profiling information beyond the instruction level. For those who wish to examine a system at the microarchitectural level, or even at a lower level, performance models or detailed cycle simulators can be attached. For example, one can switch from HGE to Multi2Sim to model the microarchitecture of GPU cores.

As illustrated in Figure 9.7, the "profile units" in HGE allow the users to profile the execution of HSAIL instructions. The instrumentation for this profiling facility is enabled by the HSAIL finalizer, which analyzes the HSAIL instructions for each code block during its code generation work and inserts a function call at the bottom of the code block to deposit the profile data when the code block is finished. For example, one can use the information to roughly estimate if a kernel function is compute-bound or memory-bound, based on the instruction mix. Moreover, the soft-MMU and soft-TLB routines in HGE are also instrumented to provide statistics on memory accesses. For example, synchronization instructions (barrier and atomic instructions), TLB misses, page faults, etc. can have a heavy impact on application performance; the statistics from HGE can provide useful indications without resorting to slow detailed simulation, as shown in Figure 9.8.

Furthermore, with more instrumentation, HGE can support debugging of applications at the level of HSAIL. For example, HGE can display the value of HSAIL registers and record event traces with barrier synchronization operations included

```
== NTHU HSAemu profile info ==
        number of compute unit = 1
        execution time = 0.143519
        total time = 0.307985
HSA profile counter info:
        total instruction     = 23203840
        barrier instruction    = 8192
        atomic instruction     = 0
        special function unit  = 1048576
        global store           = 8192
        global load            = 24576
        group store            = 16384
        group load             = 4194304
        tlb miss               = 80
        page fault             = 0
        computation/communication ratio = 0.817123
```

FIGURE 9.8

Profile data reported by HGE.

during the runtime. Such information can be further analyzed to pinpoint potential bugs in HSAIL finalizer or possible race conditions.

For a system-wide performance analysis, the user of HSAemu can leverage the profiling infrastructure, MCEmu [13]. Because the main system (CPU) emulator in HSAemu and MCEmu are both based on QEMU, we have successfully ported the "virtual performance profiling monitoring unit" (VPMU) and "virtual timing models" (VTD) of MCEmu, as well as open source cache simulators, for example, GEMS, into HSAemu. The resultant profiling infrastructure provides a unified facility for component simulators to deposit performance data and for the users to implement their own timing model for the system clock, which are useful for early stage architectural studies.

9.3 SoftHSA SIMULATOR
9.3.1 INTRODUCTION

The softHSA simulator is designed to provide a high-performance, accurate, and debuggable simulation of whole HSA-enabled programs at the HSA-API level. The simulation provides no performance modeling. Consequently, the softHSA simulator is most appropriate for compiler-writers tracking down HSAIL code generation bugs, and possibly other HSA users needing a rich, low-level debugging interface.[1]

---

[1] The simulator was developed contemporaneously with the specification, but has not kept up-to-date; consequently, the version of the HSAIL, BRIG, and HSA APIs supported is not reflective of the final standard. Hopefully, this issue will be addressed in a future revision of the simulator. Until then, these deficiencies will require some work-arounds from a motivated end user.

9.3.2 HIGH-LEVEL DESIGN

Unlike some other simulators that only operate at the HSAIL level, the softHSA simulator is intended to be a drop-in replacement for an HSA device, including the runtime. Consequently, the simulator reads BRIG files directly. Ideally, the simulator should have reused a library for reading and verifying BRIG, but at the time the simulator was developed, these libraries were not available. The simulator replicates BRIG's file-layout in memory as though the file were mmaped. A series of helper classes facilitate higher-level analysis and protect against changes to the underlying BRIG format.

The simulator analyzes the BRIG code and creates LLVM IR that replicates the global data structures, functions, and function control flow. The simulator also imports all available HSA debugging information to LLVM IR. Preserving the debugging information is critical to providing source level debugging. Individual instructions are not translated to equivalent LLVM IR. Instead, each instruction is translated to a call to a specific function that implements the HSAIL instruction.

Implementing instructions as functions rather than through direct translation greatly simplifies the translation process from BRIG to LLVM, and allows each instruction to be tested independently. The translator also generates code for reading and modifying registers and for handling the various HSAIL addressing modes. The simulator does not maintain a centralized map from HSAIL instructions to simulator functions. Instead, the simulator mangles the instruction's name and type information to produce the name of a function. If a function that implements a particular instruction is missing, the simulator can fail dynamically at runtime, when and if the simulator tries to execute the missing function.

Potentially, the overhead of calling functions to implement each instruction could be avoided by compiling all of the instruction simulation functions to LLVM IR and then inlining them. Inlining these functions would dramatically improve LLVM's ability to optimize the simulator code. For example, in many circumstances, LLVM could promote simulated HSA registers from stack-allocated data structures in physical registers. We believe that modifying the simulator to inline the functions implementing instructions would be relatively simple and could appear in future versions of the simulator.

To execute the LLVM IR, the simulator uses LLVM's JIT functionality. The simulator will use the JIT to compile an entire module at finalization time. Consequently, when the simulator executes an HSA kernel, no simulation or emulation actually occurs. The kernel has already been JITed, so it executes natively. One of the great benefits of LLVM's JIT is that it will dynamically generate DWARF debugging information from LLVM debug information. The GDB debugger can load dynamically generated DWARF information and use it to enable source-level debugging. The flow of debugging information flows from a high-level language to HSAIL to LLVM to DWARF to GDB. Consequently, GDB can map from symbol names to the appropriate memory address or ISA register. Since the simulator code is really native code with symbolic debugging information, GDB provides a full-featured debugging experience including breaking on specific lines of code, modifying variables, and printing call traces.

9.3.3 BUILDING AND TESTING THE SIMULATOR

The latest version of The softHSA simulator is always available at: https://github. com/HSAFoundation/HSAIL-Instruction-Set-Simulator. The instructions for building the simulator are available in laborious detail in the README file, but generally, the project uses a standard CMAKE-style build system. The simulator has been tested on a wide variety of platforms, including numerous permutations of i386, ×86-64, CentOS, Ubuntu, gcc, and clang. If you run into trouble on your platform of choice, bug reports, and better yet, pull requests for bug fixes are always welcome.

After building the simulator, please take the time to try the simulator's various tests. Building the HSA simulator will generate nine test cases. The two most important tests are brig_reader_test and brig_runtime_test. Both are based on Google Test [14]. brig_runtime_test tests individual instructions for on a wide array of inputs. brig_runtime_test contains several long-running test cases that are disabled by default. Depending on the host, these tests can take between hours and days. To enable these tests, run brig_runtime_test with the -gtest_filter=* option. brig_reader_test tests instructions and kernels in the context of a full HSA simulation. If both brig_reader_test and brig_runtime_test pass, the simulator is probably working correctly. The remaining tests are more idiosyncratic, as explained below.

barrierTest tests the barrier instructions.

brig_reader_test tests inter-operability between the HSAIL assembler and simulator. Starting with HSAIL, the brig_reader_test assembles the programs to BRIG, then simulates the programs for various test inputs to ensure semantic consistency.

brig_runtime_test verifies each instruction has been implemented in accordance with the HSA PRM using automatic test vector generation.

debug tests the HSA runtime debug interface.

fcos is a standalone application that reports the the cos of angles form -pi radians to pi radians at half pi intervals. Due to rounding error, the cosine of pi/2 may be reported as a very small negative number instead of zero, as pi/2 is not precisely representable as a floating point number.

fib is a recursive Fibonacci implementation based on an example in the HSA PRM. This program demonstrates correct scoping for argument variables and recursion.

hsa_runtime_test tests the implementation of the HSA runtime API.

vectorCopy performs a vector copy using the HSA simulator.

The simulator was built in accordance with various draft HSA specifications that are not publicly available. Consequently, the simulator's API does not presently match the HSA runtime API exactly. As always, patches are welcome, but until this deficiency is corrected, programmers can consult the examples in the simulator's demo directory for examples of how to use the draft APIs.

9.3.4 DEBUGGING WITH THE LLVM HSA SIMULATOR

The GDB debugging interface is possibly the most useful feature of the softHSA simulator. A debugging session can be started simply by using gdb to run an HSA binary built against the simulator's HSA API implementation. The simulator's GDB-based debugging interface supports printing and modifying local variables, registers, and arguments. Here is an example debugging session using the fib program included with the simulator:

```
1 $ gdb ./fib**
2 Reading symbols from fib … done.
3 (gdb) break fib
4 Function "fib" not defined.
5 Make breakpoint pending on future shared library load? (y or [n]) y
6 Breakpoint 1 (fib) pending.
7 (gdb) run
8 Starting program: ./fib
9 [Thread debugging using libthread_db enabled]
10 Using host libthread_db library "/lib/x86_64-linux-gnu/
   libthread_db.so.1".
11 Fib sequence: [New Thread 0x7ffff6bb9700 (LWP 1752)]
12 [Switching to Thread 0x7ffff6bb9700 (LWP 1752)]
13
14 Breakpoint 1, fib (n = @0x7ffff6bb8810: 1, r = @0x7ffff6bb8814: 0)
15     at test/fib. hsail : 13
16 13        ld_arg_s32 $s1, [%n];
17 (gdb) p n # Print an argument
18 $1 = (s32 &) @0x7ffff6bb8810: 1
19 (gdb) p hsa$s1 # Print a register
20 $2 = {b32 = 0, f32 = 0}
21 (gdb) n # Single step an HSA Instruction
22 14        cmp_lt_b1_s32 $c1, $s1, 3; // if n < 3 go to return
23 (gdb) p hsa$s1
24 $3 = {b32 = 1, f32 = 1.40129846e-45}
25 (gdb) n # Single step an HSA Instruction
26 15        cbr $c1, @return;
27 (gdb) p hsa$c1 # Print an HSA register
28 $4 = true
29 (gdb) p hsa$c1 = 0 # Modify an HSA register
30 $5 = false
31 (gdb) p hsa$s1 = 4 # Modify an HSA register
32 $6 = {b32 = 4, f32 = 5.60519386e-45}
33 (gdb) p n = 4 # Modify a parameter
34 $7 = 4
35 (gdb) c # Continue until the next break point
36 Continuing.
37
38 Breakpoint 1, fib (r = @0x7ffff6bb81f4 : 0, n = @0x7ffff6bb81f8 : 2)
```

```
39     at test/fib.gsail : 13
40 13         ld_arg_s32 $s1, [%n];
41 (gdb) bt # Print a stack trace
42 #0 fib (r=@0x7ffff6bb81f4 : 0, n = @0x7ffff6bb81f8: 2) at test/fib.
   hsail : 13
43 #1 0x00007ffff7ff60cb in fib (r = @0x7ffff6bb882c: 0,
   n = @0x7ffff6bb8828: 4)
44     at test/fib.hsail: 23
45 #2 0x00007ffff7ff620f in
46     fibKernel (r_ptr=@0x1dc5500: 31571312, n_ptr=@0x1dc5508 : 1)
47     at test/fib.hsail : 51
48 #3 0x00007ffff7ff62c1 in kernel.fibkernel ()
49 #4 0x000000000084aee4 in hsa : : brig : : workItemLoop (vargs =
   0x1def7c0)
50     at src/brig211vm/brig_engine.cc : 256
51 #5 0x00007ffff79c0f6e in start_thread (arg=0x7ffff6bb9700)
52     at pthread_create. c:311
53 #6 0x00007ffff6cb49cd in clone ()
54     at ../sysdeps/unix/sysv/linux/x86_64/clone.S:113
55 (gdb) p/x b8Value # Print an HSA global variable
56 $8 = 0x31
57 (gdb) p/x b16Value # Print an HSA global variable
58 $9 = 0x3141
59 (gdb) p/x b32Value # Print an HSA global variable
60 $10 = 0x31415926
61 (gdb) p/x b64Value # Print an HSA global variable
62 $11 = 0x3141592653589793
63 (gdb) p p = 7 # Modify an HSA local variable
64 $12 = 7
65 (gdb) p b32Value = 13 # Modify an HSA global variable
66 $13 = 13
```

After the user starts the debugging session, they place a break point on the fib function (line 3). The fib function is an HSA function, but GDB cannot locate this function, as the relevant code has not been finalized. Using a pending breaking point (line 5) will cause the GDB to insert the relevant hardware break point once the code is finalized. After the user starts the program (line 7), GDB breaks when the fib function first executes and prints line and source code information related to the original HSAIL source code (lines 14-16). The mapping between HSAIL instruction and source code was created by the assembler and encoded in the BRIG binary read by the simulator. The mapping doesn't depend on the specific semantics of the language being mapped, so any compiler that generates BRIG with appropriate debugging information will enable source line debugging in the simulator.

The user continues the debugging session by printing the value of local variables by name (lines 17-18), as well as registers (lines 19-20). Internally, the simulator represents HSA registers as local variables. This is appropriate, as HSA register values are undefined at function entry. The simulator must provide a unique name to each

HSA register that is distinct from any possible symbol name in the original program; a collision between a local variable named s1 and the corresponding HSAIL register would be confusing to users. To avoid this confusion, the simulator prepends hsa$ to the name of each register. HSA registers are untyped and can be used as integer or floating point values. The simulator reports the types of these registers as unions, so a $s register is a union of a uint32_t and a float; a $d register is the union of a uint64_t and a double.

The user advances the program by a single HSAIL instruction (line 21), and prints the value of the s1 register (line 23). The value of the register has changed, as it was last printed (line 19) by the load instruction that just executed. Advancing the program by another single step (line 25), the user examines the value of the recently modified predicate register c1 (line 27-28). The user modifies the value of register c1 from true to false (line 29), the value of register s1 from one to four (line 31), and the value of the formal parameter n from one to four (line 33). Finally, the user continues execution until the next breakpoint is reached (line 35).

At the next breakpoint, the user prints a backtrace (line 41). Printing a backtrace shows the fib and fibKernel HSA function and kernel on the stack, as well as several functions internal to the simulator. The user prints global values of HSAIL types b8 (lines 55-56), b16 (lines 57-58), b32 (lines 59-60), and b64 (lines 61-62). Note that the simulator reflects the type of these functions correctly, as well as value of their arguments. Finally, the user modifies and prints a local variable (lines 63-64) and a global variable (lines 65-66).

The demonstrated functionality, setting breakpoints, examining backtraces, controlling execution, and modifying and printing variables and registers, serves as the basis of a productive debugging environment. This functionality will be especially convenient for compiler writers trying to debug the translation of high-level languages to HSAIL.

REFERENCES

[1] R. Ubal, B. Jang, P. Mistry, D. Schaa, D. Kaeli, Multi2Sim: a simulation framework for CPU-GPU computing, in: Proc. of the 21st International Conference on Parallel Architectures and Compilation Techniques, 2012.

[2] HSA Foundation, HSA Programmers Reference Manual: HSAIL Virtual ISA and Programming Model, Compiler Writers Guide, and Object Format (BRIG), 2014. provisonal 1.0 edition.

[3] HSA Foundation. HSAIL-Tools. https://github.com/HSAFoundation/HSAIL-Tools, 2015.

[4] HSA Foundation, HSA Runtime Programmers Reference Manual, 2014. provisonal 1.0 edition.

[5] HSA Foundation. Okra Interface to HSA Devices. https://github.com/HSAFoundation/Okra-Interface-to-HSA-Device, 2015.

[6] HSA Foundation, HSA Platform System Architecture Specification, 2014. provisional 1.0 edition.

[7] J.E. Stone, D. Gohara, G. Shi, Opencl: a parallel programming standard for heterogeneous computing systems, IEEE Des. Test 12 (3) (2010) 66–73.

[8] Open Source Project. Aparapi – API for Data Parallel Java. Allows Suitable Code to be Executed on GPU via OpenCL. https://code.google.com/p/aparapi/, 2015.

[9] F. Bellard, Qemu, a fast and portable dynamic translator, in: Proceedings of the Annual Conference on USENIX Annual Technical Conference, ATEC '05, USENIX Association, Berkeley, CA, USA, 2005, pp. 41.

[10] J.-H. Ding, W.-C. Hsu, B.-C. Jeng, S.-H. Hung, Y.-C. Chung, Hsaemu: a full system emulator for hsa platforms, in: Proceedings of the 2014 International Conference on Hardware/Software Codesign and System Synthesis, CODES '14, ACM, New York, NY, USA, 2014, pp. 26:1–26:10.

[11] N. Binkert, B. Beckmann, G. Black, S.K. Reinhardt, A. Saidi, A. Basu, J. Hestness, D.R. Hower, T. Krishna, S. Sardashti, R. Sen, K. Sewell, M. Shoaib, N. Vaish, M.D. Hill, D.A. Wood, The gem5 simulator, SIGARCH Comput. Archit. News 39 (2) (2011) 1–7.

[12] J.-H. Ding, P.-C. Chang, W.-C. Hsu, Y.-C. Chung, Pqemu: a parallel system emulator based on qemu, in: Proceedings of the 2011 IEEE 17th International Conference on Parallel and Distributed Systems, ICPADS '11, IEEE Computer Society, Washington, DC, USA, 2011, pp. 276–283.

[13] C.-H. Tu, S.-H. Hung, T.-C. Tsai, Mcemu: a framework for software development and performance analysis of multicore systems, ACM Trans. Des. Autom. Electron. Syst. 17 (4) (2012) 36:1–36:25.

[14] Google. Google Test. https://code.google.com/p/googletest/, 2008.

Index

Note: Page numbers followed by *b* indicates boxes, *f* indicates figures, and *t* indicates tables.

A

Activelaneid HSAIL instruction, 28
Activelanepermute instruction, 28
Architected Queuing Language (AQL) packets
  in active and launch state, 43–44
  agent dispatch packet, 43, 85–86, 85*t*
  barrier-AND/OR packet, 86, 86*t*
  barrier-AND packet, 43
  barrier-OR packet, 43
  building packets, 86–87
  in complete and error state, 43–44
  description of, 42–43
  error codes, 44
  invalid packet, 84
  kernel dispatch packet, 43, 84–85, 84*t*
  packet header, 82, 83*t*
  in queue state, 43–44
  types, 82–86
  types of, 43
  vendor-specific packets, 43, 83
Arg segment, HSAIL, 26
Array-of-Structure (AoS) layout, 151–152, 153*f*
Array of Structure of Tiled Arrays (ASTA),
    131–132, 152, 153*f*
Asynchronous notification, HSA runtime, 39–40
Atomic conflict, 70
Atomic operations, HSA memory model, 24–25

B

Base profile, HSAIL, 29
Breadth-first search (BFS) algorithm, 4–5, 131, 132
  baseline implementation, 144
  description, 142–143
  execution time, 145, 145*f*
  global barrier synchronization on GPU, 144*f*
  HSA implementation, 147–150, 148*b*
  legacy implementation, 145–147, 146*b*, 148–150
  sequential implementation, pseudocode of,
      143, 144*b*

C

C++ Accelerated Massive Parallelism
    (C++ AMP), 4
  array_view, 99 100
  conceptual mapping, 102–104
  description, 98

generic C++ code example, 114, 114*f*
generic C++ pointer variables, 114
Kalmar compiler
  components, 102
  HSAIL kernel code, 107, 108*f*
  limitations, shared virtual memory, 115–116
  multi-step compilation process, 104, 106*f*
kernel invocation, 100–102
memory segment annotation, 111–113
new/delete operators, compiler support for
  global memory segment, 126
  implementation, 124–125
  library functions, 123, 124*t*
  wait API/HSAIL signal instruction,
    126–128
parallel_ for_each construct
  captured variables, 101
  compute domain, 100
  extent object, 100
  Lambdas/functors, 100
  restrict(amp) modifier, 101–102
  restrict(cpu) specifier, 101
platform atomics, compiler support for,
    116–123, 118*t*
tile_static, 110–111
tiling
  address space and barriers, 110–111
  explicit approach, 107–109
  implicit approach, 107–109
  tidx.barrier.wait method, 110
  tiled_extent, 109
  tiled_index, 109–110
vector addition program, 98, 99*f*
C++ AMP kernels
  C++11 atomic operations inside, 132–134, 133*f*
  C++11 std atomic member functions, 134
CL Offline Compilation (CLOC), 32–33
Coherency, 9
Consumer electronic gaming, 1
Core runtime API
  AQL packets, 42–44
  asynchronous notification, 39–40
  code objects, 45–47
  executables, 45–47
  HSA system and agent information, 40
  initialization and shutdown, 38–39
  memory management, 44–45

Core runtime API *(Continued)*
  packet state diagram, 39–40, 39*f*
  purpose/goal of, 36
  queues, 41–42
  signals, 40–41
  synchronous notification, 39
CUDA unified memory, 138

D

Data layout conversion, 4–5, 131–132
  AoS layout, 151–152, 153*f*
  ASTA layout, 131–132, 152, 153*f*
  PTTWAC algorithm, 154*b*
    HSA implementation, 155–157
    in-place SOA-ASTA conversion,
      153–154
  SoA layout, 151, 153, 153*f*
Data-race-free memory model, 61
Data races, 61
Direct scope synchronization, 67, 67*f*
Dual source programming, 10
Dynamic execution queueing scheme,
  135–136, 136*b*

E

Extended runtime API, 36

F

Full profile, HSAIL, 29, 30
Full system simulator, 160

G

Global segment, HSAIL, 26
GPU computing
  address conversion, 8
  coherency, 9
  context switching, 14
  discrete GPU cards, 7, 8*f*
  dual source programming, 10
  HSA enabled SOC, 11–12, 12*f*
  HSA Foundation, 17–18
  HSAIL virtual ISA, 14
  HSA software execution stack, 15–17
  HSA specifications
    platform system architecture, 14–15
    programmer's reference manual, 15
    runtime specification, 15
  memory model, 13
  memory paging, 8–9
  NUMA, 8
  queuing model, 13–14

SOCs, 11, 11*f*
  task initiation overhead, 9
Group segment, HSAIL, 26

H

Heterogeneous system architecture (HSA)
  agents, 20, 25, 40–42, 170, 171, 174
  atomics in
    C++11 atomic operations, 132–134, 133*f*
    C++ interface of, 132
    memory_order_acq_rel, 134
    memory_order_acquire, 134
    memory_order_release, 134
    memory_order_seq_cst, 134
  description, 2
  kernel agents, 40, 44–45, 165, 175
  platform atomics, 13, 131, 134
    compiler support for, 116–123
    new/delete operator implementation, 124–125
  task queue system, 134–142
Heterogeneous system architecture intermediate
    language (HSAIL), 3
  activelaneid HSAIL instruction, 28
  activelanepermute instruction, 28
  assembler/disassembler, 33
  Base profile, 29, 30
  benefits of, 19
  BRIG format, 19
  CL Offline Compilation, 32–33
  compiler frameworks, 32, 33*f*
  cross-lane instructions, 28
  description, 19
  execution model
    kernel, 21–22
    levels of, 22, 22*f*
    parallelism, 23
    wavefront, 23
    work-groups, 23
    work-items, 23–24
  fast and robust compilation, 20
  finalization flow, 30
  finalization routines, 47–48
  fixed-size register file, 20
  flat memory address, 27
  Full profile, 29, 30
  HSA runtime support for, 30, 31*f*
  instruction set
    arg segment, 26
    atomic operations, 24–25
    global segment, 26
    group segment, 26
    kernarg segment, 27

private segment, 26
readonly segment, 27
registers, 25–26
specification, 24
spill segment, 26
ISA and machine code assembler/disassembler, 34
just-in-time compiler, 19
large machine model, 29
loading flow, 30–32
profiles, 29
sample compilation flow, 20–21, 21*f*
small machine model, 29
specification of, 36
wavefronts, 28–29, 28*f*
HSAemu framework
design of, 171–174
modeled HSA components
hardware queues, 170
HSA agent, 170, 171
HSAIL, 170–171
HSA packet processor, 170
shared virtual memory model, 170
topology table, 171
user mode queues, 170
multithreaded HSA GPU emulator
code cache, 175
computer unit, 175–176
debugging and performance models, 176–177
HSA agent and packet processor, 174
kernel agent and work scheduling, 175
profiling, 176–177
schematic illustration, 174, 175*f*
soft-MMU, 176
soft-TLB, 176
OpenCL applications, 169
HSA Foundation, 17–18
HSAIL. *See* Heterogeneous system architecture intermediate language (HSAIL)
hsailasm tool, 33
HSAIL virtual ISA, 14
HSA memory model, 13
HSA platform system architecture, specification of, 14–15, 35, 43
HSA queuing model, 13–14
HSA runtime, 3
classification of, 35
core runtime API
AQL packets, 42–44
asynchronous notification, 39–40
code objects, 45–47
executables, 45–47

HSA system and agent information, 40
initialization and shutdown, 38–39
memory management, 44–45
packet state diagram, 39–40, 39*f*
purpose/goal of, 36
queues, 41–42
signals, 40–41
synchronous notification, 39
description of, 35
extended runtime API, 36
extensions
HSAIL finalization, 47–48
images and samplers, 48–50
implementation of, 37
software architecture stack with, 37, 37*f*
specification of, 36
HSA software execution stack, 15–17

I
Inclusive scope synchronization, 67, 68, 68*f*
Instruction level simulator, 160
I/O device model, 2

J
Just-in-time (JIT) compiler, 19

K
Kalmar compiler, C++ AMP
components, 102
HSAIL kernel code, 107, 108*f*
limitations, shared virtual memory, 115–116
multi-step compilation process, 104, 106*f*
Kernarg segment, HSAIL, 27

L
ldimage instruction, 49–50

M
Memory model, 4, 53
arg memory, 56
coarse-grained runtime-controlled allocations, 58
conflicts and races, 60–61
fences, 72, 73, 73*f*
flat address space, 57
global segments, 55–56
group memory, 56
HSA race freedom analysis, 70–71
images, 59
kernarg memory, 56
lock variable, 54

Memory model (*Continued*)
   memory scopes
      agent and system, 66, 66*f*
      direct scope synchronization, 67, 67*f*
      inclusive scope synchronization, 67, 68, 68*f*
      motivation, 65–66
      transitive scope synchronization, 67, 68, 69*f*
      wave-front scope, 66, 66*f*
      work-group scope, 66, 66*f*
      work-item scope, 66, 66*f*
   observations and considerations, 71
   ownership, 58–59, 73–74
   private memory, 56
   readonly segments, 55–56
   relaxed atomics, 72–73
   segments, 69
   sequential consistency, 60, 61*f*
   shared virtual addressing, 57–58
   for single memory scope
      acquire operation, 63
      atomic with acquire-release
         semantics, 63
      race-free memory model framework, 62
      races, 64–65
      release operation, 62, 63
      synchronization operations, 62–63
      transitive synchronization, 63–64, 64*f*
   spill memory, 56
Memory paging, 8–9
Memory races, 61
Multi2Sim simulator
   application-only simulation scheme, 160
   basic I/O support, 164
   components of, 160–161, 160*f*
   description of, 159–160
   emulator design
      hierarchical design, 165–166
      memory systems, 166–167
      segment management system, 166*f*
   feature of, 159–160
   future prospects, 168
   HSA runtime implementation, 164
   HSA runtime interception, 163–164
   HSA simulation, 161–162
   installation and support, 168–169
   kernel launch and execution, 162–163
   logging and debugging, 167–168
   Okra, 162–163
   program entry, 163
   timing simulator, 161
Multithreaded HSA GPU emulator, HSAemu
   code cache, 175
   computer unit, 175–176

   debugging and performance models,
      176–177
   HSA agent and packet processor, 174
   kernel agent and work scheduling, 175
   profiling, 176–177
   schematic illustration, 174, 175*f*
   soft-MMU, 176
   soft-TLB, 176

N
Non-Uniform Memory Access (NUMA), 8

O
OpenMP, 20, 21
Ordinary conflict, 70

P
Platform atomics, 131, 134
Private segment, HSAIL, 26

Q
QEMU, 169, 177
Queuing model, 4
   AQL packets
      agent dispatch packet, 85–86, 85*t*
      barrier-AND/OR packet, 86, 86*t*
      building packets, 86–87
      invalid packet, 84
      kernel dispatch packet, 84–85, 84*t*
      packet header, 82, 83*t*
      types, 82–86
      vendor-specific packet, 83
   submission and scheduling of packets
      compare-and-swap operations, 90
      function for multiple consumers, 92, 93*f*
      packet processor scheduler, 93, 94*f*
      pop function, 93, 95*f*
      queue structure and read/write access, 89, 90*f*
      read index, 88
      write index, 88, 89, 91–92
   user mode queues
      callback parameter, 79–80
      error codes, 80
      group_segment_size parameter, 80
      hsa_queue_t, 80, 80*t*
      for particular agent, 77
      private_segment_size parameter, 80
      size of, 79, 81
      soft *vs.* hard queues, 81
      type parameter, 79
      types, 78–79, 79*f*

R

rdimage instruction, 49–50
Readonly segment, HSAIL, 27
Registers, HSAIL, 25–26
Relaxed atomics, 72–73

S

Sequential consistency, 60, 61*f*
Soft-HSA simulator, 177
  barrierTest, 179
  brig_reader_test, 179
  brig_runtime_test, 179
  building instructions, 179
  debugging with LLVM HSA simulator, 180–182
  debug tests, 179
  fcos, 179
  fib, 179
  high-level design, 178
  hsa_runtime_test, 179
  vectorCopy, 179
Soft *vs.* hard queues, 81
Spill segment, HSAIL, 26
Static execution queueing scheme, 135, 136*b*

stimage instruction, 49–50
Structure of Array (SoA) layout, 151, 153, 153*f*
Synchronization races, 61
Synchronous notification, HSA runtime, 39

T

Task queue system, 4–5, 131, 132
  average execution times, 141–142, 141*f*
  code segment of synthetic experiment, 140–141, 140*f*
  dynamic execution, 135–136, 136*b*
  experiment with synthetic input data, 140–142
  on GPU, 136–137
  histogram computation, 142
  HSA implementation of, 138*f*, 139*b*
  legacy implementation of, 136, 137*f*
  load balancing, 134
  static execution, 135, 136*b*
Transitive scope synchronization, 67, 68, 69*f*
Transitive synchronization, 63–64, 64*f*

V

Video manipulation, 1

Printed in the United States
By Bookmasters